Artificial Intelligence in Education and Teaching Assessment

Wei Wang · Guangming Wang · Xiaoming Ding ·
Baoju Zhang

Editors

Artificial Intelligence in Education and Teaching Assessment

 Springer

Editors
Wei Wang
College of Artificial Intelligence
Tianjin Normal University
Tianjin, China

Guangming Wang
Faculty of Education
Tianjin Normal University
Tianjin, China

Xiaoming Ding
College of Aritificial Intelligence
Tianjin Normal University
Tianjin, China

Baoju Zhang
College of Electronic and Communication
Engineering
Tianjin Normal University
Tianjin, China

ISBN 978-981-16-6504-2   ISBN 978-981-16-6502-8   (eBook)
https://doi.org/10.1007/978-981-16-6502-8

This Springer imprint is published by the registered company Springer Nature Singapore Pte Ltd.
The registered company address is: 152 Beach Road, #21-01/04 Gateway East, Singapore 189721,
Singapore

Contents

Chapter 1
A Review of Content Analysis on China Artificial Intelligence (AI) Education Policies

Shaofang Wang, Guangming Wang, Xia Chen, Wei Wang, and Xiaoming Ding

Abstract This paper analyzes the content of education policy about artificial intelligence (AI) issued by our country in recent years which demonstrated the direction of the AI education development clearly. Four aspects can be focused in these policies and will be the trends and promising aspects in the next few years, including intelligent campus construction, teachers team professional development, online intelligent education platform and lifelong learning environment, ranging from elementary school education to highschool education.

Keywords Education policies · Content analysis · AI in the policies

1.1 Introduction

At the 2019 Artificial Intelligence and Education Conference, President Xi Jinping pointed out that China government attaches great importance to the profound impact of AI on education, actively promotes the deep integration between AI and education to lead educational reform and innovation [1]. In recent years, the Ministry of Education has initiated a series of AI-related education policies to plan for the deep integration of AI and education from a macro perspective, then exploratory practices for intelligent teaching and learning has been carried out. By sorting out the policy documents from the perspective of policy changes, it's obvious that the nation has strong reform determination on intelligence campus, teacher education, online education and life-long education. AI is placed in high hopes of reforming traditional education. Important policy documents were launched including "Ten-year Development Plan for Educational Informatization (2011–2020)" "The 12th Five-year Plan for the Development of Education" "The 13th Five-Year Plan for the Development of Education", "New Generation of Artificial Intelligence Development Plan" "The

S. Wang · G. Wang (✉) · X. Chen
Faculty of Education, Tianjin Normal University, Tianjin 300387, China

W. Wang · X. Ding
College of Artificial Intelligence, Tianjin Normal University, Tianjin 300387, China

Action Plan for Artificial Intelligence Innovation in Colleges and Universities" "Education Informatization 2.0 Action Plan" "Notice on the Pilot Work of the Action to Promote the Construction of AI Teacher Team" "China Education Modernization 2035" etc.

By sorting out the policy documents contents, it can be seen that AI education policies improve the campus environments from campus informatization to wisdom campus construction, and also make accelerate move in teacher professional intelligent competence. At the same time, AI education policies create a new context for education system including elementary education, higher education and life-long education. The artificial intelligence education policy promotes the pilot work of policies tailored to local conditions, continuously promoting the education fairness through multi-domain, hierarchical, and cyclical experiments and explorations, so as to finally realize the deep integration of AI and education under the guidance of the value of "providing an education that satisfies the people".

1.2   A Intelligent Campus

Intelligent campus is a new type of intelligent learner-centered learning environment, which essentially stands for the reconstruction of the teachers' ability and quality, with its sight on fragmented teaching source's integration, laying out the space transformation from physical to the mixed.

The construction of intelligent campus is an important opportunity for the deep integration of AI and school education and teaching activities. It is a key step for intelligent education to link the school education with family education, collaborate with physical space teaching and virtual space teaching. Therefore, in the policy documents, the construction of wisdom campus is an important way to transform students' learning methods and reform teachers' teaching methods. In 2012, the Ministry of Education launched the "Ten-Year Development Plan for Educational Informatization (2011–2020)" [2], which proposed to improve the information construction of all schools according to the actual needs of elementary education in the aspects of infrastructure, teaching resources, software tools and so on, building an intelligent teaching environment. The nation initially put forward the embryonic form of the construction of intelligent campus. In the same year, "The 12th Five-Year Plan for the Development of National Education" [3] proposed to integrate education informatization into the national informatization development strategy and "explore the construction of digital campus and intelligent classroom". In 2017, the State Council issued the "New Generation of AI Development Plan" [4], which proposed to accelerate the in-depth application of AI, and made overall deployment for the development of AI. Education policies on AI were also released in full force. In the same year, the Ministry of Education issued the "The 13th Five-Year Plan for the Development of National Education" [5], which clearly proposed to vigorously promote the deep integration of information technology and education and teaching and support schools at all levels and of all kinds to build smart campuses and explore new models of education and teaching in the future by comprehensively utilizing Internet, big data, AI and virtual reality technology. In this document, there has been a relatively clear planning and implementation path for the construction of intelligent campus including deepening the promotion of network learning space for everyone, forming a new network ubiquitous learning model combining online and offline organically, schools and teachers relying on the network learning space to record the learning process of students. The schools make use of big data technology to collect, analyze and feedback the data of educational and teaching activities and students' behavior, strengthen the exploration and promotion of new models of information education and teachers training, such as "Expert Teacher Classroom", "Elite Online Class" "Courier Class" and "Online Open Course" and so on. The construction of intelligent campus should be improved mainly in terms of changing learning methods, creating new media environment and creating new space–time environment.

In 2018, the Ministry of Education issued the "AI Innovation Action Plan for Colleges" [6], proposing to promote the transformation and demonstration application of scientific and technological achievements in the field of AI in colleges, which clearly pointed out that we should promote the development of intelligent education and teaching reform, realize a transformation from digital campus to intelligent campus, construct a intelligent teaching environment from aspects of detection, diagnosis, evaluation, optimization of management and service mechanism. Therefore, the document clearly puts forward the goal and action guide for the construction of a smart campus, that is, exploring a new teaching model based on artificial intelligence and reconstruct the teaching process, carrying out teaching process detection, learning situation analysis and academic level diagnosis, establishing a multi-dimensional comprehensive intelligent evaluation based on big data, accurately assessing teaching and learning performance, and realizing individualized teaching, promoting the reform of school governance, supporting schools to change the organizational structure and management system, optimizing the operation mechanism and service mode, achieving accurate campus management, personalized services in order to comprehensively improve the level of school governance based on AI.

In 2018, the Ministry of Education issued the "Education Informatization 2.0 Action Plan" [7], proposing to build Internet + education platform to further promote the specific implementation of Internet + education, emphasizing the development of intelligent education popularizing the construction of the digital campus, and launching innovation demonstration of intelligence education. Building intelligence learning support environment and speeding up for the next generation network intelligent learning system construction of colleges gradually push the digital campus upgrade in the direction of intelligent campus.

"A New Generation of AI Development Plan" distributed by the State Council in 2017 put forward the idea of intelligent education for the first time. In 2018 the Ministry of Education kicked off "AI Innovation Action Plan for Colleges", a top-level policy aiming to design the advancing strategic plan of technological innovation and education practice, make full use of the technology of AI resource to accelerate the construction of campus intelligent facilities, strengthen the development of high-quality education resources, build an all-around integrated AI education platform, and improve the service efficiency and quality of educational technology.

1.3   The Professional Development of Teachers Team

In the area of AI + education, the professional development of teachers Team is also an important aspect. The deep integration of AI and education cannot be separated from teachers' teaching practice. The construction of intelligent campus in the intelligent teaching environment, the integration of intelligent network resources and the innovation of new teaching mode under the background of intelligence requires teachers to adapt to the change of intelligent technology. In 2018, China released a landmark policy document entitled "Opinions of the CPC Central Committee and the State Council on Comprehensively Deepening the Reform of Teacher Team Development in the New Era" [8], which clearly points out that teachers should take the initiative to adapt to new technological changes such as information technology and AI. In 2018, the Ministry of Education issued the Education Informatization 2.0 Action Plan to implement the requirements of teacher team building in conjunction with the deployment of major strategic tasks such as the national "Internet +" big data and a new generation of artificial intelligence etc.

"Education informationization 2.0 action plan" provides a strong operational guidance. The "AI + Teacher Team developing Action" will be launched to promote a new path for AI to support teacher governance, teacher education and teaching, targeted poverty and promote teachers to update their ideas, reshape their roles, improve their literacy and enhance their capabilities. In 2018, the Ministry of Education also issued the "Notice on the Pilot Work of AI to Promote Teacher Team development" [9], which put forward more detailed guidelines on the integration of AI and teacher team development. It is mainly carried out in the aspect of external environment and teachers' intelligence literacy. The construction of external environment refers to the gradual improvement of teaching facilities, the construction of intelligent classrooms and intelligent laboratories for teachers. The document proposes to establish an intelligent laboratory for teacher development to achieve intelligent assessment and diagnosis of education and teaching, which can be used to support activities such as demonstration, simulation and virtual teaching and research in teaching, thereby ultimately enhancing teachers' teaching capacity and promoting their professional development. The Teacher Development Intelligence Lab captures information on teachers' teaching, science and management to form teacher big data, build a digital portrait of teachers and carry out teacher big data mining to support school decision-making, improve teacher management and optimise teacher services. The file broadly outlines the basic path of AI boosting the teachers team developing, the application of intelligent equipment, intelligent teachers training and the improvement of teachers' intelligent literacy.

In 2019, the Ministry of Education issued the "Implementation Opinion of the National Elementary School Teachers' Information Technology Application Ability Promotion Project 2.0" [10], which proposes to establish teachers' information literacy development mechanisms based on the school and classroom specific circumstance, making full use of new technologies such as AI achievement to improve the innovation ability of headmasters and teachers for the future, meanwhile, extending AI to education in poor areas according to the actual demand from rural school in minority border and poor areas, organising 'double teachers' teachers training mode in the condition of expert teachers online classroom to assist remote collaborative teachers training and offer actively information technology support in elementary schools. It can be seen that China is actively exploring the application of AI in the development of rural teacher teams by policies. In 2020, the Ministry of Education and other six departments issued the "Opinions on Strengthening the Development of Rural Teacher Teams in the New Era" [11], which proposed to give full play to the boosting role of 5G, AI and other new technologies and build intelligent teacher training platforms, which can intelligently select the data, precisely deliver research content and resources, and can support teachers to choose their own learning resources and provide teachers with synchronized, customized and precise high-quality training and research services. Obviously, China attaches great importance to the role of AI in narrowing the gap between urban and rural teacher training, providing high-quality training resources for teachers, building a learning and research community for urban and rural teachers, and is making gradual progress.

1.4   Online Intelligent Education Platform

With the increasing abundance of intelligent network resources, online intelligent education platform is also developing gradually. National policies have successively emphasized the importance of online education. The construction of ubiquitous intelligent learning environment not only accelerates the innovation of education mode, but also provides a guarantee for the supply of learning resources. By making using of 5G network technology, traditional classroom can be upgraded to a remote interactive classroom, so as to solve the problems of education resources distribution imbalance and schools' cross-regional communication platform deficiency. Online intelligent education platform not only for students according to their aptitude, but also education in the mountain areas, promote the education fairness. Especially during the COVID-19 epidemic, online learning and education platforms played an irreplaceable role. In 2017, in order to speed up the process of education informatization, strengthen education power construction, the Ministry of Education issued "Opinions about Digital Education Resources Construction and Application of Guidance" [12], which pointed out that promote the interaction between teachers teaching and research, parents and school, colleges and enterprise activity online on the basis of new teaching pattern.

In 2018, the Ministry of Education issued the "Notice on the Population of Online Learning Space Applications" [13], which demonstrated and promoted typical cases and successful experiences of online learning space in online teaching, resource sharing, education management, and comprehensive quality evaluation, and guided the construction and application of online learning Spaces in each region.

In 2019, the Ministry of Education jointly issued "Guiding Opinions on Promoting the Healthy Development of Online Education" [14], which pointed out that online education takes advantage of the Internet, AI and other modern information technologies to enable teacher-student interaction in teaching and learning, which is an important part of education services. The development of online education is conducive to the construction of a digital, personalized and life-long education system, and is helpful to the construction of a learning society in which everyone can learn whenever and wherever they want. The document emphasizes tapping online education resources in English, mathematics, music, physics and art for poor areas to make up for the lack of basic public services in education and to promote the integration of online and offline education. At the same time, qualified online courses should be brought into the education teaching system in order to integrate information technology and intelligent technology into education teaching process.

As the supplement of the traditional off-line education, open and flexible online education mode is expected to bridge the education fair gap. In 2019, the Ministry of Education, together with other eight departments, issued "opinions on orderly and healthy development of education's mobile Internet application" [15], which regulates problems such as rampant applications, platform monopoly, mandatory usage, excessive advertising, and harmful information dissemination. The guideline calls for building a normal governance system and creating a good ecosystem for the development of online education. In 2020, the Ministry of Education issued "Guidance on Strengthening the Application of 'Three Classrooms'" [16] which proposed to create Internet + education ecology and more fair and more quality education system. "Three Classrooms" refers to "Mail Classroom" which provides high-quality educational resources according to the teaching schedule, "Expert Teacher Online Classroom" which explores new forms of teaching and research activities in the network environment and "elite school network classroom" which promotes the sharing of high-quality educational resources at a regional or national level.

1.5   Lifelong Learning System

AI has promoted education modernization, at the same time triggered a change in the concept of learning. Online education platforms, collection and enrichment of educational resources, and the trend of digitization of educational resources create conditions for lifelong learning.

National public service platforms such as "One Teacher, One Excellent Course, One Class, One Expert Teacher", MOOC China, School Online, I-course Online, Good University Online and other MOOC websites in China, ranging from the national public service platform for educational resources, to the catechism resource network used for teaching in universities, to the educational learning websites and APPs developed by enterprises, have been optimized and innovated constantly with the rapid update of technology and the needs of educational reform and development, providing convenient conditions for lifelong learning. With the rapid update of technology and the demand of education reform and development, the system is constantly optimized and innovated, which provides convenient conditions for lifelong learning.

In 2018, the Ministry of Education issued "Education Informationization 2.0 Action Plan" [17] which clearly pointed out that education informatization has the unique advantages of breaking time and space constraints and will be the effective way to promote education fair and improve the quality of education. Education informatization will built a ubiquitous learning environment, finally realizing the lifelong learning. In 2020, the Ministry of Education issued "National Comprehensive Reform for Open University" [18], which proposed to build a national lifelong learning education system. With the rapid development of the AI, 5G, virtual reality, chain blocks, big data, cloud computing and other new technologies, a online national lifelong learning education platform can be established, "Vertically connected and horizontally integrated learning network" promotes the digitalization, intelligence, life-long and integration of open education, and opens up a new path for the construction of a lifelong learning system for the whole people.

1.6   Conclusion

Nowadays, AI is playing an increasingly important role in China's education policy, reshaping educational areas such as intelligent campus, teachers team development, online intelligent education platforms and lifelong learning. By June 2021, the government has issued several policy documents for the deployment of AI education, reflecting the main development path of AI education promoted by the nation. As the national level gradually deepens the understanding of the form and connotation of AI, the key points involved in the policies will become more and more rich.

Acknowledgements The work was supported by the National Social Science Foundation of 2017 Education Key Project "Research on Teachers Core Literacy and Ability Construction" (AFA170008) and TJNU "Artificial Intelligence + Education" United Foundation.

References

1. *International Conference on Artificial Intelligence and Education.* http://www.moe.gov.cn/jyb_xwfb/gzdt_gzdt/moe_1485/201905/t20190518_382468.html
2. Ten-year development plan for educational informatization (2011–2020). http://www.moe.gov.cn/srcsite/A16/s3342/201203/t20120313_133322.html
3. The 12th five-year plan for the development of national education. http://www.moe.gov.cn/srcsite/A03/moe_1892/moe_630/201206/t20120614_139702.html
4. New generation of AI development plan. http://www.gov.cn/zhengce/content/2017-07/20/content_5211996.htm
5. The 13th five-year plan for the development of national education. http://www.moe.gov.cn/jyb_xxgk/moe_1777/moe_1778/201701/t20170119_295319.html
6. AI innovation action plan for colleges. http://www.moe.gov.cn/srcsite/A16/s7062/201804/t20180410_332722.html
7. Education informatization 2.0 action plan. http://www.moe.gov.cn/srcsite/A16/s3342/201804/t20180425_334188.html
8. Opinions of the CPC Central Committee and the State Council on comprehensively deepening the reform of teacher team development in the new era. http://www.gov.cn/zhengce/2018-01/31/content_5262659.htm
9. Notice on the pilot work of AI to promote teacher team development. http://www.moe.gov.cn/srcsite/A10/s7034/201808/t20180815_345323.html
10. Implementation opinion of the National Elementary School Teachers' information technology application ability promotion project 2.0. http://www.moe.gov.cn/srcsite/A10/s7034/201904/t20190402_376493.html
11. Opinions on strengthening the development of rural teacher teams in the new era. http://www.gov.cn/zhengce/zhengceku/2020-09/04/content_5540386.htm
12. Opinions about digital education resources construction and application of guidance. http://www.moe.gov.cn/srcsite/A16/s3342/201802/t20180209_327174.html
13. Notice on the population of online learning space applications. http://www.moe.gov.cn/srcsite/A16/s3342/201810/t20181018_352052.html
14. Guiding opinions on promoting the healthy development of online education. http://www.gov.cn/xinwen/2019-09/30/content_5435245.htm
15. Opinions on orderly and healthy development of education's mobile internet application. http://www.moe.gov.cn/srcsite/A16/moe_784/201908/t20190829_396505.html
16. Guidance on strengthening the application of "three classrooms". http://www.gov.cn/zhengce/zhengceku/2020-03/16/content_5491791.htm
17. Education informationization 2.0 action plan. http://www.moe.gov.cn/srcsite/A16/s3342/201804/t20180425_334188.html
18. National comprehensive reform for open university. http://www.moe.gov.cn/srcsite/A07/zcs_zhgg/202009/t20200907_486014.html

Chapter 2
Analyzing Policy Documents of Labor Education and Study Tour in China

Zhipeng Zhu, Jiajia Zhou, Yueyuan Kang, and Xin Zhang

Abstract In this chapter, the policy documents of the Ministry of Education (ME) and 7 provincial administrative regions (PAR)s about labor education and study tour are analyzed and discussed. Text analysis method is applied to identify the top keywords from the documents. The discussion of policy documents are comprised of four parts. First, the release time of documents are analyzed in chronological order. Second, a sequence of keywords is extracted from the documents to stand for the policies. Word frequency is given to show the structure of the documents. Then, the consistency between ME and 7 PARs are discussed with respect to five aspects. Finally, the uniqueness of the documents is discussed. Following a brief overview of the policy document of the ME and related works in Sect. 2.1, Sect. 2.2 presents policy documents of provincial administrative regions of China. Section 2.3 gives the proposed method used to analyze the policy documents. Section 2.4 defines the proposed evaluation criteria to analyze the documents, and shows the text analysis results. The chapter is summarized in Sect. 2.5.

Keywords Educational data mining · Labor education · Study tour · Text analysis

2.1 Policy Overview and Related Works

Both the State Council and the ME released their policy documents about labor education. "Labor education will be incorporated into the education system to foster citizens with an all-round moral, intellectual, physical and aesthetic grounding, in addition to a hard-working spirit [1]". Study tour is also called research travel to emphasize research and learning purpose in the activity. As defined in policy document from the ME, "study tour refers to a kind of extracurricular education activity,

Z. Zhu · J. Zhou · X. Zhang (✉)
Tianjin Key Laboratory of Wireless Mobile Communications and Power Transmission, Tianjin Normal University, Tianjin, China
e-mail: ecemark@tjnu.edu.cn

Y. Kang
Faculty of Education, Tianjin Normal University, Tianjin, China

which is organized and arranged by education departments and schools in a planned way [2]". Labor education is an old and gradually reborn content. Labor is the key to our survival and development. And its spirit is particularly important in carrying forward the work of frugality, struggle, innovation and dedication among the students of all grades [3]. In order to promote the universal labor education, the ME has formulated various policy measures in the past few years. The number of policy documents published by the ME is shown in Fig. 2.1. It can be seen from the figure that the period between 1977 and 1998 has larger number of policy documents than the other periods.

With the development of the times, these policies are in the continuous iteration. The ME recently issued the relevant policy is the "primary and secondary school labor education guidelines (trial)," the policy clearly defined the concept of labor education "to students love labor, love the people's education activities." At the same time, the main contents of labor education are put forward: "Daily labor education, production labor education and service-oriented labor education" [4]. The purpose of labor education is to cultivate the ability of primary and secondary school students to strengthen themselves independently, to better deal with personal life and health habits, to develop good labor habits and quality, and then to create material wealth through their own hands, to establish a correct concept of labor, and finally to guide primary and secondary school students through their own knowledge, to provide services to others and society, enhance social responsibility, and carry forward the spirit of selfless dedication [4, 5].

Study tour is an emerging concept, which first appeared in 2013, and has since become a new initiative linking tourism development and quality education reform [6]. The ME has its specific definition of study tour: "The out-of-school education activities, combining research learning and travel experience carried out through group travel and centralized accommodation under the systematic organization of education departments and schools, are innovative forms of school education and out-of-school education convergence. They are an important part of education and

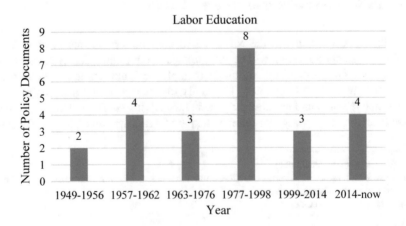

Fig. 2.1 The number of policy documents of labor education published by the ME

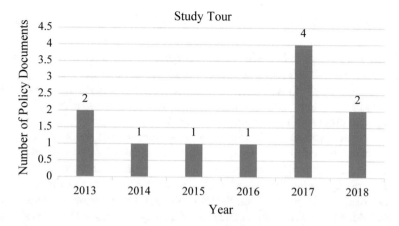

Fig. 2.2 The number of policy documents of study tour published by the ME

teaching, and an effective way to educate people in comprehensive practice" [6]. The development of study tour is still in the exploratory stage, and the ME has relatively few policy documents on study tour [7]. The number of policy documents of study tour published by the ME is shown in Fig. 2.2. It can be seen from the figure that the year 2017 has larger number of policy documents than the other.

Labor education and study tour are all important measures put forward by the ME to strengthen the comprehensive quality education of students, which is of great significance and value in strengthening the coordinated development of moral, intellectual and physical beauty and labor, and promoting the comprehensive reform of quality education in primary and secondary schools. From the concept of both, the nature of labor education is hands-on practice, the nature of study tour is life experience, although labor education is more mature than the development of study tour, but the two are still in the stage of exploration and adjustment, scholars at home and abroad have put forward their own views and thinking on these two important measures.

Regarding labor education, the majority of scholars discussed what labor education is, what to teach and how to teach, the problems in the development of labor education, the solution and the prospect of the future are the focus of most scholars. The discussion of scholars on study tour is more reflected in the progress of the development of primary and secondary school study tour, implementation strategies and scholars' reflection. At present, there is relatively little research, discussion and attention on "how the policy strategies proposed by each province are consistent and different from those proposed by the ME" in the labor education and study tour. This chapter analyzes the labor education and study tour policy documents of the selected 7 PARs. The study will use text analysis methods, and compares with the policy documents of the ME with 7 PARs to visually reflect the consistency and uniqueness of policies.

2.2 Policy Documents of Provincial Administrative Regions

After the ME put forward the relevant policies of labor education and study tour, the response degree of each province and city is different. After the ME, the policy of labor education in each provincial administrative region (PAR) is more rapid, while the policy of study tour in each PAR is more scattered, which has a lot to do with the development process of the two mentioned above.

The labor education policy is a long process of innovation, its ideological approach is more mature than study tour. On the other hand, the study tour is in the preliminary exploration stage. It will still take a long time for research and practical testing. We looked up policy documents related to labor education and study tour on the official websites of the ME and the seven PARs. Tables 2.1 and 2.2 show the release time of policy documents about labor education and study tour, respectively. Both tables contain document information for the ME and 7 PARs. For labor education policy, the document of the ME has 10,305 words, which is much more than the 7 PARs; while the document of Tianjin has 1,074 words, which is the least as shown in Table 2.1.

For study tour policy, the document of Hainan has 6,651 words, which is much more than the ME and the other 6 PARs; while the document of Tianjin has 1,970

Table 2.1 Summary of policy documents about labor education

Number	Province/Department	Release date	Word count
1	ME	2020.7.7	10,305
2	Tianjin	2021.1.12	1,074
3	Shandong	2020.9.9	3,772
4	Shanxi	2021.3.31	4,112
5	Hainan	2021.5.27	5,516
6	Sichuan	2020.11.10	6,386
7	Jiangxi	2021.1.7	4,437
8	Guangxi	2020.9.16	4,762

Table 2.2 Summary of policy documents about study tour

Number	Province/Department	Release date	Word count
1	ME	2016.12.19	3706
2	Tianjin	2017.11.3	1970
3	Shandong	2017.7.4	3639
4	Shanxi	2017.4.12	5213
5	Hainan	2017.12.29	6651
6	Sichuan	2017.11.22	5645
7	Jiangxi	2017.7.6	4778
8	Guangxi	2019.4.25	4727

words, which is the least as shown in Table 2.2. It is observed that the documents of 5 PARs have more words than the document of the ME.

2.3   Text Analysis Method

This section presents the text analysis method. The analysis is based on policy documents between ME and each provincial administrative region (PAR).

The procedures of the text analysis method are shown in Fig. 2.3. First, the policy document of ME doc^{ME} is input to the method and processed by document preparation method. The document preparation method is shown in Fig. 2.4, which will be introduced in the following. After text preparation, a list of important words T^{ME} of ME policy document is obtained. Then for policy document of each PAR doc_i^{PAR}, the document is input to the method. A list of important words T_i^{PAR} of doc_i^{PAR} is obtained by using text preparation method. Then a comparison is done between T^{ME} and T_i^{PAR}. The comparison criteria will be introduced in the next section.

The procedures of the data preparation method are shown in Fig. 2.4. First, a document is input to the method. The document could be policy document of ME or a PAR. The tokenization of a document is done by using Unicode Stand [8] and Annex and International Components for Unicode libraries [9].

Fig. 2.3 Procedures of the text analysis method

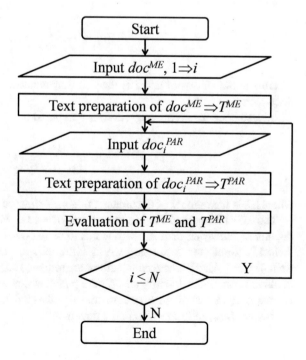

Fig. 2.4 Procedures of
document preparation

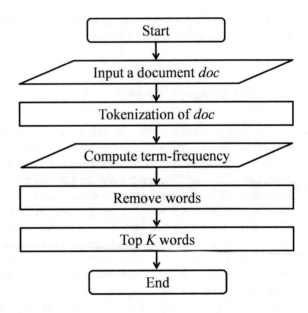

To compute term frequency of a document, term frequency-inverse document frequency (TF-IDF) is a commonly used metric [10, 11]. Term frequency (TF) is computed by:

$$\text{TF}_{i,j} = \frac{n_{i,j}}{\sum_k n_{i,j}} \tag{2.1}$$

where i is the i-th word and j is the j-th document; $n_{i,j}$ is the count of word i in document d_j.

Inverse document frequency (IDF) is computed by:

$$\text{IDF}_i = \lg \frac{|D|}{\left|\{j : t_i \in d_j\}\right|} \tag{2.2}$$

where $|D|$ is the number of documents; t_i is the i-th word.

The TF-IDF method could return a list of words with frequency counter of a document. However, there are step words to be removed from the list such as "the", "which", "want", etc. In this step, words with similar meaning have been combined to a single word. Also Chinese punctuations are removed due to the tokenization method could not completely identify all Chinese punctuations. Finally, the top K words are chosen from the list. Such words are considered as the first K most important words as they are frequently repeated in the documents.

2.4   Document Analysis Results and Discussion

This section presents there criteria for evaluating policy documents between the ME and each PAR. For each criterion, the results are reported and discussed. Text analysis is performed by Matlab software.

2.4.1   Execution Analysis of Policy Documents

Generally, the policy document of the ME is released first. Then each PAR would release the policy document by taking the ME policy as on the baseline. The releasing time of policy documents of a PAR is later than that of the ME. The time interval is appropriate to reflect the enthusiasm of a PAR responding to the appeal of the ME.

For labor education policy, the time interval of 7 PARs later than the ME is presented in Fig. 2.5. For example, Shandong and Guangxi PARs released their policies after 2 months after the ME released the policy. Sichuan, Jiangxi, and Tianjin released their policies after 4, 6 and 6 months after the policy of the ME. Shanxi and Hainan are the second last and the last to publish the labor education policy among the 7 PARs.

For study tour policy, the time interval of 7 PARs later than the ME is presented in Fig. 2.6. For example, Shanxi and Jiangxi PARs released their policies after 4 and 7 months after the ME released the policy. Tianjin, Sichuan and Hainan released their policies after 11, 11 and 12 months after the policy of the ME. Guangxi and Shandong are the second last and the last to publish the labor education policy among the 7 PARs. Time gap of Guangxi and Shandong is much bigger than the other 5 PARs.

Fig. 2.5 Time interval of 7 PARs for releasing labor education policies

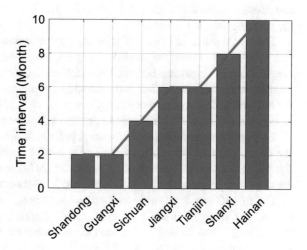

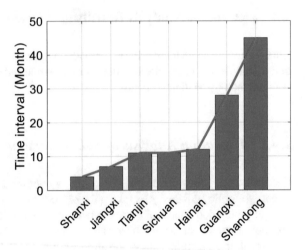

Fig. 2.6 Time interval of 7 PARs for releasing study tour policies

It can be seen from Figs. 2.5 and 2.6 that Shandong and Guangxi ranks first and second with respect to time interval for labor education policy; whereas both ranks the last and the second last with respect to time interval for study tour policy. Shanxi ranks the second last for labor education policy; while it ranks first for study tour policy. Hainan ranks the last for labor education policy and the third last for study tour policy. Sichuan, Jiangxi, and Tianjin have similar ranks for both policies.

2.4.2 Word Frequency Analysis of Policy Documents

Based on the method given in Fig. 2.4, it is able to extract top K words in policy documents. In the simulation, K is set to 20. The K words for the ME and all PARs are given in Tables 2.3 and 2.4.

The top 20 words of labor education policy documents are given in Table 2.3. The first column is the words of the ME policy document; while the remaining columns are for Tianjin, Shandong, Shanxi, Hainan, Sichuan, Jiangxi, and Guangxi. It can be seen from the table that labor and education are the first and second terms among the top words. This means that policy documents of the ME and 7 PARs refers to the same topic and discusses the topic in details in documents.

The word frequency of labor education policies is shown in Fig. 2.7. In the figure, the curve of the ME roughly overlaps with the curves of 7 PARs. This means that the policy documents are written in similar style. Moreover, it can be seen that the curve of Tianjin shows larger gap for the top 3 words compared with other PARs.

The top 20 words of study tour policy documents are given in Table 2.4. The structure of Table 2.4 is similar to that in Table 2.3. It can be seen from the table that tour and study are the first and second terms among the top words. This means that policy documents of the ME and 7 PARs refers to the same topic and discusses the

Table 2.3 Top 20 words of labor education policies of the ME and 7 PARs

ME	Tianjin	Shandong	Shanxi	Hainan	Sichuan	Jiangxi	Guangxi
Labor	Labor	Labor	Labor	Labor	Labor	Labor	Labor
Education	Education	Education	Education	Education	Education	Education	Education
Student	School	School	Practice	School	School	Practice	Student
Practice	Teacher	Society	School	Practice	Practice	School	School
School	Occupation	Student	Student	Student	Student	Curricular	Organize
Service	Normal	Strengthen	Carry out	Society	Service	Student	Society
Society	Construct	Practice	Society	Service	Society	Strengthen	Carry out
Spirit	Evaluation	Comment	Service	Carry out	Strengthen	Society	Practice
Activity	All-around	Service	Curricular	Occupation	Carry out	Evaluation	Strengthen
Carry out	Student	Teacher	Activity	Activity	Construction	Construct	Service
Occupation	Tianjin	All-around	Construct	Curricular	Construct	System	Occupation
Awareness	Practice	Combine	Occupation	Hainan	Volunteer	Carry out	Activity
Life	Profession	Safety	Strengthen	All-around	Teacher	Organize	Curricular
Organize	Measure	Carry out	Content	Cultivate	Implementation	Department	Implementation
Create	Bring into	New era	Construction	Combine	Organize	Construction	Teacher
Profession	Overall	Organize	Profession	Construction	System	Combine	Combine
Guide	Quality	System	Basis	Construct	Occupation	Implementation	Improve
Process	System	Shandong	Important	Skill	Curricular	Basement	Normal
Normal	Combine	Resource	Institution	Organize	Basement	Place	Spirit
Pay attention to	Development	Construct	Skill	Basis	Mechanism	Work	Awareness

Table 2.4 Top 20 words of study tour policies of the ME and 7 PARs

ME	Tianjin	Shandong	Shanxi	Hainan	Sichuan	Jiangxi	Guangxi
Tour	Study	Tour	Tour	Tour	Tour	Tour	Tour
Study	Tour	Study	Study	Study	Study	Study	Study
Student	Student	Student	Student	Student	Student	Student	Student
School	Work	Work	Education	Education	Safety	Education	Education
Education	Education	Safety	Department	Activity	Education	Safety	Activity
Safety	Activity	School	Work	Safety	Activity	Department	Safety
Department	Base	Shandong	Safety	Department	Sichuan	Activity	Department
Responsibility	Region	Implementation	School	Work	School	Responsibility	School
Carry out	ME	Activity	Base	School	Work	Carry out	Administration
Activity	School	Carry out	Carry out	Base	Department	School	Carry out
Development	Safety	Education	Culture	Responsibility	Administration	Work	Responsibility
Region	Culture	Construct	Activity	Administration	Carry out	Base	Base
Work	Resource	Department	Responsibility	Society	Responsibility	Culture	Work
Institution	Safeguard	Improve	Society	Carry out	Develop	Administration	Organize
Important	Design	Responsibility	Administration	Practice	Strengthen	Region	Guangxi
Society	Curricular	Mechanism	Shanxi	Hainan	Region	Jiangxi	Curricular
Mechanism	Parents	Base	Organize	Plan	Parents	Curricular	Culture
Safeguard	Department	Plan	Safeguard	All	Transportation	Safeguard	Parents
Administration	History	Curricular	Mechanism	Organize	Organize	Organize	Responsibility
Parents	Administration	Guide	Strengthen	Culture	Base	Red	Society

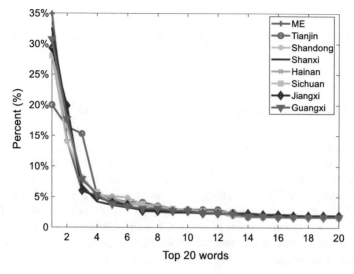

Fig. 2.7 Top 20 words for labor education policies

topic in details in documents. The third term is "student" for all documents, which means that the dominant position of students is highlighted in study tour policies.

The word frequency of labor education policies is shown in Fig. 2.8. In the figure, the curve of the ME roughly overlaps with the curves of 7 PARs. This means that the policy documents are written in similar style. Moreover, it can be seen that the curve of Tianjin shows larger gap for the top 2 words compared with other PARs.

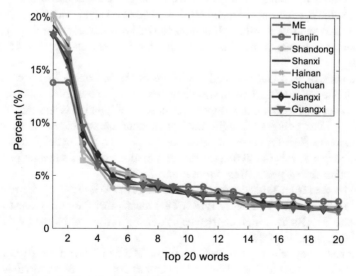

Fig. 2.8 Top 20 words for study tour policies

It can be seen from the two tables and figures that the word frequency of the ME and 7 PARs are very similar. Tianjin has lower word frequency for the top 2 or 3 words.

2.4.3   Consistency Analysis of Policy Documents

The consistency refers to the similarities between policies of the ME and each PAR. If a PAR developed a policy document to a large extent following the policy of the ME, then the consistency of the PAR would maintain greater consistency; otherwise, the consistency of a PAR would be less compared with the policy of the ME.

Based on top K words, consistency C is quantified from five aspects. The five aspects include (1) content, (2) purpose, (3) implementation, (4) support and (5) evaluation. Each aspect is assumed to be of the same importance. Hence, consistency is a form of percentage [0, 100]%. Mathematically, consistency is defined as:

$$C = \sum_{j=1}^{5} a_j. \tag{2.3}$$

The value of a aspect a_i is computed by:

$$a_i = \frac{number\ of\ words\ belong\ to\ the\ aspect}{K}. \tag{2.4}$$

The number of words belongs to a aspect is counted based on top K words. Then the value a_i is computed based on (2.4). The consistency value C is computed based on (2.3) and five a_i values. It is probably that a_i value computed by (2.4) may be greater or less than 20%. This means that the five aspects may not have equal percentage.

The consistency of labor education policies of the ME and 7 PARs are given in Table 2.5. For policy of the ME, the implementation aspect has 25%, which is greater than the other four aspects; the support aspect has 10%, which is less than the other four aspects. For policy of Tianjin, the implementation aspect has 35%, which is greater than the other four aspects; the support aspect has 5%, which is less than the other four aspects. It is found that the implementation aspect has greater percentage than the other four aspects. This is true for all 7 PARs.

It can be seen from Table 2.5 that the percentage of the five aspects is greater than or equal to 5% for the ME and 7 PARs. This means that the policy documents of the ME and 7 PARs have high consistency. All aspects are considered by 7 PARs to follow the suggestion of the ME.

The consistency of study tour policies of the ME and 7 PARs are given in Table 2.6. For policies of the ME and Tianjin, the support aspect has 30%, which is greater than the other four aspects. For the remaining 6 PARs, the implementation aspect has

Table 2.5 Consistency of labor education policies of the ME and 7 PARs

ME/PAR	a_1^{PAR} (%)	a_2^{PAR} (%)	a_3^{PAR} (%)	a_4^{PAR} (%)	a_5^{PAR} (%)	C (%)
ME	20	20	25	10	15	90
Tianjin	15	20	35	5	20	95
Shandong	15	10	45	15	10	95
Shanxi	20	15	25	20	10	90
Hainan	15	15	35	15	10	90
Sichuan	15	10	40	20	5	90
Jiangxi	15	5	45	25	10	100
Guangxi	15	20	40	10	10	95

Table 2.6 Consistency of study tour policies of the ME and 7 PARs

ME/PAR	a_1^{PAR} (%)	a_2^{PAR} (%)	a_3^{PAR} (%)	a_4^{PAR} (%)	a_5^{PAR} (%)	C (%)
ME	15	10	25	30	20	100
Tianjin	15	10	20	30	10	90
Shandong	25	5	40	20	10	100
Shanxi	15	10	35	25	15	100
Hainan	20	10	40	20	10	100
Sichuan	15	10	40	20	10	95
Jiangxi	20	10	35	15	15	95
Guangxi	20	10	30	25	10	95

greater percentage compared with the other four aspects. It is found that the purpose aspect has smaller percentage than the other four aspects. This is true for the ME and 7 PARs.

It can be seen from Table 2.6 that the percentage of the five aspects is greater than or equal to 5% for the ME and 7 PARs. This means that the policy documents of the ME and 7 PARs have high consistency. All aspects are considered by 7 PARs to follow the suggestion of the ME.

2.4.4 Uniqueness Analysis of Policy Documents

The uniqueness refers to the dissimilarities and specificities between policies of the ME and each PAR. If a PAR developed a policy document having differences from the policy of the ME, then the differences of the PAR would be the specificities compared with the ME.

Alike to consistency metric, uniqueness of policies U_i is defined based on top K words. Mathematically, uniqueness is defined as:

Table 2.7 Uniqueness of labor education policies of ME and 7 PARs

ME (%)	Tianjin (%)	Shandong (%)	Shanxi (%)	Hainan (%)	Sichuan (%)	Jiangxi (%)	Guangxi (%)
10	5	5	10	10	10	0	5

Table 2.8 Uniqueness of study tour policies of the ME and 7 PARs

ME (%)	Tianjin (%)	Shandong (%)	Shanxi (%)	Hainan (%)	Sichuan (%)	Jiangxi (%)	Guangxi (%)
0	10	0	0	0	5	5	5

$$U_i = \frac{number\ of\ words\ not\ belong\ to\ the\ five\ aspects}{K}, \tag{2.5}$$

where i stands for the ME and 7 PARs.

The uniqueness of labor education policies of the ME and 7 PARs are given in Table 2.7. For policies of the ME, Shanxi, Hainan and Sichuan, the uniqueness takes 10%; the uniqueness takes 5% for Tianjin, Shandong and Guangxi. The uniqueness of Jiangxi takes 0%, which means that the policy of Jiangxi does not have uniqueness compared with the five aspects in the last subsection.

For the ME, the uniqueness refers to keywords "occupation" and "pay attention to" as listed in Table 2.4. Hence, the U_i value for the ME is 10%. For Tianjin and Guangxi, the uniqueness refers to "occupation". For Shanxi, the uniqueness refers to "occupation" and "institution". For Hainan, the uniqueness refers to "occupation" and "skill". For Sichuan, the uniqueness refers to "volunteer" and "occupation". It can be seen that keyword "occupation" causes high uniqueness. It differs from the five aspects as mentioned in the last subsection.

The uniqueness of study tour policies of the ME and 7 PARs are given in Table 2.8. For policies of Tianjin, the uniqueness takes 10%; the uniqueness takes 5% for Sichuan, Jiangxi and Guangxi. The uniqueness of the ME, Shandong, Shanxi and Hainan takes 0%, which means that their policy does not have uniqueness compared with the five aspects in the last subsection.

For Tianjin, the uniqueness refers to "design" and "history" keywords as listed in Table 2.4. Hence, the U_i value for Tianjin is 10%. For Sichuan, the uniqueness refers to "transportation". For Guangxi, the uniqueness refers to "responsibility".

2.5 Summary

In this chapter, the policy documents of the ME and 7 PARs about labor education and study tour are analyzed and discussed. Text analysis method is applied to identify the top keywords from the documents. Matlab software is used to implement word cutting, keyword extraction and word frequency computation. A sequence of 20 keywords is extracted from each document. The policy documents of each PAR and the policy documents of the ME have the same keywords, but also have different keywords. Based on the observation and contents, the same keywords are classified as "consistency", and the different keywords are classified as "uniqueness". Then the frequency of these keywords and the proportion of the 20 keywords extracted from the documents are shown in tables and figures.

It is concluded that the 7 PARs keep s high consistency with the ME in policy-making. Moreover, more uniqueness is observed compared the labor education policies and study tour policies. There are 34 provincial administrative regions in China, which means that most regions are not discussed in the chapter. This is because that the remaining regions do not publish their policy documents of both labor education and study tour. A further discussion about more regions would be continued in future.

Acknowledgements This paper was supported by the Tianjin Normal University "Artificial Intelligence + Education" United Foundation.

References

1. Xinhua: China to promote labor education in schools. https://global.chinadaily.com.cn/a/201907/09/WS5d2479dea3105895c2e7c8e0.html (2019)
2. Xinhua: Study tours, camps gaining in popularity. http://www.chinadaily.com.cn/cndy/2019-09/13/content_37509866.htm (2019)
3. H. Wang, X. Wang, Review and reflection on the development of labor education in primary and secondary schools in China. J. Hebei Normal Univ. (Edu. Sci.) **22**(3), 36–45 (2020)
4. Ministry of Education of the People's Republic of China: Guidelines for labor education in primary, middle school and university. http://www.moe.gov.cn/srcsite/A26/jcj_kcjcgh/202007/t20200715_472808.html (2020)
5. L. Huang, C. Gu, Q. Ma, Time-space diversion and future prospects of the development of labor education in China. Vocat. Tech. Edu. **41**(10), 6–12 (2020)
6. J. Li, A review on research of study tour in China in the past five years. J. Beijing Inst. Edu. **31**(6), 13–19 (2017)
7. Z. Li, Reflections on study tour services in public libraries in the era of culture and tourism integration. Library Word and Study **10**, 18–24 (2019)
8. Davis, M., Chapman, C.: Unicode Standard Annex #29 Unicode text segmentation. https://www.unicode.org/reports/tr29/ (2020)
9. International components for unicode documentation: boundary analysis. https://unicode-org.github.io/icu/userguide/boundaryanalysis (2021)
10. N.S. Mohd Nafis, S. Awang, An enhanced hybrid feature selection technique using term frequency-inverse document frequency and support vector machine-recursive feature elimination for sentiment classification. IEEE Access **9**, 52177–52192 (2021)
11. J. Rashid et al., Topic modeling technique for text mining over biomedical text corpora through hybrid inverse documents frequency and fuzzy k-means clustering. IEEE Access **7**, 146070–146080 (2019)

Chapter 3
Classroom Teaching Behavior Analysis Based on Artificial Intelligence

Sumeng Shi, Jie Gao, and Wei Wang

Abstract The integration of information technology and education has effectively promoted the improvement of the quality of education and teaching. However, traditional classroom teaching behavior analysis still uses manual observation methods, which is not only inefficient, but also subjectively affected by observers. To solve this problem, this paper uses the Mini-XCEPTION Networks model and the Long Short-Term Memory (LSTM) Networks model to put forward the classroom teaching behavior analysis based on artificial intelligence around two aspects of teacher expression and classroom atmosphere in the teaching process. This method greatly reduces the workload of statistical data and the impact of subjective judgment. In face expression recognition, we use the separable convolution depth and face recognition technology, real-time analysis of changes in the expression of teachers. For speech emotion recognition, we fused Mini-XCEPTION network model and the LSTM network model, by extracting features of speech mel-spectrogram, real-time analysis of changes in the classroom atmosphere. Through the final analysis results, teachers can fully grasp the classroom dynamics, create positive emotional communication in teacher-student interaction, and better optimize their classroom teaching behavior.

Keywords Classroom teaching behavior · Mini-XCEPTION · LSTM · Facial expression recognition · Speech emotion recognition

3.1 Introduction

With the popularization of education informatization and the update of emerging technologies, AI promote the development of the field of education. The "Notice of the State Council on Issuing the Development Plan for the New Generation of Artificial Intelligence" emphasizes to construct a new education system that includes intelligent learning and interactive learning. Classroom is an important place for

S. Shi · J. Gao · W. Wang (✉)
College of Artificial Intelligence, Tianjin Normal University, Tianjin 300387, China
e-mail: weiwang@tjnu.edu.cn

teaching research and teaching activities. Discovering teaching problems in real classrooms is the primary task of current research.

The teacher's emotional literacy is embodied in the teacher's understanding of students' emotional experience, the maintenance of the teaching emotional environment, and the process of emotional interaction with students [1]. Teaching is not only a cognitive activity, but also an emotional practice. Teachers' emotional state has an important impact on students' learning status and classroom teaching effectiveness. A positive classroom atmosphere can promote students' acceptance of teaching content and shorten the distance between teachers and students [2].

In the mid-1990s, teachers' emotion is presented as a formal research question. Sutton, Becker and Arguedas [3–5] studied the influence of different teachers' emotions in the classroom on students. Sutton explored the relationship between teachers' emotion and classroom teaching effectiveness and proved negative emotions will directly decline teaching effectiveness [6]. Mostly traditional measure of teachers' emotions based on subjective experience. Therefore, the results will inevitably be affected by the impact. With the development of computer technology and the popularization of education informatization, some scholars apply AI technology to research. Evaggelos collected the classroom teaching voice data and used Support Vector Machines (SVM) algorithm to detect the emotions of students to help teacher master class status [7]. But he ignored the impact of teacher's emotion on the classroom. Liang used the Recurrent Neural Networks (RNN) algorithm to establish a teacher evaluation system by extracting Mel Frequency Cepstral Coefficients (MFCC) [8].

Our research uses the analysis of classroom teacher's teaching behavior as a breakthrough, aims at the emotional communication in the teacher-student interaction in classroom teaching and constructs a classroom teaching analysis system based on AI technology. Under the existing classroom teaching behavior analysis framework, facial expression recognition technology and speech recognition technology are used to identify and analyze teacher emotions and interactive atmosphere respectively. It promotes the application of new AI technology in classroom teaching analysis, and reduce the difficulty of classroom teaching analysis. By actively optimizing classroom teaching behavior, teachers can improve the quality of classroom teaching and promote the sound development of education.

The rest of the paper is arranged as follows. Section 3.2 introduces the emotion recognition based on expressions and introduces the Mini-XCEPTION Networks model and teacher expression recognition system flow and implementation code in detail. Section 3.3 introduces the speech emotion recognition, LSTM Networks structure, speech recognition system flow and implementation code. Section 3.4 shows the application of the system in teaching videos, and analyzes the teacher's facial expressions and the classroom atmosphere generated during the teaching process. Section 3.5 concludes the research work of this paper, reflects on the deficiencies in the research, and looks forward to the future research work.

3.2 Classroom Teacher Teaching Analysis System Based on Emotion Recognition of Expressions

With the rapid development of deep learning and AI technology, more and more researchers are applying deep learning to emotion recognition. For emotion recognition, the most important part is feature extraction. Traditional methods need to design a feature by themselves. Deep learning can select appropriate features according to the target's loss function, no longer rely on complex image preprocessing, and has better robustness in the face of problems caused by lighting, posture, and occlusions. The performance of deep learning is related to the size of its neural network and the amount of training data. In recent years, innovations in the structure of neural networks have promoted the development of deep learning, such as Convolutional Neural Networks (CNN), RNN, and LSTM Networks.

3.2.1 Mini-XCEPTION Networks Model

Mini-XCEPTION [9] is one of the current mainstream convolutional neural network models. The XCEPTION model is an improved lightweight network model based on Inception V3 [10]. It uses deep separable convolution to replace traditional convolution operations, greatly reducing network parameters. For a M*M pixel, the number of channels is N (N = 1, 2, 3…) images through k*k (k = 1, 3, 5…) convolution kernel layer, under the condition that the number of output channels is N + 1, the number of parameters of this convolution layer:

$$S_C = k \times k \times N(N+1) = k^2(N^2 + N) \tag{3.1}$$

The depth Separable Convolution parameter is obtained by adding two parts of Depthwise Convolution and Pointwise Convolution, where:

$$S_{depthwise} = k \times k \times N = k^2 N \tag{3.2}$$

$$S_{pointwise} = 1 \times 1 \times N(N+1) = N^2 + N \tag{3.3}$$

$$S_{sep} = S_{depthwise} + S_{pointwise} = N^2 + k^2(N+1) \tag{3.4}$$

It can be seen from Eqs. (3.1) and (3.4) that when N > 0, the number of parameters brought by the traditional convolution operation is greater than the number of parameters brought by the depth separable convolution.

When the depth of the neural network increases, the depth separable convolution can greatly reduce the number of parameters in the network. In addition,

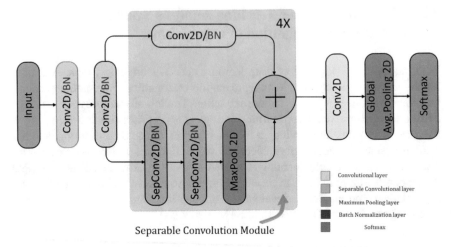

Fig. 3.1 Mini-XCEPTION structure diagram

XCEPTION introduces a residual connection mechanism [11], which has significantly improved the convergence speed and recognition accuracy of the network. The Mini-XCEPTION model is compressed on the basis of XCEPTION, and the model structure is shown in Fig. 3.1.

It contains four deep Separable Convolution modules. After each convolution layer, a Batch Normalization layer is used. The Batch Normalization layer can accelerate the network training and convergence. In addition, the Relu function is used as the activation function; The Maximum Pooling layer is connected behind each convolutional layer. The last layer of convolutional layer is added with a Global Average Pooling layer, which can prevent the network from overfitting and reduce the parameters; then the softmax layer is used for expression classification.

3.2.2 Teacher Expression Recognition System

In the teacher facial expression recognition system, we can use the facial expressions collected by the terminal to preprocess the collected data and send it to our trained Mini-XCEPTION network for feature extraction, and finally output predictions through classification result. The flow of the facial expression recognition system is shown in Fig. 3.2.

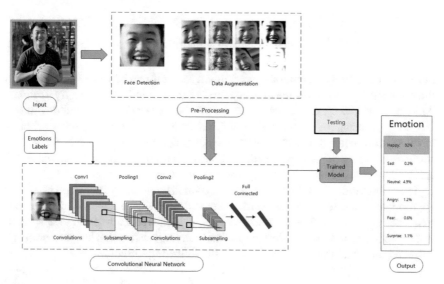

Fig. 3.2 Face expression recognition schematic illustration

The main code of the program is as follows:

Input: A image **X**, $X \in R^{m \times m}$, Mini-XCEPTION neural network weights **W**

Output: The prediction P, emoticon recognition result image Y

Begin:

1. Read image **X**
2. Image grayscale processing:

$$x_{Gray}(i, \; j) = \frac{\left[x_{Red}(i, \; j) + x_{Green}(i, \; j) + x_{Bule}(i, \; j) \right]}{3}$$

3. Detect the face information in the image $y' = (x_1, x_2 \ldots x_n)$
    if $y' > 0$ then
        sort x_n from smallest to largest, $y' = x_{largest}$
    end if
4. Through cv2.resize(), convert y' to y, $y \ni R^{48*48}$
5. Load the weights, send y to the neural network for prediction, get **P** and **Y**

End

3.3 Classroom Teacher Teaching Analysis System Based on Speech Emotion Recognition

For speech emotion recognition, the common features can be roughly divided into three categories: prosodic features, spectral features, and voice quality features. Among them, the spectrum feature is one of the most popular artificial features. Due to the outstanding performance of CNN in image processing, some scholars have begun to convert speech signals into spectrograms and use CNN for feature extraction. Figure 3.3 shows the spectrograms of different emotions, in which the speech data comes from CASIA Chinese emotion corpus.

The information contained in the spectrogram is huge, and it is difficult to extract appropriate voice features. Converting the ordinary frequency scale to the Mel frequency scale can reduce the sensitivity to the high-frequency part of the speech, thereby reducing redundant information. The mapping relationship between ordinary frequency and Mel frequency is shown in the following formula:

$$mel(f) = 2595 \times \lg\left(1 + \frac{f}{700}\right) \tag{3.5}$$

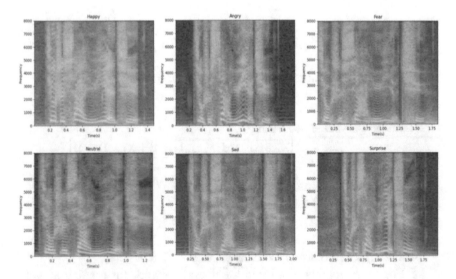

Fig. 3.3 Spectrograms of different emotions

3.3.1   LSTM Networks Model

CNN has a good effect when processing single-frame images, but for time series data such as voice information, we need to consider the time series relationship that exists between the frames. RNN has more advantages when processing sequence information, but it will have problems such as gradient explosion and gradient disappearance when processing sequence information with a long time. Hochreiter [10] proposed an LSTM model on the basis of RNN, LSTM increases gate structure composed of a more complex unit cell.

There are three gates in the LSTM unit: input gate σ_i, forget gate σ_f and output gate σ_o. Usually the gate structure is realized by Sigmoid function and dot multiplication. The LSTM unit controls the forgetting and storage of information transfer between units through these gate structures, and the status information of the unit is recorded by the cell status. x_t is the input of the current LSTM unit, h_t is the output of the current LSTM unit, c_t is the current state of the cell, h_{t-1} is the output of the previous LSTM unit, c_{t-1} is the state of the previous cell unit, i_t controls how much information can be stored in the current state of the cell. Among them W_{xi} is the weight of the input gate, W_{hi} is the cyclic weight of the input gate, and b_i is the bias of the input gate.

$$i_t = \sigma_i (W_{xi}x_t + W_{hi}h_{t-1} + b_i) \tag{3.6}$$

f_t determines how much information needs to be forgotten, as shown in Eq. (3.6). By Sigmoid function, forget gate can map the input to the interval [0, 1] at time t, 0 means that no information can be passed, 1 means all information can be passed. W_{xf} is the weight of the forget gate, W_{hf} is the cyclic weight of the forget gate, and b_f is the bias of the forget gate.

$$f_t = \sigma_f \left(W_{xf}x_t + W_{hf}h_{t-1} + b_f \right) \tag{3.7}$$

The update of the cell state requires the forgetting gate and the input gate to cooperate with each other. After forgetting part of the information, add new information through the input gate. The update process is as follows:

$$c_t = i_t \cdot \tanh(W_{xc}x_t + W_{hc}h_{t-1} + b) + f_t \cdot c_{t-1} \tag{3.8}$$

After c_t update, o_t decides to output the state characteristics of the current cell state according to h_{t-1} and x_t (Fig. 3.4).

$$O_t = \sigma_o(W_{xo}x_t + W_{ho}h_{t-1} + b_o) \tag{3.9}$$

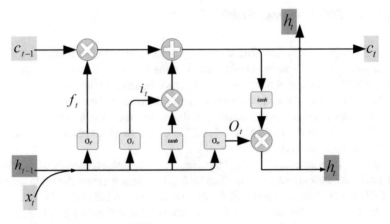

Fig. 3.4 Schematic diagram of LSTM unit

$$h_t = O_t \cdot \tanh(C_t) \tag{3.10}$$

3.3.2 Speech Emotion Recognition System

In speech recognition, we first perform endpoint detection on the speech data and remove the silent part. The processed speech is converted into a mel-spectrogram, which is split using a rolling window and then sent to CNN for feature extraction. Then the output of the CNN is sent to the LSTM network to obtain the relevant information of the context, and finally the emotion detected in the speech is predicted through the fully connected layer. The system flow is as follows (Fig. 3.5).

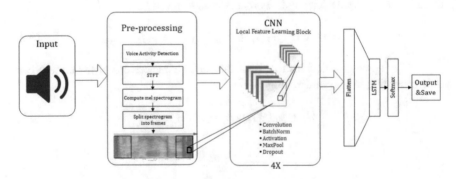

Fig. 3.5 Speech recognition schematic illustration

The main code of the program is as follows:

Input: Audio signal **X**, the weight of LSTM **W**
Output: The prediction P
Begin:
  1.   Remove the silent part of x by endpoint detecting
  2.   Compute the spectrogram of y
  3.   Convert to y mel-spectrogram y'

$$y' = 2595 \times \lg\left(1 + \frac{y}{700}\right)$$

  4.   Framing the signal through the Hamming window, win_step=64, win_size=128
  5.   Load **W**, send y' to the neural network for prediction, get **P**
  6.   Save the predictions
End

3.4   Experimental Results and Analysis

This paper studies an AI-based classroom teaching analysis system. The operating system used by the experimental institute is Windows10, the programming language is Python3.7, the experimental hardware parameters are R5-3600CPU and 16GDDR4 memory. The deep learning framework is Tensorflow2.0. The system is mainly divided into facial expression recognition module and voice emotion recognition module.

In this paper, we select the videos of the 2019 "One Teacher One Excellent Class, One Class One Teacher" activity as the research object. Among them, 40 high school math concept lessons are selected for teacher emotional analysis, with a total time of 1,800 min. Among them, high-quality video lessons are distributed in many provinces China to ensure the quality of samples and the diversity of national distribution. Taking into account the characteristics of facial expression changes and the reasonableness of data statistics, before starting the experiment, we adjusted the number of video frames, and the adjusted frame number was one frame per second.

According to the actual teaching situation, we have counted the number of teachers' "happy" and "natural" expressions. Combining the stages divided by the teaching framework, the system counts the number of times of "happy" and "natural" expressions in each stage. Figure 3.6 shows the average number of different facial expressions of teachers at each stage of the 40 high school math concept classes.

In speech recognition, we use teacher-student interaction data to characterize the classroom atmosphere for analysis. The classroom atmosphere is divided into three categories: "positive", "neutral" and "negative". The positive classroom atmosphere

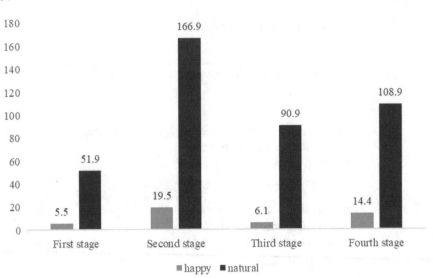

Fig. 3.6 The statistical average of the number of teacher expressions at different stages

is represented by 1, the neutral classroom atmosphere is represented by 0, and the negative classroom atmosphere is represented by −1. In the process of data statistics, we conduct observation and statistics every 30 s. Figure 3.7 shows the comprehensive scores of classroom atmosphere at different moments of 40 high school math video lessons. The abscissa in the image is the observation moment during the teaching process, and the ordinate is the score of the classroom atmosphere.

Figure 3.8 shows the teacher's facial expression changes at each stage of the teaching process in the "Trigonometric Function of Arbitrary Angle" lesson in high

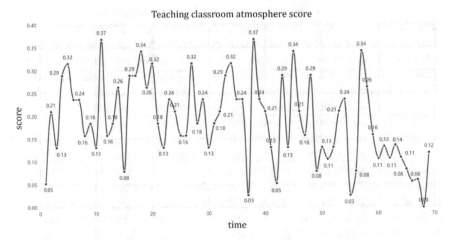

Fig. 3.7 Comprehensive scores of classroom atmosphere at different moments

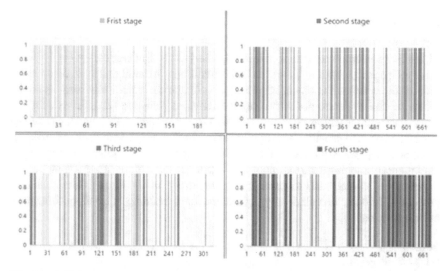

Fig. 3.8 A "Trigonometric Function of Arbitrary Angle" classroom teacher's expression changes

school mathematics of a school. Through the statistical data, we can intuitively see the change trend of the teacher's expression during the teaching process, which is helpful to grasp the teacher's emotional change in each stage of teacher-student interaction.

Figure 3.9 shows the difference between the classroom atmosphere score of the class and the overall classroom atmosphere score, which can help teachers visually see the teacher-student interaction at each moment and create a positive classroom atmosphere.

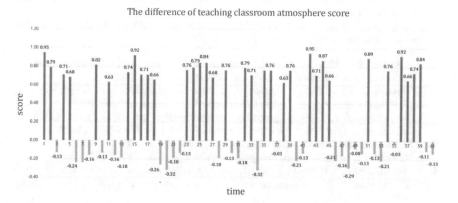

Fig. 3.9 Classroom atmosphere score of "Trigonometric Function of Arbitrary Angle"

3.5 Conclusion

This paper constructs a classroom teaching analysis system based on AI technology and applies it to practice. Compared with traditional manual analysis, this system reduces the workload of teachers' statistical data and can help teachers focus on the reflection and evaluation of classroom teaching. At the same time, the system can make classroom teaching behavior analysis normalized and scaled, and the accumulated data can also provide data support for teaching management decision-making. In the next step, we will increase the number of samples to supplement multiple types of classroom teaching samples and we will optimize the feature extraction method to improve the accuracy and robustness of recognition; finally, through the intelligent processing of data, we will deeply dig into the inner meaning of teaching behaviors, better serve teaching.

Acknowledgements The work was supported by the Natural Science Foundation of China (61731006, 61971310).

References

1. M. Zembylas, Emotional ecology: the intersection of emotional knowledge and pedagogical content knowledge in teaching. Teach. Teach. Educ. **23**, 355–367 (2007)
2. P. Ekman, W. Friesen, *The Repertoire of Nonverbal Behavior: Categories, Origins, Usage, and Coding Semiotica*, vol. 1, pp. 49–98 (1969)
3. R.E. Sutton, Teachers' anger, frustration, and self-regulation, in *Emotion in Education*, pp. 259–274 (Academic Press, 2007)
4. E.S. Becker, T. Goetz, V. Morger et al., The importance of teachers' emotions and instructional behavior for their students' emotions–an experience sampling analysis. Teach. Teach. Educ. **43**, 15–26 (2014)
5. M. Arguedas, A. Daradoumis, F. Xhafa, Analyzing how emotion awareness influences students' motivation, engagement, self-regulation and learning outcome. Educ. Technol. Soc. **19**, 87–103 (2016)
6. R.E. Sutton, K.F. Wheatley, Teachers' emotions and teaching: a review of the literature and directions for future research. Educ. Psychol. Rev. **15**, 327–358 (2003)
7. E. Spyrou, R. Nikopoulou, I. Vernikos et al., Emotion recognition from speech using the bag-of-visual words on audio segment spectrograms. Technologies **7**, 20 (2019)
8. L. Jie, Z. Xiaoyan, Z. Zhaohui, Speech emotion recognition of teachers in classroom teaching, in *2020 Chinese Control and Decision Conference (CCDC)*, pp. 5045–5050 (2020)
9. F. Chollet, Xception: deep learning with depthwise separable convolutions, in *IEEE Conference on Computer Vision and Pattern Recognition (CVPR)*, pp. 1800–1807 (2017)
10. S. Xie, R. Girshick, P. Dollár, Z. Tu, K. He, Aggregated residual transformations for deep neural networks, in *IEEE Conference on Computer Vision and Pattern Recognition (CVPR)*, pp. 5987–5995 (2017)
11. S. Hochreiter, J. Schmidhuber, Long short-term memory. Neural Comput. **9**, 1735–1780 (1997)

Chapter 4
Research on the Control of Redundancy Effect of Decorative Icons in Instructional PPT

Hui Yang Li, Qing Li, and Xue Wang

Abstract This study explored whether different correlations between decorative icons and text content in instructional PPT would have affect learners' learning experiences and learning outcomes, and whether some redundancy effect occurs. A sample of 120 college students were randomly divided into four groups: text-only group, icon-text low-related group, medium-related group, and high-related group. The results showed that: (1) learning material with decorative icons would generate higher cognitive load than text-only learning materials when correlation between icons and text was low, thus resulting in redundancy. (2) Learners would gain higher learning satisfaction and perceived achievement when icons are highly correlated with text. (3) Learners learn best when decorative icons are more relevant to text. (4) The higher the cognitive load learners experienced, the worse the learning experience and learning outcomes. Finally, suggestions are provided on the control of redundancy effect of decorative icons in designing instructional PPT.

Keywords Redundancy effect · Decorative icons · Cognitive load · Learning outcomes · Instructional PPT

4.1 Introduction

PowerPoint is the most important teaching method of multimedia teaching in the internet age. The intuitive and convenient features it offers make it a valuable demonstration tool for instruction. The decorative icons, with their image and concise features, are easy to attract people's attention, promote learners' interest in learning, and gradually become the "darling" of instructional PPT designers. At present, many instructional PPT designers pay more attention to the application of icons from visual

H. Y. Li · X. Wang (✉)
Faculty of Education, Tianjin Normal University, Tianjin 300387, China

Q. Li
Department of Foreign Languages, Chongqing University of Science and Technology, Chongqing, China

University of North Texas, Denton, USA

© The Author(s), under exclusive license to Springer Nature Singapore Pte Ltd. 2021   37
W. Wang et al. (eds.), *Artificial Intelligence in Education and Teaching Assessment*,
https://doi.org/10.1007/978-981-16-6502-8_4

aesthetics to make up for the empty image, and pay little attention to the relevance of icons to the text content, and less attention to the cognitive law of learners, so the icons selected do not necessarily help learners understand what they are learning, and may even cause redundancy effects.

Research by Han-Chin Liu and Hsueh-Hua Chuang found that decorative icons do attract learners' attention, making it harder for them to process the target content [1]. Paul's experiments showed that icons with decorative value but lack of distinguishability and clarity are too abstract to convey information accurately [2]. The redundancy effect was first proposed by Professor Mayer, who found that on-screen text of concise narrated animation caused redundancy [3]. Sweller demonstrated the redundancy effect within the cognitive load framework, and the experiments he conducted indicate that when images and text appear simultaneously, cognitive resources may be used for images rather than text, making learning effect worse [4]. Research on redundancy effect has mainly focused on instructional video, courseware and teaching animation, but quite few on the control of redundancy effect of decorative icons in instructional PPT.

This experimental research intends to explore whether decorative icons, when not related to text content, have any impact on learners' learning experience and learning outcomes, and cause a certain redundancy effect. Based on the research findings, some feasible suggestions will be proposed to help control redundancy effect of decorative icons in instructional PPT design.

In this experiment, data indicators of learning effectiveness, cognitive load, learning satisfaction and perceived achievement were used to evaluate the redundancy effect of decorative icons in PPT. Therefore, the following hypotheses are proposed.

H1: Learning materials with decorative icons (i.e. low relevance, medium relevance, high relevance) produce higher cognitive load for learners than text-only learning materials.

H2: Learning materials with decorative icons (i.e. low relevance, medium relevance, high relevance) produce higher learning satisfaction and perceived achievement for learners than text-only learning materials.

H3: Learning materials with decorative icons (i.e. low relevance, medium relevance, high relevance) lead to better learning outcomes.

H4: The higher the cognitive load, the worse the learning experience and learning effect.

4.2   Method

4.2.1   Experimental Design

4.2.1.1   Independent Variables

Control group: text-only group.

Experimental group: icon-text low-related group, medium-related group and high-related group.

4.2.1.2   Dependent Variables

This experiment measures the effect of redundancy by two indicators: learning experience and learning effect.

Learning effect: including retention test and transfer test.

Learning experience: including cognitive load, learning satisfaction, and perceived achievement. Cognitive load covers perceived material difficulty and mental effort. Learning satisfaction includes learning process satisfaction and decorative icon design satisfaction.

4.2.1.3   Control Variables

The participants' prior knowledge level.

4.2.2   Experimental Materials and Measures

There are four learning materials, the topic of which is geography (weather and climate) for 7th grade students. The content is mainly about the formation causes of various natural phenomena. The four learning materials were all produced with the software of PowerPoint, and the content is about the causes of hail, clouds, thunderstorm, sleet, and dust storms. All four materials are comprised of six slides with identical text of 480 words, one of which was designed in a full text mode, while the other three were presented with icons of varying degrees of relevance. The icon size, type, and position of the icons were set to be exactly the same.

Basic information questionnaires: To find out demographic information including the age, sex, and major, and to understand students' recognition and attention to the decorative icons in the instructional PPT.

Prior knowledge test questionnaires: to ensure that the level of the prior knowledge of the four groups was basically identical, and the prior knowledge of the participants had no influence on the experimental results. In the first part of the questionnaire, 5 questions were set, and the participants were required to choose according to their familiarity with the theme, from "not at all" (0 points) to "very familiar" (4 points); in the second part, 6 questions were set, the first 5 being single choice questions, and the 6th a question-and-answer item. The first part is a total of 20 points and the second part has a total of 10 points.

Learning effectiveness test questionnaires: The questionnaires were designed according to the contents of the instructional PPT, including retention test and transfer test. Types of questions included single-choice questions, fill-in-the-blank, and question-and-answer questions. The retention test consisted of 7 single-choice questions, each with a score of 5 points. The transfer test consisted of 5 question-and-answer questions, each with a score of 10 points. The total test was 85 points.

Cognitive load questionnaires: The cognitive load scale was designed by Pass, comprising of two aspects: the perceived material difficulty (on a scale of 1–9, 1 indicating "very simple", 9 meaning "very difficult"), and mental effort (on a scale of 1–9, 1 indicating least effort, 9 meaning "the most effort").

Learning satisfaction questionnaires: Using a 7-point Likert scale (1–7, 1 indicating "strongly dislike", 7 meaning "strongly like") were used to investigate the satisfaction level of "Learning process of studying instructional PPT materials" and "design of decorative icon design in the instructional PPT".

Perceived achievement questionnaires: Using a 7-point Likert scale (1–7, 1 indicating "very bad", 7 being "very good"), with the question "How do you think you performed on the test?".

4.2.3 Participants

As the subjects of the experiment, 120 students recruited from Tianjin Normal University were randomly divided into four groups, each containing 30 participants. There was no difference in the level of prior knowledge among the subjects ($F = 0.037$, $p = 0.990 > 0.05$). The majority of the subjects showed a high degree of attention and recognition to the decorative icons, believing that they were simple and easy to understand, interesting, and more conducive to learning compared with materials without any icons.

4.2.4 Experimental Procedures

Participants were randomly selected to fill basic information questionnaires and the prior knowledge test questionnaires, which were used to screen the subjects who had a level of prior knowledge too high or too low, and to ensure their pre-test knowledge level was basically consistent.

Participants were asked to read PPT learning materials and study the content according to specific requirements.

After the learning, the participants completed the corresponding learning effectiveness test questionnaires, cognitive load questionnaires, learning satisfaction questionnaires, and perceived achievement questionnaires. They were informed of some matters needing attention before filling in the questionnaires.

The experiment was over.

4.3 Results

The average scores of learning performance, cognitive load, learning satisfaction and perceived achievement of each group were shown in Table 4.1. The correlation analysis was shown in Table 4.2.

4.3.1 Cognitive Load

To investigate the effect of the correlation between decorative icons and text on the cognitive load of learners, one-factorial ANOVAs and LSD test were conducted, the results showed that the correlation between decorative icons and text significantly affected the perceived material difficulty ($F = 63.587$, $p = 0.001 < 0.05$) and the mental effort ($F = 97.009$, $p = 0.002 < 0.05$), the low-related group < text-only group < medium-related group < high-related group (as shown in Table 4.1).

4.3.2 Learning Satisfaction and Perceived Achievement

To examine the effect of the correlation between decorative icons and text on learners' learning satisfaction and perceived achievement, one-way ANOVAs and LSD test were conducted, and the results showed that the degree of correlation between decorative icons and text had a significant effect on learners' learning satisfaction ($F = 6.138$, $p = 0.012 < 0.05$), perceived achievement ($F = 24.889$, $p = 0.001 < 0.05$), and the low-related group < text-only group < medium-related group < high-related group (as shown in Table 4.1).

4.3.3 Learning Outcomes

To investigate the effect of the correlation between decorative icons and text on learners' learning outcomes, one-way ANOVAs and LSD test were conducted, the

Table 4.1 Experiment results of each group

Measure			The degree of correlation between decorative icons and text							
			Plain text		Low correlation		Moderate correlation		High correlation	
			M	SD	M	SD	M	SD	M	SD
Learning performance	Retention		16.83	10.379	12.50	7.628	17.83	8.375	22.33	9.072
	Transfer		12.93	4.835	9.13	8.705	18.97	10.186	21.17	11.709
Learning experience	Cognitive load	Effort	17.17	2.705	29.27	5.099	16.40	5.834	12.03	6.322
		Difficulty	17.13	2.700	27.43	6.699	15.90	5.498	10.90	6.666
	Learning satisfaction	Process	3.87	0.819	3.23	1.569	4.87	0.937	5.60	1.499
		Icons	–	–	2.60	1.499	5.00	0.788	6.47	0.629
	Perceived achievement		3.17	1.147	2.63	0.999	3.80	1.297	4.73	1.680

Table 4.2 Correlations analysis

		Retention	Transfer	Learning satisfaction	Perceived achievement
Perceived material difficulty	Pearson correlation	−0.302	−0.311	−0.551	−0.482
	Sig. (two-side)	0.001	0.001	0.000	0.000
	N	120	120	120	120
Mental effort	Pearson correlation	−0.318	−0.341	−0.475	−0.564
	Sig. (two-side)	0.000	0.000	0.000	0.000
	N	120	120	120	120

results showed that the correlation between decorative icons and text significantly affected the retention ($F = 6.138, p = 0.001 < 0.05$) and transfer ($F = 10.734, p = 0.012 < 0.05$), the low-related group < text-only group < medium-related group < high-related group (as shown in Table 4.1).

4.3.4   Correlation Analysis

A Correlation Analysis between cognitive load and learning effect, learning satisfaction, and perceived achievement was shown in Table 4.2.

There was a significant negative correlation between cognitive load and learning effect (perceived material difficulty and retention test: $r = −0.318 < 0, p = 0.000 < 0.05$, mental effort and retention test: $r = −0.318 < 0, p = 0.000 < 0.05$, perceived material difficulty and transfer test: $r = −0.311 < 0, p = 0.001 < 0.05$, mental effort and transfer test: $r = −0.341 < 0, p = 0.000 < 0.05$).

Then, there was a significant negative correlation between cognitive load and learning satisfaction (perceived material difficulty and learning satisfaction: $r = −0.482 < 0, p = 0\ 0.005 < 0.05$, mental effort and learning satisfaction $= −0.475 < 0, p = 0\ 0.000 < 0.05$).

Besides, a significant negative correlation between cognitive load and perceived achievement was revealed (perceived material difficulty and perceived achievement: $r = −0.482 < 0, p = 0\ 0.005 < 0.05$, mental effort and perceived achievement: $r = −0.564 < 0, p = 0\ 0.001 < 0.05$).

4.4   Discussion and Conclusion

4.4.1   Empirical Findings

This study explored whether different correlation between decorative icons and text content in instructional PPT have an impact on the learners' learning experience and learning outcomes, and whether some redundancy effect occurs. The experimental results showed that when the correlation between decorative icons and text was low, the learning materials with decorative icons had higher cognitive load than the text-only learning materials, which resulted in the redundancy effect. When the correlation between decorative icons and text was high or medium, the learning materials with decorative icons tend to produce higher learning satisfaction and perceived achievement for learners. When the relationship between decorative icons and text was low, the group that studied materials with decorative icons had lower learning satisfaction and perceived achievement compared with the text-only group. When the correlation between decorative icons and text was high or medium, the group with decorative icons had the highest retention and transfer scores, and when the correlation between decorative icons and text was low, the retention and transfer scores of the decorative icons group were significantly lower than the text-only group. There was a significant negative correlation between cognitive load and learning effect, learning satisfaction and perceived achievement. The experimental results verified hypothesis 4, and hypothesis 1, 2 and 3 were partially confirmed. Therefore, it could be concluded that if the decorative icons were highly related to the text content in the instructional PPT, the use of icons would not cause redundancy effect, but would be beneficial to the effective transmission of instructional information and improving the learners' learning experience and learning outcomes; if the correlation between icon and text was low, the extraneous cognitive load would increase, which would produce a certain redundancy effect.

4.4.2   Theoretical Implications

Theoretically, the findings of our study support dual coding theory and cognitive load theory. According to the dual coding theory, when the presented material is textual content, the learner would construct a mental representation of the textual information in short-term memory, i.e., semantic encoding. Similarly, when the material was presented by decorative icons, the learner constructed mental representations of the decorative icon in short-term memory, i.e., representation coding [5]. It was difficult to establish a correlation between the psychological representation of the text by the semantic system and the psychological representation of the decorative icon by the representation system when the text content in the instructional PPT picture was matched with low-related icons, which in turn makes the learning task more difficult, with limited cognitive resources to consume for the learners, and the thus formed extraneous cognitive load [4]. As learners use more cognitive resources thinking about what the icons meant, they paid less attention to the text content, which resulted in lower learning effect.

4.4.3   Practical Implications

The results of this research revealed that when the relationship between decorative icons and text was high, the learners have lower cognitive load and better learning satisfaction, perceived achievement and learning effect. Therefore, when designing instructional PPT, priority should be given to application of decorative icons that are highly relevant to the content of the text. However, for text content that is more abstract or difficult to find decorative icons with higher relevance, it would be more beneficial to learner's learning experience and learning outcomes to not apply any icons. Since instructional PPT is one of the most important multimedia learning and teaching mediums in the internet age, designers should take the learner-centered approach, taking full consideration of the characteristics of the learner's cognitive law, and aim at promoting the learner's learning to ensure that the selection of decorative can both be highly compatible with the text and produce aesthetic effect to effectively transfer instructional information and reduce the redundant effect.

4.5   Limitations and Future Research

In this study, only 120 participants were selected and the population was not sufficiently diverse. Future research directions might be toward expanding the sample size, giving more consideration to learners' characteristics (such as age, ethnicity, culture background). In addition, this study only set up the cognitive-behavior experiment due to time and space limitation, and did not incorporate the eye-tracking approach, which to some extent neglected the real situation of the learners' cognitive processing.

Acknowledgements Thanks are due to funding by MOE (Ministry of Education in China) Project of Humanities and Social Sciences (foundation no. 19YJC880090) and Key Cultivation Projects of Tianjin Teaching Achievement Award (foundation no. PYGJ-014).

References

1. H.C. Liu, H.H. Chuang, An examination of cognitive processing of multimedia information based on viewers' eye movements. Interact. Learn. Environ. **19**(5), 503–517 (2011)
2. P.R. Seesing, Icons-communication tool or decorative art? in *International Professional Communication Conference' Communicating to the World* (IEEE, 1989), pp. 142–146
3. R.E. Mayer, Multimedia learning. Psychol. Learn. Motiv. **41**, 85–139 (2002)
4. J. Sweller, Cognitive load theory[M]//Psychology of learning and motivation. Academic Press **55**, 37–76 (2011)
5. J.M. Clark, A. Paivio, Dual coding theory and education. Educ. Psychol. Rev. **3**(3), 149–210 (1991)

Chapter 5
Research on the Influence of Quantity and Emotion of Danmaku in Online Instructional Video on Learning

Yu Wei Cheng, Qing Li, and Xue Wang

Abstract This study explored the influence of Danmuku (bullet-screen comments) on learning experience and learning outcomes based on the number of comments and the emotional information contained. A sample of 107 college students were randomly divided into 4 groups: group with more bullet comments, group with less bullet comments, group with positive emotion, and group with neutral emotion. Learners' learning experience (emotion, cognitive load, social presence, learning satisfaction) and learning outcomes (retention test scores, transfer test scores and total test scores) were measured. The results showed that: (1) In terms of learning experience: instructional videos with a large number of bullet comments could significantly improve learner's positive emotions and psychological effort; instructional video with bullet comments containing positive emotion could suppress the learner's negative emotions. (2) In terms of learning effects: instructional videos with a large number of bullet comments could significantly improve learners' retention test scores, transfer test scores and total test scores. (3) Correlation analysis results showed that: the more positive emotion a learner experiences, the better the learning experience and learning outcomes. Finally, suggestions are provided on selection and optimization of bullet comments attached to online instructional video.

Keywords Online instructional video · Danmaku · Emotion · Learning outcomes

5.1 Introduction

The origin of "Danmaku" (also known as bullet screen or bullet comments) is from Niconico, a Japanese animation website. It was firstly applied to entertainment videos in China, and now has become a feature widely used in classroom teaching and online

Y. W. Cheng · X. Wang (✉)
Faculty of Education, Tianjin Normal University, Tianjin 300387, China

Q. Li
Department of Foreign Languages, Chongqing University of Science and Technology, Chongqing, China

University of North Texas, Denton, USA

© The Author(s), under exclusive license to Springer Nature Singapore Pte Ltd. 2021
W. Wang et al. (eds.), *Artificial Intelligence in Education and Teaching Assessment*,
https://doi.org/10.1007/978-981-16-6502-8_5

instruction. Under the influence of the global pandemic, online education and online learning have been carried out worldwide. How to improve and optimize online instruction to catch up with the development of times and learners has become an important research question that needs to be addressed in the epidemic context.

Danmaku's use in online teaching has been found to direct learners' attention, enhance their presence, and improve their performance due to its immediate inter-activity [1]. Most of the existing research on the number and emotion of Danmaku focused on online video communication. For example, Wang found that the amount of Danmaku can reflect the user's willingness to participate in discussions to some extent [2]. Chen said that the more Danmaku floating across a video, the more inter-esting it turned out to be [3]. Bai and Hu have classified the emotional information contained in Danmaku into three categories: neutral, positive and negative based on the emotional analysis of Danmaku text [4]. Li demonstrated through experiment that Danmaku can have different emotional effects on different videos [5]. Research at home and abroad shows that the intersections between Danmaku quantity and emotion with the field of online teaching require further exploration.

This study adopts the method of experimental research, exploring whether the number of Danmaku (more and less) and the emotions contained in Danmaku (positive and neutral) in online instructional videos have an impact on learners' learning experience (emotion, social presence, cognitive load, learning satisfaction) and learning outcomes. The purpose of this work is to provide a reference for the selection and management of Danmaku attached to an online instructional video.

On the basis of previous studies, three hypotheses are put forward:

H1: The number and emotion of Danmaku would significantly affect the learners' learning experience.

H2: The number and emotion of Danmaku would significantly affect the learners' learning outcomes.

H3: Positive emotions are positively correlated with learning outcomes.

5.2   Method

5.2.1   Experimental Design

5.2.1.1   Independent Variables

Number of Danmaku: more Danmaku, less Danmaku

Emotional information contained in Danmaku: Danmaku with positive emotion, Danmaku with neutral emotion.

5.2.1.2   Dependent Variables

Learning experience: emotion, cognitive load, social presence, learning satisfaction.

Learning outcomes: retention test scores, transfer test scores and total test scores.

5.2.1.3   Control Variables

Learners' prior knowledge.

5.2.2   Materials and Measures

The first material provided for the experiment is a set of four instructional videos with a duration of five minutes. All videos are about "How can Nucleic Acid Amplification Testing Efficiently Screen for the Presence of COVID-19?" Based on Python's emotional propensity analysis, Danmaku of the videos were categorized into three groups: positive, neutral, and negative. The group with more Danmaku had 650 bullet comments while the group with less had 100 bullet comments, both groups controlling for 60% of positive emotions. For the group with positive emotions, the share of positive emotion was 90%, and that of neutral emotions was 10%; for the group with neutral Danmaku, the share of neutral was 90%, 10% was positive emotions, and the number control of Danmaku was 200.

The second material is a prior knowledge questionnaire.

The third is a learning outcomes questionnaire, consisting of a retention test and a transfer test. The question items are comprised of single choice, multiple choice, and short answer questions. (Internal consistency reliability of the questionnaire is 0.773).

The fourth material is a learning experience questionnaire, including positive–negative emotion scale (positive internal consistency reliability is 0.85, negative internal consistency reliability is 0.84), social presence scale (the internal consistency reliability is 0.73), cognitive load scale (the internal consistency reliability is 0.74), and a learning satisfaction scale (the internal consistency reliability is 0.91).

5.2.3   Participants

As the subjects of the experiment, 107 undergraduates and graduate students with low prior knowledge levels were recruited from Tianjin Normal University. Prior knowledge and emotion among the four groups did not differ significantly.

5.2.4 Experimental Procedures

Step 1: Participants were asked to complete a prior knowledge test.
Step 2: Participants watched the instructional videos.
Step 3: Participants completed the tests on learning experience and learning outcomes.

5.3 Results

Data of the learning experiences and learning outcomes of participants from each group are shown in Table 5.1.

5.3.1 The Influence of the Danmaku Number and Emotion on Learners' Learning Experience

In order to explore the effects of the number of Danmaku (more or less) on learners' learning experience (emotion, cognitive load, learning satisfaction, social presence), an independent-samples T-test was adopted. The results showed that positive emotion ($t = 1.724, p = 0.091 < 0.1, d = 0.47$) and psychological effort ($t = 2.058, p = 0.045 < 0.05, d = 0.56$) were significantly affected. The negative emotion ($t = 0.849, p = 0.4 > 0.05$), material difficulty ($t = -1.333, p = 0.188 > 0.05$), related concept understanding ($t = -0.647, p = 0.521 > 0.05$), learning satisfaction ($t = 0.722, p = 0.649 > 0.05$), social presence ($t = -0.459, p = 0.649 > 0.05$) had no significant effect.

In order to explore the effect of Emotional information contained in Danmaku (positive, neutral) on learners' learning experience (emotion, cognitive load, learning satisfaction, and social presence), an independent-samples T-test was adopted. The results showed that there was no significant effect of Danmaku on the learning experience. By means of the rank sum test of paired samples before and after the experiment, it was found that the negative emotion ($z = -2.164$ c, $p = 0.03 > 0.05, d = 0.22$) in the positive Danmaku group had significant influence on the negative emotion before and after the experiment.

As can be seen from Table 5.1, the group with more Danmaku scored better than the one with less Danmaku on both positive emotion and psychological effort, indicating that more Danmaku in the online instructional video can stimulate learners' positive emotion, and the fact that learners put more psychological effort into learning with the instructional video with more Danmaku to achieve their learning goals. In the group categorized as positive emotion, the before and after test shows that negative emotions tended to decrease, which indicates that the learners had less negative emotions when watching online instructional video with Danmaku containing positive emotion.

Table 5.1 The results of each group

Measure			Number of Danmaku			
			More Danmaku		Less Danmaku	
			M	SD	M	SD
Learning experience	Emotion	Positive emotion	30.59	6.846	27.12	7.82
		Negative emotion	19.3	7.615	17.69	6.018
	Cognitive load	Material difficulty	5.63	1.757	6.27	1.733
		Psychological effort	6.26	1.403	5.42	1.554
		Understanding of related concepts	5.78	1.739	6.08	1.623
	Learning satisfaction		3.85	0.662	3.69	0.928
	Social presence		31.07	5.65	31.85	6.589
Learning outcomes	Retention test scores		5.67	2.602	4.23	2.286
	Retention test scores		5.11	2.736	3.77	2.944
	Total test scores		10.78	4.552	8	4.808
Measure			Emotions of Danmaku			
			Danmaku with Positive Emotion		Danmaku with Neutral Emotion	
			M	SD	M	SD
Learning experience	Emotion	Positive emotion	28.43	5.633	28.81	7.009
		Negative emotion	18.46	8.289	17.27	5.696
	Cognitive load	Material difficulty	6.07	1.609	5.69	1.543
		Psychological effort	5.89	1.707	5.77	1.306
		Understanding of related concepts	5.96	1.29	5.69	1.408
	Learning satisfaction		3.54	0.576	3.77	0.652
	Social presence		32	6.771	31.58	5.565
Learning outcomes	Retention test scores		4.5	2.755	4.65	2.712
	Retention test scores		3.79	2.2	4.15	2.203
	Total test scores		8.29	4.569	8.88	4.549

5.3.2   The Influence Danmaku Number and Emotion on Learners' Learning Outcomes

To explore the effect of the number of Danmaku (more or less) on learners' learning effect (retention test scores, transfer test scores and total test scores), an independent-samples T-test was adopted. The results showed that there were significant differences in the number of Danmaku in retention score ($t = 2.131, p = 0.038$

$< 0.05, d = 0.58$), transfer score ($t = 1.72, p = 0.092 < 0.1, d = 0.47$), total score ($t = 2.16, p = 0.035 < 0.05, d = 0.59$).

An independent-samples T-test was performed to examine the effect of Danmaku emotion (positive, neutral) on learners' learning effect (retention test scores, transfer test scores and total test scores). Danmaku did not appear to have an impact on retention, transfer, or performance in total.

As illustrated by Table 5.1, the group with more Danmaku scored higher on retention test scores, transfer test scores, and total test scores than the group with less Danmaku, which suggests that the more Danmaku there are, the better the learner's learning effects, and the more meaningful learning it results in.

5.3.3 Correlation Analysis

5.3.3.1 The Correlation Between Cognitive Load, Social Presence, and Learning Satisfaction

A correlational analysis of the experiment in terms of the Danmaku number found that there was a significant positive correlation between psychological effort and social presence ($r = 0.290, p = 0.035 < 0.05$), and a significant positive correlation between psychological effort and learning satisfaction ($r = 0.271, p = 0.04 < 0.05$). There was a significant positive correlation between concept comprehension and material difficulty ($r = 0.665, p < 0.000 < 0.01$), and a significant negative correlation between concept comprehension and learning satisfaction ($r = -0.473, p < 0.000 < 0.01$).

Based on a correlation analysis of the experiment regarding the Danmaku emotion, there was a positive correlation between material difficulty and psychological effort ($r = 0.380, p = 0.005 < 0.01$), and a significant positive correlation between material difficulty and understanding of related concepts ($r = 0.580, p < 0.000 < 0.01$), and a significant positive correlation between psychological effort and understanding of related concepts ($r = 0.320, p = 0.018 < 0.05$).

5.3.3.2 Correlation Between Emotion, Learning Outcomes, and Cognitive Load

A correlational analysis of the number of Danmaku experiment revealed that positive emotion was negatively correlated with material difficulty ($r = -0.316, p = 0.021 < 0.05$), positively correlated with psychological effort ($r = 0.402, p = 0.003 < 0.01$), and negatively correlated with concept understanding ($r = -0.383, p = 0.005 < 0.01$). Negative emotion was negatively correlated with retention score ($r = -0.375, p = 0.006 < 0.01$), transfer score ($r = -0.298, p = 0.03 < 0.05$) and total score ($r = -0.374, p = 0.006 < 0.01$).

A correlational analysis of the experiment regarding Danmaku emotion showed that positive emotion was negatively correlated with material difficulty ($r = -0.367$,

$p = 0.006 < 0.01$), positively correlated with transfer score ($r = 0.294$, $p = 0.031 < 0.05$), and negatively correlated with material difficulty ($r = 0.270$, $p = 0.048 < 0.05$).

5.4   Discussion and Conclusion

5.4.1   Empirical Findings

The present study examined the effects of the number and emotion of Danmaku in online instructional video on learning experience and learning outcomes. Compared with online instructional videos with fewer Danmaku, online instructional videos with more Danmaku could stimulate positive emotions and encourage learners to put in more psychological efforts. Additionally, learners were able to achieve higher retention, transfer, and total test scores and meaningful learning was more likely to occur when they were experiencing positive emotions. Compared with Danmaku emotionally neutral, online instructional videos with positive Danmaku can reduce learners' negative emotions after learning, while negative emotions show negative correlation with learning experiences such as social presence and learning satisfaction. The results partially verified the first, second and third hypothesis. Therefore, it can be inferred that online instructional videos with positive Danmaku and a larger number of Danmaku can improve the learning experience, and online instructional videos with more Danmaku can help improve the learning effectiveness. This study expands on the discussion of Danmaku number and emotion in the context of online instructional videos.

5.4.2   Theoretical Implications

Overall, the findings obtained from this research are partially consistent with previous studies. In terms of learning experience, positive emotions are found to be associated with multiple learning experiences. Analyzed from the perspective of cognitive effects of multimedia learning, emotions are influenced by motivation and difficulty of learning material, while positive emotions can facilitate the multimedia learning experience by manipulating the cognitive process. Social presence in online instructional videos reflects the degree of learner's emotional communication expression, and this study validates the findings of Gunawardena et al. that there is a correlation between social presence and learning satisfaction [6]. As for learning outcomes, this research found that Danmaku with positive emotion contributed to a reduction in learners' negative emotions, but did not find a positive effect on learning effectiveness, which is inconsistent with Stark et al.'s finding that either positive or negative emotional text design can facilitate learning [7].

5.4.3 Practical Implications

From the perspective of improving learning experience, learners who watched online instructional video with a large number of Danmaku received higher positive emotion scores, while learners who watch video with Danmaku containing positive emotions scored lower on test of negative emotions. The research reveals that "the higher the positive emotion, the more psychological effort will be put into the study experience; the higher the negative emotion, the lower the social existence and the study satisfaction", therefore it is important to regulate the amount and length of the emotional factors in the study experience.

Therefore, for online instructional videos that introduce Danmaku, bullet comments with positive emotions can be selected and the number of comments can be increased according to the actual needs in order to improve learners' learning experience.

From the perspective of improving learning outcomes, learners watching online instructional videos with more Danmaku put in more mental effort. According to the research finding, "the more the psychological effort, the higher transfer test scores." It is found that psychological effort reflected the performance of transfer score test, and the significant difference is also found that the learning outcomes (retention test scores, transfer test scores, and total test scores) of learners who watch online instructional videos with more Danmaku is significantly better, which suggests that more Danmaku help meaningful learning to occur.

Therefore, for online instructional videos that have introduced Danmaku, a relatively large amount of Danmaku can be designed to improve learners' learning outcomes and promote meaningful learning.

5.5 Limitations and Prospects

Although this study was conducted in strict accordance with the scientific research process, the control of irrelevant variables such as experimental environment and status of subjects was not precise enough due to the use of online experiments and subjective questionnaires. Future research can adopt methods of conducting experiments in laboratory and combining objective measurements such as EEG, eye tracker, etc.

Acknowledgements Thanks are due to funding by MOE (Ministry of Education in China) Project of Humanities and Social Sciences (foundation no. 19YJC880090) and Key Cultivation Projects of Tianjin Teaching Achievement Award (foundation no. PYGJ-014).

References

1. J. Leng, J. Zhu, X. Wang, X. Gu, Identifying the potential of Danmaku video from eye gaze data, in *2016 IEEE 16th International Conference on Advanced Learning Technologies (ICALT)* (2016), pp. 288–292
2. L. Wang, Z. Liu, H. Han, Research on Danmaku knowledge discovery service under computational communication, in *6th International Conference on Humanities and Social Science Research (ICHSSR 2020)* (2020)
3. Y. Chen, Q. Gao, P. Rau, Watching a movie alone yet together: understanding reasons for watching Danmaku videos. Int. J. Human Comput. Interact. **33**, 731–743 (2017)
4. Q. Bai, Q.V. Hu, L. Ge, L. He, Stories that big Danmaku data can tell as a new media. IEEE Access **7**, 53509–53519 (2019)
5. Chen, How danmaku influences emotional responses: exploring the effects of co-viewing and copresence. (2018)
6. C. Gunawardena, F. Zittle, Social presence as a predictor of satisfaction within a computer-mediated conferencing environment. Am. J. Distance Educ. **11**, 8–26 (1997)
7. L. Stark, Facial recognition, emotion and race in animated social media. First Monday **23**(9), (2018)

Chapter 6
Cluster Analysis of College Students' Online Classes Experience

Junda Lian, Bo Zhang, Xiaoyang Gong, and Linpeng Ban

Abstract To understand college students online learning experience quickly and accurately, a BERT (Bidirectional Encoder Representation from Trans-formers) model and a Bidirectional Long Short-Term Memory (BiLSTM) layer were used to analyse the data. The effectiveness of the proposed methods are verified by representative design examples.

Keywords Deep learning · Online course reviews · Online teaching · Training model

6.1 Introduction

Students' evaluation have been paid more and more attention over the years. The importance is emphasised in [1], and organizing various student evaluations is considered as the most effective way to improve teaching quality and select outstanding teachers in [2]. In [3], students' evaluation of classroom experience not only promotes the transformation of teacher-student relationship from authority to democracy, but also highlights the concept of students' rights. In [4], students' evaluation can help teachers review classroom teaching from students' perspective, and promote teachers' self-reflection and self-improvement effectively. In [5], the combination of classroom experience quality evaluation and the comprehensive evaluation results of

J. Lian · B. Zhang (✉) · L. Ban
Tianjin Key Laboratory of Wireless Mobile Communications and Power Transmission, College of Electronic and Communication Engineering, Tianjin Normal University, Tianjin 300387, China
e-mail: b.zhangintj@tjnu.edu.cn

X. Gong (✉)
Faculty of Education, Tianjin Normal University, Tianjin 300387, China
e-mail: xgong@tjnu.edu.cn

teachers and students is more conducive to improving teaching quality than teacher self-evaluation.

The remaining part of this paper is structured as follows. A review of text pre-processing is given in Sect. 6.2. The proposed method with design examples are introduced in Sect. 6.3. Conclusions are drawn in Sect. 6.4.

6.2 A Review of Text Pre-processing

6.2.1 Chinese Word Segmentation

A core technology in natural language processing. Here, we use a statistically-based word segmentation method to segment Chinese words. The main idea is to treat each word as a combination of characters. If the connected characters appear more often in different texts, then the connected characters is probably a word.

6.2.2 Stop Words Removal

Stop words are functional words that have less semantic information and have little effect on the classification results, including prepositions, conjunctions, punctuation, etc. The common method is to use a list of stop words and delete the stop words by matching strings after completing the aforementioned word segmentation.

6.3 Proposed Design Method

6.3.1 Cluster Analysis

The original data is collected in Chinese. Here, the English version of a part of data extracted from questionnaires is shown in Fig. 6.1. After calculating the word frequency of the processed text, the corresponding high relevance keywords are classified in 6 groups and are shown in Fig. 6.2, where the second column represents the corresponding relevant keywords, and the third column represents the name of classification group. Here, we can see that the name of the first group is "willingness of online lessons", including the keywords "going back to school, clocking in, going to school, and school". The name of the second group is "platform experience" with the words "webpage, sign-in" etc. Similarly, the name of the third, fourth, fifth and sixth group are named after "teaching site", "personal equipment", "tasks", "learning status", respectively.

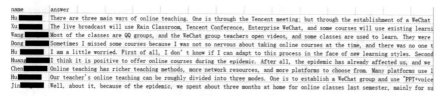

name	answer
Hu	There are three main ways of online teaching. One is through the Tencent meeting; but through the establishment of a WeChat
Xu	The live broadcast will use Rain Classroom, Tencent Conference, Enterprise WeChat, and some courses will use existing learni
Wang	Most of the classes are QQ groups, and the WeChat group teachers open videos, and some classes are used to learn. They were
Dong	Sometimes I missed some courses because I was not so nervous about taking online courses at the time, and there was no one t
Hu	I am a little worried. First of all, I don't know if I can adapt to this process in the face of new learning styles. Second
Huang	I think it is positive to offer online courses during the epidemic. After all, the epidemic has already affected us, and we
Chen	Online teaching has richer teaching methods, more network resources, and more platforms to choose from. Many platforms use 1
Hu	Our teacher's online teaching can be roughly divided into three modes. One is to establish a WeChat group and use "PPT+voice
Jin	Well, about it, because of the epidemic, we spent about three months at home for online classes last semester, mainly for su

Fig. 6.1 Comment data collection example

category	Highly relevant keywords	Type definition
1	Back to school, class, happy, why, clock in, voice, every day, at home, don't want to, school, end of get out of class, not use, teach, go to school, evening	Willingness to learn online
2	Webpage, learning, online, course, superstar, sign-in, answer, can't get in, tell, trash, open, physical education, teaching, software	Platform experience
3	Guan Mai, cute, heard, teacher, classmate, roll call, answer, voice, question, lecture, group, live broadcast, lecture, screen, bad	Teaching site
4	Classroom, at home, MOOC, campus, not used, school, student, camera, time, system, computer, mobile phone, WeChat	Personal equipment
5	Video, eyes, homework, arrangement, like, submit, hope, after class, record, watch, not, physical education class, home, scene, end	Tasks
6	Posture, going to school, understanding, surfing, status, don't want, campus, notice, sharing, a lot, happy, eyes, bullying, notes, rollover	Learning Status

Fig. 6.2 High relevance keywords

	Willingness to learn online	Platform experience	Teaching site	Personal equipment	Tasks	Learning Status
Comment one	0	0	1	1	0	1
Comment two	1	1	0	1	0	1
Comment three	0	0	0	1	1	1
...	...	...	...	...	...	...

Fig. 6.3 Word frequency matrix

Based on these highly relevant keywords, comments in Fig. 6.1 are transformed to a word frequency matrix, as shown in Fig 6.3. Number 1 in the matrix represents the belonging of the groups (labels), and each comments can have more than one label. Number 0 represents non-belonging to this category.

6.3.2 Classification

Here, we use BERT model for text vectorization. The benefit is that the information on the left and right sides of the word can be considered. After converting the text data into vectors through the BERT model, we select BiLSTM model, including a forward and a backward LSTM layer to learn the left and right contextual information of each word. Figure 6.4 shows the total number of comments for each label. Here, we can see that the first group "willingness of online lessons" includes the most comments, followed by "video teaching", while students concern "personal equipment" the least.

6.4 Conclusions

In this paper, text pre-processing including word segmentation and stop word removal are reviewed, and a BERT model with a BiLSTM layer selected for better understanding the left and right contextual information of each word is proposed for students' evaluations. As shown in the given design examples, students concern more about online lessons, video teaching and school tasks than platform experience, personal equipment and learning status.

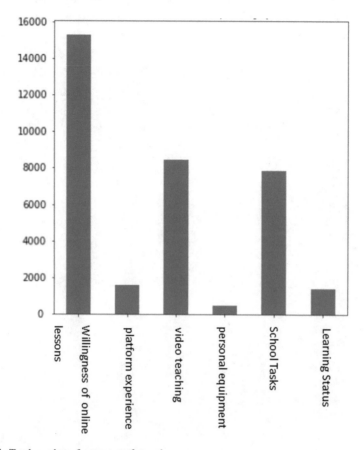

Fig. 6.4 Total number of comments for each group

References

1. H.W. Marsh, Students' evaluations of university teaching: dimensionality, reliability, validity, potential baises, and utility. J. Edu. Psychol. **76**(5), 707–754 (1984)
2. C.T. Chau, A bootstrap experiment on the statistical properties of students' ratings of teaching effectiveness. Res. Higher Edu. **38**, 497–517 (1997)
3. F. Ye, Xue sheng ping jiao: jiu jing xin feng na zhong jiao yu zhe xue? [Student evaluation of teaching: what kind of educational philosophy do you believe in?]. J. Shanghai Educ. Res. **10**, 36–38 (2006)
4. D. Zhao, Cu jin jiao shi fa zhan de xue sheng ping jiao [Students' evaluation of teaching to promote teachers' development]. J. Chinese Soc. Edu. **12**, 64–67 (2006)
5. H.W. Marsh, L.A. Roche, Making students' evaluations of teaching effectiveness effective: the critical issues of validity, bias, and utility. Am. Psychol. **52**(11), 1187–1197 (1997)

Chapter 7
Study in Intelligent Exam Based on RNN and LSTM

Rui Li, Xiaoyang Gong, Bo Zhang, Chen Liang, Menglin Li, and Hui Guo

Abstract According to the learning basis of different students, two intelligent exam paper generation models are introduced: recurrent neural network (RNN) and long short-term memory (LSTM). Compared to RNN, LSTM based structure can obtain long-term information by using cyclic memory function and selective forgetting function, and it can better capture the correlation between the results of similar questions in the student's answering behavior.

Keywords Intelligent exam paper · LSTM architecture · RNN architecture

7.1 Introduction

In traditional education model, exam papers are usually developed by teachers and the same exam paper is used for all students. However, according to the different learning basis of different students, the same exam paper for all students do not satisfy the new teaching requirement "Teaching varies from person to person". To solve the problem, artificial intelligence technology has entered people's vision, which can provide different design schemes according to different users' needs. In [1], shallow Bayesian knowledge tracking has been trained and analyzed to obtain students' mastery of different knowledge points. In [2–4], RNN is introduced as a dynamic machine learning model for processing different sequence data. All cyclic units of the RNN are connected in a chain, and the sequence data is used as input. It performs

R. Li · B. Zhang (✉) · C. Liang · M. Li · H. Guo
Tianjin Key Laboratory of Wireless Mobile Communications and Power Transmission, College of Electronic and Communication Engineering, Tianjin Normal University, Tianjin 300387, China
e-mail: b.zhangintj@tjnu.edu.cn

X. Gong (✉)
Faculty of Education, Tianjin Normal University, Tianjin 300387, China
e-mail: xgong@tjnu.edu.cn

cyclic recursion during the evolution of the sequence to make the information persistent, and is a great solution to the problems of using knowledge tracking technology in intelligent education to process students' answer records. LSTM stands for long short-term memory and has better performance in dealing with long-term dependencies [5]. When dealing with long time series, some previous relatively unimportant information will be selectively forgotten. Although it is more complex than RNN, it is generally proven to be more powerful than RNN [6].

The rest of the paper is structured as follows. Exam research on RNN is given in Sect. 7.2, and the corresponding research on LSTM is described in Sect. 7.3. The conclusions are drawn in Sect. 7.4.

7.2 RNN architecture

The RNN network is expanded in time series, as shown in Fig. 7.1. In this single-layer RNN network, the input of RNN at time 0 is x_0, and the output is h_0. The state of the network neuron at time 0 is stored in neuron A. When the next time 1 comes, the state of the network neuron at this time is determined not only by the input x_1 at time 1, but also by the state of the neuron at time 0. In the study of intelligent exam, the learning basis of different students (a student answers the right and wrong questions) is the input. When the input time sequence enters the hidden layer, a weighted transformation is used to obtain a prediction of the student overall answering situation and finally output test papers suitable for the student.

The standard RNN layer usually uses a hyperbolic tangent function, as shown in Fig. 7.2. We can see the same truth from Eq. 7.1, where the output is not only related to the input at the current moment, but also related to the output of the previous hidden layer and the weight of each layer.

$$h_t = \tanh(W_x^* x_t + W_h^* h_{t-1} + b) \tag{7.1}$$

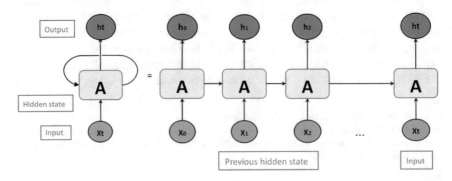

Fig. 7.1 A single layer of RNN

Fig. 7.2 RNN architecture

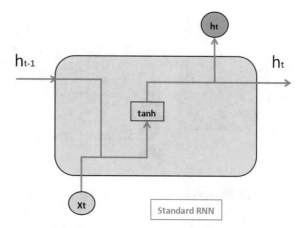

The state of neuron A mentioned above at time t is the value of the hyperbolic tangent function of the neuron state at time $t - 1$ and the network input at time t. This value is not only used as the output of the network at that moment, but also as the state of the network at that moment and passed into the network state at the next moment. The RNN model can be trained by inputting a large number of answer records to obtain a relatively suitable answer test paper. However, the designed RNN exam model has two problems: short memory distance and difficult to train.

Short memory distance: The traditional RNN can only memorize the temporal logic relationship within a very limited time sequence. When RNN needs to predict a certain sequence with a long time sequence, the content of a long time ago is likely to be forgotten; in other words, a test paper output is more likely to be affected by nearby values, rather than values far from it.

Difficult to train: RNN training mainly uses gradient descent method, and the neural network adopts backward-propagation. If it is a long sequence, then it is easy to cause gradient explosion or gradient disappearance. In detail, in the case of gradient disappearance the weight update of the hidden layer close to the input layer will become slow, resulting in the weight of the hidden layer close to the input layer almost unchanged and still close to the initialized weight. While in the case of gradient explosion, when the initial weight is too large, the weight near the input layer changes faster than that near the output layer, which will cause the problem of gradient explosion.

7.3 Exam Research Based on LSTM

The LSTM architecture is shown in Fig. 7.3. It is controlled by setting a "forgotten gate", keeping the required values in the hidden unit and explicitly deleting some useless information in the forgetting unit. Equation 7.2 represents the discarded

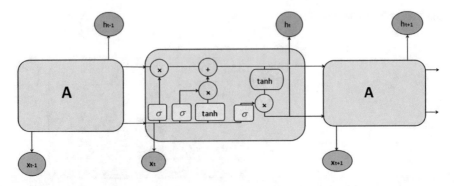

Fig. 7.3 LSTM architecture

information in LSTM. Equations 7.3 and 7.4 represent updated information, with the update status demonstrated in Eq. 7.5, and the final output information in Eq. 7.6. To generate test papers automatically, the input of LSTM is a fixed-length time series vector, which is transformed by the student's answer. Moreover, LSTM uses its special structure to block the gradient length whose norm is higher than the threshold to effectively prevent the exploding gradient, achieving an effect that cannot be achieved by traditional RNN.

$$f_t = \sigma(W_f \cdot [h_{t-1}, x_t] + b_f) \tag{7.2}$$

$$i_t = \sigma(W_i \cdot [h_{t-1}, x_t] + b_i) \tag{7.3}$$

$$\tilde{C}_t = \tanh(W_c \cdot [h_{t-1}, x_t] + b_c) \tag{7.4}$$

$$C_t = f_t * C_{t-1} + i_t * \tilde{C}_t \tag{7.5}$$

$$o_t = \sigma(W_o h_{t-1}, x_t + b_o) \tag{7.6}$$

$$h_t = o_t * \tanh C_t. \tag{7.7}$$

7.4 Conclusions

In this paper, the RNN and LSTM architectures for generating exam papers are both introduced. Compared to RNN, LSTM can obtain long-term information by using the cyclic memory function and selective forgetting function, and it can well capture the correlation between the results of similar questions in the student's answering behavior. Based on the advantages of LSTM, the structure can also be extended to the course selection system, where students' ability and their interest can be seen as input, and the system will tell students their most suitable courses.

References

1. M. Zhang, Ji yu ren zhi zhen duan de bei ye si zhi shi zhui zong mo xing gai jin yu ying yong [Improvement and application of bayesian knowledge tracking model based on cognitive diagnosis]. Ph.D. dissertation, East China Normal University (2019)
2. H. Cao, J. Xie, Lstm-based learning achievement prediction and its influencing factors. J. Beij. Univ. Posts Telecommun. (Social Science Edition) **22**(6), 90–100 (2020)
3. L. Yang, Y. Wu, J. Wang, Y. Liu, Xun huan shen jing wang luo yan jiu zong shu [Summary of recurrent neural network research]. J. Comput. Appl. **38**(S2), 1–6+26 (2018)
4. H. Liu, T. Zhang, P. Wu, G. Yu, Zhi shi zhui zong zong shu [Overview of knowledge tracking]. J. East China Normal Univ. (Nat. Sci.) **05**, 1–15 (2019)
5. X. Bai, Text classification based on lstm and attention, in *Thirteenth International Conference on Digital Information Management (ICDIM)*, vol. 2018, pp. 29–32 (2018)
6. K. He, Ji yu zi ran yu yan chu li de wen ben fen lei yan jiu yu ying yong [Research and application of text classification based on natural language processing]. Ph.D. dissertation, Nanjing University of Posts and Telecommunications (2020)

Chapter 8
Teacher Facial Expression Recognition Based on GoogLeNet-InceptionV3 CNN Model

Yan Tian, Tingting Han, and Libao Wu

Abstract Teacher expression recognition based on deep learning is an important application of deep learning in the field of education, which can quickly and accurately obtain teacher expressions, and save time and resources comparing with traditional manual classroom evaluation. In this paper, the GoogleNet-InceptionV3 convolutional neural network (CNN) model was proposed for teacher facial expression recognition. Contrast Limited Adaptive Histogram Equalization (CLAHE) was used for CK+ dataset image enhancement. After training, a classification accuracy rate of 81.4% was achieved. Furthermore, we selected a teachers' lecture video from MOOC website and analyzed it using the trained model. The correct recognition rate of the teachers' facial expressions in this video is 90%. Teacher facial expression recognition technology based on deep learning provides a new idea and scheme for contemporary classroom teaching management and quality assessment.

Keywords Deep learning · Teacher facial expression recognition · Image enhancement · CLAHE · GoogLeNet-InceptionV3

8.1 Introduction

Teachers' teaching emotions affect teachers' subjective consciousness and play an important role in classroom teaching activities. In 2014, Prosen [1] analyzed the teachers' emotions by their language and the students' reactions to teachers' emotions such as happiness, anger and sadness. They found that happy emotions have a better effect on teacher-student interaction. Therefore, teachers' expression is a factor that cannot be ignored in contemporary classrooms. Analyzing changes in teachers' facial expressions is of extremely significance to classroom evaluation.

Y. Tian · T. Han (✉)
Tianjin Key Laboratory of Wireless Mobile Communications and Power Transmission, Tianjin Normal University, Tianjin 300387, China
e-mail: hanting608@163.com

L. Wu
Faculty of Education, Tianjin Normal University, Tianjin 300387, China

The traditional classroom evaluation is mainly based on subjective evaluation such as other teachers' evaluation and students' survey, which lacks objective and scientific data support [2]. With the development of computer vision, deep learning technology and the gradual maturity of related hardware, facial expression recognition based on deep learning is getting more attention in the field of "artificial intelligence + education".

Pramerdorfer and Kampel [3] demonstrated that CNN is superior to traditional methods in FER2013. The abstract features extracted by CNN have stronger robustness and better generalization ability. In 2017, Li et al. [4] designed the Deep Locality-Preserving CNN (DLP-CNN) algorithm based on RAF-DB dataset. This model solves the problem of facial expression recognition in uncontrolled environment. Wen et al. [5] combined the Convolutional Block Attention Module (CBAM) with ResNet in 2020, which improved the network's feature extraction capability. In 2011, Feng [6] introduced facial expression recognition technology into intelligent online teaching systems, which was the first implementation of facial expression recognition and emotion judgment system in the online environment. Zhan et al. [7] combined facial recognition and eye-tracking technology to develop the emotional and cognitive recognition model for distance learners, which greatly improved the accuracy of learners' state judgment in the network environment.

The above facial expression recognition methods have achieved good results. However, there is little research on teachers' facial expression recognition. In this paper, we demonstrated a GoogLeNet-InceptionV3 CNN model for teacher facial expression recognition. The main works were shown as follows: (1) In order to get more detailed facial expression data, the CLAHE method was used to enhance the CK+ dataset. (2) Construct GoogLeNet-InceptionV3 CNN model to train the enhanced CK + dataset. (3) Select a teacher's lecture video from MOOC [8] and make a detailed analysis of the teacher's facial expressions.

8.2   Image Enhancement

The Extended Cohn–Kanade Dataset (CK+) is most extensively used for facial expression intensity. CK+ was expanded on the Cohn–Kanade dataset in 2010 and contains 593 sequences across 123 subjects, and 327 of the 593 sequences have expression labels [9]. These expression sequences are encoded from 0 to 7, which represent seven kinds of expressions and neutral expression (i.e. $0 =$ neutral, $1 =$ anger, $2 =$ contempt, $3 =$ disgust, $4 =$ fear, $5 =$ happiness, $6 =$ sadness, $7 =$ surprise). Figure 8.1 shows the visualization of the eight expressions in CK+ dataset.

In the CK+ dataset, some images are exposed excessive or low brightness. The image enhancement can make the image clearer and the character details more prominent, thereby ensuring higher model accuracy. In this paper, the method of Contrast Limited Adaptive Histgram Equalization (CLAHE) was used to enhance the CK+ dataset.

0 = neutral   1 = anger   2 = comtempt   3 = disgust   4 = fear   5 = happiness   6 = sadness   7 = surprise

Fig. 8.1 The visualization of the eight expressions in CK+ dataset

Histogram Equalization (HE) is usually used for contrast enhancement. The main principle is to map the gray distribution of the image to another distribution. Thus, the dynamic range of the gray distribution becomes flat and extended, thereby improving the overall contrast of the image, which make the image clearer. Due to the light and dark distribution of the image, the traditional HE method may cause the loss of local details of the image. By dividing the image into several sub-blocks, the Adaptive Histogram Equalization (AHE) method was used for the sub-blocks to optimize the equalization effect. Nevertheless, this will cause excessive noise amplification. CLAHE is an improvement of AHE. The main difference is that CLAHE sets a limit on the contrast of local images. By limiting the height of local histogram, the enhancement amplitude of local contrast is reduced, which limits the increase of image noise and excessive enhancement of local contrast. This method not only makes the image clearer, but also preserves the image's local details. The CLAHE algorithm flow was shown as follows [10]:

The input image is assumed to consist of discrete gray levels in the dynamic range of $[0, L - 1]$, The gray level is r_k.

(1) Divide the image into non-overlapping equal sub-blocks, and mark the number of pixels contained in each sub-block as N.

(2) Calculate the histogram of each sub-block. The histogram of the sub-block is $h(r_k)$.

(3) Calculate the shear threshold, limiting the number of pixels contained in each gray level cannot exceed ncl times the average number of pixels (N/L). *clipLimit* is expressed as a shear threshold, which is used to control the magnitude of contrast enhancement.

$$\text{clipLimit} = ncl\frac{N}{L}, \tag{8.1}$$

In Eq. (8.1): *ncl* is a variable value that can be set flexibly according to the actual situation of the image.

(4) For each sub-block, use the corresponding clipLimit value for $h(r_k)$ cutting, the number of pixels being cut will be uniform again assigned to each gray level of the histogram.

$$\text{sumR} = \sum_{k=0}^{L-1} (\max(h(r_k) - \text{clipLimit}, \ 0)), \tag{8.2}$$

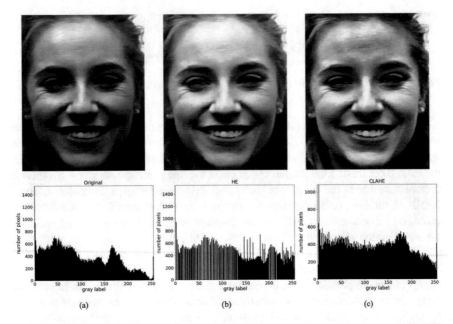

Fig. 8.2 a Histogram of original image **b** Histogram of HE processed image **c** Histogram of CLAHE processed image

In Eq. (8.2): sumR represents the total number of pixel values that exceeds *clipLimit*.

$$\text{avgN} = \text{sumR/L}, \tag{8.3}$$

In Eq. (8.3): avgN represents the average number of pixels increased by each gray level in the histogram.

Repeating the above allocation steps until all the cut pixels were allocated. Use $h'(r_k)$ to represent the histogram of $h(r_k)$ after redistribution processing, then

$$h'(r_k) = \begin{cases} \text{clipLimit}, & h(r_k) > \text{clipLimit} - \text{avgN} \\ h(r_k), & h(r_k) \leq \text{clipLimit} - \text{avgN} \end{cases} \tag{8.4}$$

(5) The gray histogram of each sub-region after redistribution was processed separately, and the result was represented by $p(r_k)$.

(6) According to $p(r_k)$, the gray value of the center pixel of each sub-block was taken as the reference point, and the bilinear interpolation technique was used to calculate the gray value of each point in the output image.

The comparison among the images processed by CLAHE and HE algorithms and the Original image were shown in Fig. 8.2, which shows the histogram of original image (a), the HE processed image (b) and the CLAHE processed image (c).

It can be clearly seen from Fig. 8.2 that the dynamic distribution range of the CLAHE image histogram is wider and more uniform than that of the HE image and the original image. And the CLAHE image has higher definition and more local details.

8.3 GoogLeNet-IncepionV3 CNN Model

Typically, the performance improvement of CNN relies on improving the depth and width of the network, which will inevitably result in a larger parameter space and computational pressure. The deeper the network, the harder it is to optimize, and the gradient is easy to disappear. To solve these problems, Szegedy et al. [11] proposed the GoogLeNet CNN with Inception structure, which can reduce the amount of computation while increasing the width and depth of the network. Inception is the core of GoogLeNet, which is a sparse and high-performance network structure.

The inceptionV1 structure contains 4 channels and $1 \times 1, 3 \times 3, 5 \times 5$ convolution kernels. 4 channels are allocated with different sizes of convolution kernels. Information can be extracted from different levels, and finally aggregated at the output, to get richer feature information. A single 3×3 or 5×5 convolution kernel will have a large amount of calculation, so a 1×1 convolution kernel is added in front of these convolution kernels to achieve dimensionality reduction. Additionally, pooling operations are essential for current convolutional networks, so an alternative parallel pooling path is added at each such stage [11]. GoogLeNet uses a large number of inception blocks to increase the convolutional layer, but reducing the computational complexity. Figure 8.3 shows the structure of InceptionV1 model.

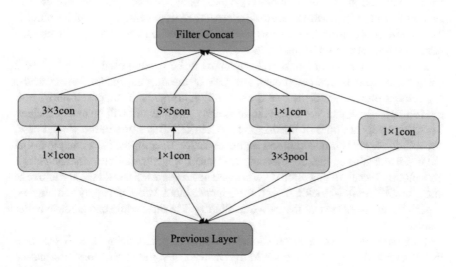

Fig. 8.3 The structure of InceptionV1 model

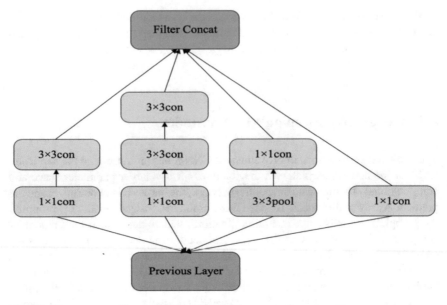

Fig. 8.4 The structure of InceptionV3 model-block1

GoogLeNet's better performance is mainly due to the extensive use of dimension reduction. This is a special kind of efficient decomposing convolution. Through proper decomposition, the parameters will be more decoupling and less, so as to accelerate the training.

In the first case, according to the ideas in VGGNet, the large 5×5 convolution kernel in inceptionV1 is decomposed into two small 3×3 convolution kernels [12], as seen from Fig. 8.4, **which shows the structure of InceptionV3 model-block1**. Two small convolution kernels use the ReLU activation function to enhance the nonlinear representation of the model.

If the 3×3 convolution kernel continues to be decomposed into two 2×2 convolution kernels, the parameters are 89% of the original model. However, the experiment proves that if the 3×3 convolution kernel is decomposed into 1×3 convolution kernel and 3×1 convolution kernel, the network will be more efficient. The parameters are 66% of the original model [12]. Therefore, in the second case, convolution kernels is decomposed asymmetrically. Decomposition principle is that the $n \times n$ convolution kernel is decomposed into $1 \times n$ convolution kernel and $n \times 1$ convolution kernel. In InceptionV3, n is equal to 7. Figure 8.5 **shows the structure of InceptionV3 model-block2**. InceptionV3 model-block2 does not apply to all layers, especially the front part of the network. Putting it in the middle can achieve better results.

Last case, to avoid representational bottleneck, parallelizing 1×3 convolution kernel and 3×1 convolution kernel instead of serial can reduce information loss and calculation cost. Figure 8.6 **shows the structure of InceptionV3 model-block3**. InceptionV3 model-block3 is placed on the high-level part of the network to

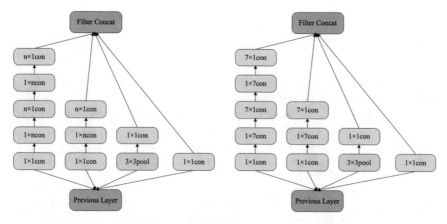

Fig. 8.5 The structure of InceptionV3 model-block2

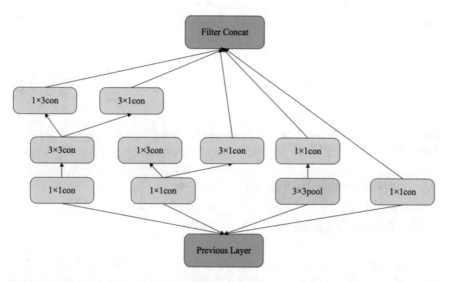

Fig. 8.6 The structure of InceptionV3 model-block3

ensure more feature information. These three inception structures together constitute GoogLeNet-InceptionV3. Compared with Inception V1, the inceptionV3 network has a faster computing speed, increases the nonlinearity of the network and reduces the probability of overfitting.

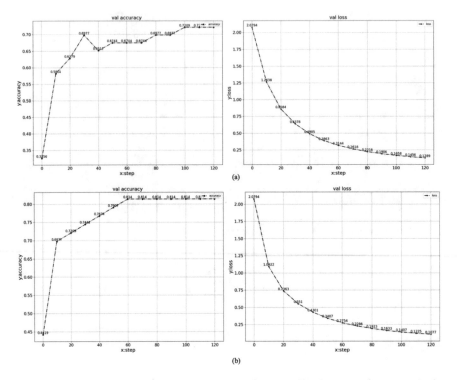

Fig. 8.7 a Loss and accuracy in the validation set of normal CK+ **b** Loss and accuracy in the validation set of enhanced CK+

8.4 Experimental Process and Analysis

8.4.1 Model Training

The experiment used the Pycharm2020 platform to build the GoogLe Net-inceptionV3 CNN based on the tensorflow framework, and used the normal CK+ dataset and enhanced CK+ dataset for training. Setting learning rate = 0.003, steps = 120, the training results are shown in Fig. 8.7, **which shows the loss and accuracy in the validation set of normal CK+ (a) and in the validation set of enhanced CK+ (b)**. Accuracy in the validation set of enhanced CK+ has significantly improved, reaching 81.4%.

8.4.2 Teacher Facial Expression Recognition

We selected a teacher's lecture video with the content of Zhao Ming Selected Works from MOOC [8]. One frame was intercepted every second (24 frames) of the teaching

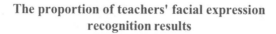

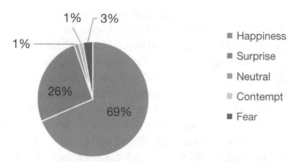

Fig. 8.8 The proportion of teachers' facial expression recognition results

The correct rate of teachers' facial expression recognition			
Expression	Total number	Correct number	Recognition accuracy
Happiness	754	745	99%
Surprise	285	233	82%
Neutral	14	10	71%
Contempt	14	6	43%
Fear	31	3	10%
	1098	997	90%

Fig. 8.9 The correct rate of teachers' facial expression recognition

video. A total of 1301 pictures were intercepted. The invalid pictures were removed, and the total number of valid pictures was 1098. Haar classifier algorithm was used to detect faces, and face pictures of the teacher were captured for test set. Finally, the teacher's facial expression recognition results in this class included five facial expressions as shown in the Fig. 8.8. The ratio of the Happiness and Surprise expressions is 95%, so positive teacher emotions are more needed in the classroom.

We also made statistics on the recognition rates of the five expressions. Figure 8.9 shows the correct rate of teachers' facial expression recognition. The correct identification rate of Happiness, Surprise and Neutral reached 99, 82 and 71%. Due to the state of the teacher's eyes and head, some expressions were recognized as Contempt and Fear. In this video, the correct recognition rate of all expressions of this teacher is 90%.

8.5   Conclusion

This paper proposed teacher facial expression recognition based on the GoogLe Net-InceptionV3 network. InceptionV3 has a deeper and wider sparse network structure than InceptionV1 and has a faster calculation speed. After training with the enhanced CK+ dataset, the recognition accuracy in the teacher's lecture video reached 90%. Through these data, this research can provide objective data for teaching evaluation, and can also analyze students' interest in the teaching content, so as to build a better learning environment. Although the study has achieved a good recognition rate, we still need to further improve the robustness of feature extraction of teachers' expressions in real scenes. Next, teachers' speech and text language will be added to the sentiment analysis research. In the future, we hope to achieve a more comprehensive teacher sentiment analysis.

Acknowledgements This work was supported by the Tianjin Science and Technology Planning Project under Grant No. 20JCYBJC00300, and the National Natural Science Foundation of China under Grant No. 11404240, and the Tianjin Philosophy and Social Science Planning Project under Grant No. TJJX17-016.

References

1. S. Prosen, H.S. Vituli, O.P. Kraban, *Teachers' Emotional Expression in the Classroom* (IEEE, 2014)
2. K. Zheng, D. Yang, J. Liu et al., Recognition of teachers' facial expression intensity based on convolutional neural network and attention mechanism. IEEE Access pp 99: 1–1 (2020)
3. C. Pramerdorfer, M. Kampel, Facial expression recognition using convolutional neural networks: state of the art. (2016)
4. S. Li, W. Deng, J.P. Du, Reliable crowdsourcing and deep locality-preserving learning for expression recognition in the wild, in *2017 IEEE Conference on Computer Vision and Pattern Recognition (CVPR)* (IEEE, 2017)
5. P. Wen, Y. Ding, Y. Wen et al., Facial Expression Recognition Method Based on Convolution Neural Network Combining Attention Mechanism. (2020)
6. F. Mantang, MA Qingyu, Wang Ruijie, Research on intelligent network teaching system based on facial expression recognition [J]. Comput. Technol. and Devel. 21 (6):193–196 (2011)
7. Z. Zehui, Remote learner emotion and cognitive recognition model based on intelligent agent: Coupling of eye movement tracking and expression recognition technology [J]. Mod. Distance Educ. Res. (05): 100–105 (2013)
8. L. Jing, Introduction to selected works of Shao Ming [EB/OL]. https://www.icourse163.org/learn/SDU-1002618005?tid=1464073444#/learn/content?type=detail&id=1242480139&cid=1265528355.2021-04-12/2021-07-30
9. L. Shan, W. Deng, Deep facial expression recognition: a survey. IEEE Trans. Affect. Comput. pp 99, (2018)
10. L. Fang, S. Tiandu, Journal of changchun university of technology. 42 (01):22–28 (2021)
11. C. Szegedy, L. Wei, Y. Jia et al., Going deeper with convolutions, in *2015 IEEE Conference on Computer Vision and Pattern Recognition (CVPR)* (IEEE, 2015)
12. C. Szegedy, V. Vanhoucke, S. Ioffe et al., Rethinking the Inception architecture for computer vision, in *2016 IEEE Conference on Computer Vision and Pattern Recognition (CVPR)* (IEEE, 2016), pp. 2818–2826

Chapter 9
An Overview Study of Importance of Artificial Intelligence in the Improvement of Online Education

Muhammad Uzair and Jin Chen

Abstract This research investigates the topic of artificial intelligence's rise in online education teaching and learning. It looks into the effects of emerging technology on how students learn and how institutions teach and change in the online teaching platform for better performance. Recent technological advances and the increased pace with which new technologies are adopted in online education are investigated. Students are unable to continue their studies on campus due to COVID-19. As a result, the institute began online teaching at that time, but students faced numerous challenges in online learning due to a lack of tactics and resources. We define some benefits and impact of AI technologies for Online teaching and learning.

Keywords Artificial intelligence · Online education · Adaptive study · Visualization of information · Virtual counselling

9.1 Introduction

Within the last few years, the definition of traditional education has changed significantly. Being physically present in a classroom is no longer the only learning option, especially with the growth of the internet and new technology. Nowadays, as long as you've got access to a computer, you can get an honest education anytime and wherever you select. We are now entering a replacement age known as the revolutions. Online education gives both the teacher and the student the ability to choose their own learning pace, as well as the added flexibility of designing a schedule that works for everyone. As a result, using an online educational platform provides for a better balance of work and study, requiring no compromises. Since the mid-twentieth century, education has emphasized specialization: studying more about fewer subjects. Students will increasingly come from a variety of ages and backgrounds [10].

M. Uzair · J. Chen (✉)
Tianjin Key Laboratory of Wireless Mobile Communications and Power Transmission, Tianjin Normal University, Tianjin 300387, China
e-mail: cjwoods@163.com

© The Author(s), under exclusive license to Springer Nature Singapore Pte Ltd. 2021
W. Wang et al. (eds.), *Artificial Intelligence in Education and Teaching Assessment*,
https://doi.org/10.1007/978-981-16-6502-8_9

COVID-19 has now forced the closure of schools all across the world. Over 1.2 billion children globally are not attending school. As a result, education is confronted with learning options, with the advent of learning in which instruction is done remotely and via digital platforms. While the students cannot go to the class-rooms almost all over the world, some students are wondering if the online learning system will continue after the pandemic, and how such a shift will impact the global education business.

Students are unable to continue their studies on campus due to COVID-19. As a result, the institute began online teaching at that time, but students faced numerous challenges in online learning due to a lack of tactics and resources. More powerful online learning solutions are required to tackle the world's problems. In this procedure, Artificial Intelligence will be quite beneficial.

The future of higher education is strongly linked to technological advancements and the internet connectivity of emerging intelligent machines. Advances in artificial intelligence in this field open up new possibilities and challenges for higher education teaching and learning, with the potential to dramatically alter governance and the internal architecture of higher education institutions. Students, whether they receive their education online or offline, want interactive classes in which they do not feel overburdened. Artificial intelligence can assist in the development of such an intriguing and helpful platform. Because there is no limit of age for learning, there are too many ways and platforms to educate itself with AI. In contrast, the use of technology in education has altered the format of instruction. Distance learning programmers have existed since the 1980s, but technological advances, content scalability, and widespread mobile adoption have made online degree programmers a feasible option for prospective students [12].

Accelerating online learning offers some benefits, but it isn't a solution. Artificial intelligence-enabled next-generation improvements, on the other hand, have the potential to completely change the virtual experience. We must completely redefine the job of an educator to improve upon the current teaching model, in which the instructor is the source of knowledge and the student is the reception [8].

AI has already had a significant impact on online education, with AI-powered modules appearing in all areas of education. Course delivery online has already decreased expenses, reduced inequity, and increased graduation rates in education. As a result of the AI revolution, online education could become even smarter, faster, and cheaper. It has already begun. AI-enabled learning management systems [7] can use surveys to group individuals into distinct learning buckets (e.g., visual, auditory, text) [9], allowing them to give effective and targeted information that corresponds to their chosen learning style. Online education will become more popular in the future.

9.2 Benefits of AI (Artificial Intelligence) in Education

Through efficiency and personalization, AI can assist fill in the gaps in learning and teaching. Artificial intelligence systems aid in the accessibility of global classrooms to all types of students, including those with special needs. These digital platforms that use AI to provide learning, assessment, and feedback discover knowledge gaps and, when necessary, shift learning to new areas. Machines can efficiently grade multiple-choice examinations, and AI has a lot of potential for making registration and admission processes more efficient [4].

AI advancements are assisting in the shaping of e-learning as the future of education. E-learning is a brand-new educational service that allows people to get an education without compromising their finances and at a far lower cost than traditional higher education institutions.

There are a variety of AI applications being explored for education, including learner mentors, smart content generation, and virtual global conferences. Education is one of the most recent industries to gain from artificial intelligence and machine learning, but the shifts are already underway and will undoubtedly continue [2].

The use of technology in education is modifying how we teach and learn all across the world. Artificial intelligence [3] is one of the disruptive technologies that can be applied to personalize the learning experiences of various learning groups, teachers, and tutors.

9.3 Current Artificial Intelligence Methods for eLearning

Online education Industry claims "An AI-based eLearning platform is a machine or system that can execute many jobs that require human intelligence. It is capable of providing solutions to human-related problems such as speech recognition, translation, decision making, and much more."

Due to COVID-19, the world needs to know the best way of online teaching. During the longer lockdown, online education platforms have become significant for education. Everyone is getting used to the unexpected new standard of completely innovative teaching and learning in the wake of the Covid-19 epidemic. The use of AI technology in e-learning enables us to better exploit e-learning solutions (LMSs, LXPs, LAPs, and so on). AI is transforming the way we learn, opening up a lot of new educational opportunities. The online education system is developing to support entire technology-mediated learning [7]. AI revolution, online education could become even smarter, faster, and cheaper. There are various AI methods that can be used for eLearning and improved performance in online education [5].

One of the most important aspects of AI is its ability to collect and analyse data from users every time they engage with the technology. When an activity previously performed by a human and believed to require the ability to learn, reason, and solve problems can now be completed by a machine, AI is demonstrated [11].

That is what can help to more efficiently outline the learner's pathways through the educational process.

- Identify the learner's next level of achievement;
- Provide appropriate stuff to guide student to that level.
- Assist in getting there in accordance with the learner's current capabilities, knowledge, and experience, as well as unique learning style and pace.

9.3.1   Adaptive Study

Adaptive learning is educational software that is customized to each student individually, with concepts presented in the sequence that each student finds easiest to understand and finished at their own pace. Adaptive learning models now work best when a large group of students is required to learn the same content, providing for a big amount of comparable data. Adaptive learning models now work best when a large group of students is required to learn the same topic, allowing for the collection of a significant amount of comparable data at the same time. They could be introduced at a much more granular level as they progress [6].

For algorithm adaptive learning Bayesian Knowledge Tracing (BKT) is a typical approach for estimating the pace at which learning happens. Item Response Theory (IRT), developed in the discipline of psychometrics to model a learner's interaction with discrete stimuli, is another well-known theory.

The use of artificial intelligence to break down a textbook into a study guide containing chapter summaries, practice quizzes, and flashcards. Adaptive learning techniques will continue to make learning faster, smarter, and more personalized in the long run.

Understanding the various ways that technology can acquire data and induce adaptivity is beneficial, and they are most successful when combined in one instrument.

- Between students and professors, some aspects promote communication and collaboration.
- Faculty can set or overrule the technology's grading scale or scores, for example.
- Sources of information (e.g., OER, publisher content, customer-generated content).

9.3.2   Intelligent Tutoring System

An intelligent tutoring system (ITS) is a computer program that tries to provide learners with instant and personalized teaching or feedback, usually without the need for human participation. ITSs share the goal of allowing meaningful and effective learning through the use of a variety of computing technologies. Mathia was created to meet your students where they are and assist them in achieving their goals.

MATHiaU was created by a team of cognitive scientists to provide each Developmental Math learner with a tailored, easy-to-use learning experience. We teamed up with OpenStax, a major producer of open educational resources, to integrate MATHiaU with their textbooks to offer a single, cost-effective learning solution for students [3].

Intelligent teaching solutions can drastically reduce that cost while also increasing the success rate. At their best, these technologies don't replace instructors; rather, they move them closer to the role of mentor [1].

9.3.3 Virtual Counselors

IBM created prototypes of AI-powered 3D settings and lifelike virtual characters for the US Army, as well as prototypes of virtual counseling. Captivating Virtual Instruction for Training (CVIT) research intends to combine live classrooms with intelligent tutors, augmented reality, and virtual instructors.

Jill Watson is IBM Watson's virtual teaching assistant. Jill, who was first introduced at Georgia Tech in a course titled "Knowledge-Based Artificial Intelligence," participates in an online discussion forum in a classroom, addressing student questions alongside other, human teaching assistants. In many circumstances, she outperforms her human colleagues by responding faster. Georgia Tech students collaborated in 2016 [4].

9.3.4 Impact of Using Artificial Intelligence in Online Education

Online education is not successful due to the flaws in the current system used for online education. Below are some of the points where we can apply artificial intelligence tools which can help us to overcome all the flaws and can provide a perfect and successful platform for online education.

9.3.4.1 Online Tutorial

AI can provide personalized digital learning interfaces such as digital textbooks, study guides, bite-sized lectures, and much more. There will be no need for searching different materials from different sources. The Artificial Intelligence tool can provide the most relevant data very easily.

9.3.4.2 Visualization of Information

AI can offer new methods of display of information, such as visualization, simulation, graphs, and web-based study environments. AI tools can be designed to automatically visualize the data in animated charts, graphs, tables, and other formats to be easily understandable.

9.3.4.3 Updates to Learning Materials

Furthermore, AI helps in the creation and updating of course content, ensuring that knowledge is up to date and adapted to different learning curves. AI tools can alert teachers/learners about the latest information about a specific topic. By using AI tools, we can easily find the latest work done on a specific topic by searching the research sites like Google Scholar, etc.

9.3.4.4 Real-Time Surveillance

One of the most important functions of an AI-based eLearning platform is its capacity to act as a tutor and deliver real-time responses to inquiries. Many students have difficulty getting clarity on a certain topic while they are learning. However, by implementing Artificial Intelligence into your learning program, you can provide the finest alternative for learners to seek clarification whenever and wherever they choose. With AI, students may quickly ask questions about the unclear subject matter and receive immediate replies [3].

9.3.4.5 Natural Language Processing

This is a dream come true for you with an Artificial Intelligence system. Natural language processing is the most important component (or sub-field) of Artificial Intelligence. Its goal is to enable systems to process human language rapidly and efficiently.

So, by incorporating AI into your eLearning program, learners will be able to interact with the system and ask questions in the style/language of their choice. This will save time and aid in the development of interesting and efficient eLearning, in addition to making learning more accessible.

9.3.4.6 Personalized Tutoring Session

Artificial intelligence is essential for assessing a learner's past performance and determining their learning style. The data is used by AI to make modifications to the fresh learning content before delivering the desired tailored learning experience.

9.4   Conclusion

This Pandemic has disturbed the education system worldwide. We should move towards online education as soon as possible to overcome waste of time and to protect the future of our students. For this purpose, we must develop a new window AI-based program so that all students around the world can easily access and get an education.

This one Window platform cannot possible without Artificial Intelligence. Hence we can do it by using the techniques given in this paper to make it more engaging and successful. AI is the future and AI is the solution.

References

1. T. Anderson, Towards a theory of online learning. Theory Pract. Online Learn. **2**, 109–119 (2004)
2. S. Aydogdu, Predicting student final performance using artificial neural networks in online learning environments. Educ. Inf. Technol. **25**, 1913–1927 (2020)
3. P.-Y. Chen, X. Peng, S. Yu, NeuroSim: a circuit-level macro model for benchmarking neuro-inspired architectures in online learning. IEEE Trans. Comput. Aided Des. Integr. Circ. Syst. **37**, 3067–3080 (2018)
4. N. Fraser, L. Brierley, G. Dey, J.K. Polka, M. Pálfy, J.A. Coates, Preprinting a pandemic: the role of preprints in the COVID-19 pandemic. BioRxiv (2020)
5. A.K. Goel, D.A. Joyner, Using AI to teach AI: lessons from an online AI class. AI Mag. **38**, 48–59 (2017)
6. S.S. Mullick, S. Datta, S. Das, Adaptive learning-based $ k $-nearest neighbor classifiers with resilience to class imbalance. IEEE Trans. Neural Netw. Learn. Syst. **29**, 5713–5725 (2018)
7. A. Palayew, O. Norgaard, K. Safreed-Harmon, T.H. Andersen, L.N. Rasmussen, J.V. Lazarus, Pandemic publishing poses a new COVID-19 challenge. Nat. Hum. Behav. **4**, 666–669 (2020)
8. B. Pérez-Sánchez, O. Fontenla-Romero, B. Guijarro-Berdiñas, A review of adaptive online learning for artificial neural networks. Artif. Intell. Rev. **49**, 281–299 (2018)
9. S.A. Popenici, S. Kerr, Exploring the impact of artificial intelligence on teaching and learning in higher education. Res. Pract. Technol. Enhanc. Learn. **12**, 1–13 (2017)
10. Stead, Clinical implications and challenges of artificial intelligence and deep learning. JAMA **320**, 1107–1108 (2018)
11. Y. Tian, X. Liu, A deep adaptive learning method for rolling bearing fault diagnosis using immunity. Tsinghua Sci. Technol. **24**, 750–762 (2019)
12. W. Wang, K. Siau, Artificial intelligence, machine learning, automation, robotics, future of work and future of humanity: A review and research agenda. J. Database Manage. (JDM) **30**, 61–79 (2019)

Chapter 10
A Review of Attention Detection in Online Learning

Libo Qiao, Zongyi Han, Wei Wang, Linlin Li, and Ying Tong

Abstract With the development of Internet technology, online courses have greatly facilitated learners' self-learning courses. However, when students study online, due to the lack of real-time interaction between teachers and students, it is easier to produce a state of inattention. Therefore, this paper focuses on analyzing the process of detecting attention technology based on artificial intelligence methods in the Internet learning scenario. Meanwhile, the advantages and disadvantages of various methods are analyzed, and the difficulties and future directions of the research are pointed out.

Keywords Online learning · Attention detection · Image processing · Artificial intelligence · Wisdom education

10.1 Introduction

The 45th "Statistical Report on Internet Development in China" shows that the number of online education users in China alone reached 423 million, an increase of 222 million from the end of 2018 [1]. With the popularization of the Internet and the continuous development of hardware equipment, network learning has gradually become an important way to obtain knowledge [2]. Online learning is also favored by students because of its rich educational resources and not limited by time and location [3].

However, compared with traditional face-to-face teaching, owing to the lack of real-time interaction between teachers and students, teachers cannot master the classroom situation at any time, and it is hard to optimize and adjust the course content and teaching progress. At the same time, students are more likely to produce a

L. Qiao (✉) · Z. Han
Faculty of Psychology, Tianjin Normal University, Tianjin 300387, China
e-mail: qlb419@126.com

W. Wang · L. Li · Y. Tong
Tianjin Key Laboratory of Wireless Mobile Communications and Power Transmission, Tianjin Normal University, Tianjin 300387, China

concentrated state of inattention, which leads to irritability and weariness of learning, resulting in a decline in learning efficiency [4]. So, carrying out this research can promote students to enter the learning state more easily and indirectly improve the learning efficiency. Simultaneously, it provides effective and scientific data to further explore the visual cognitive process and cognitive laws during learning.

After the advent of artificial intelligence (AI) technology, it has gradually become one of the hot topics in the education field. AI has been applied in the teaching environment, instructional design, teaching analysis and teaching reflection stages [5]. In the form of a literature review, this paper combs the literature on Internet learning attention based on artificial intelligence methods since 2015 from three aspects: research principles, existing problems and development trends. Summarize the research status from different perspectives, discover problems and make suggestions for future research directions.

10.2 Implementation Principle and Related Processing Methods

The main principle of attention detection is to distinguish the current learning state of the learner. And Fig. 10.1 is the basic process of attention detection. It is roughly divided into three steps: digital image preprocessing, detection of face position, and recognition of facial key features. Most studies for this research [6–30] are based on this basic process. This section will summarize the three key technologies in turn.

10.2.1 Digital Image Preprocessing

Images collected through camera devices can inevitably have noise interference. In order to improve the accuracy of subsequent face detection and recognition algorithms, the image needs to be preprocessed to enhance the quality of the image. Binarization, histogram equalization, and morphological operations are three common preprocessing methods, and the processing results are shown in Fig. 10.2.

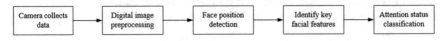

Fig. 10.1 The basic process of attention detection

(a) original image (b) Binarization (c) histogram equalization (d) morphological operation (corrosion) (e) morphological operation (dilation)

Fig. 10.2 Image preprocessing effect chart

10.2.1.1   Binarization

Binarization [31] is the process of adjusting the image to an obvious black and white effect, that is, the color of each pixel in the image is either black or white. It can not only reduce the data volume of the original image and increase the subsequent calculation speed, but also highlight the target area and reflect the overall and local characteristics of the image.

10.2.1.2   Histogram Equalization

The core of histogram equalization [32] is to stretch the image non-linearly. The grayscale histogram of the input image is adjusted from a state relatively concentrated in a certain grayscale interval to a uniformly distributed state within the entire grayscale range. The processed image is clearer in subjective perception. Objectively, it is more conducive as input data for image segmentation, object recognition and boundary detection.

10.2.1.3   Morphological Operation

Morphological operations [33] apply structural elements to input images through neighborhood operations to generate output images. There are mainly four processing methods: corrosion, expansion, open operation and closed operation. Among them, corrosion and expansion are basic operations, and open operation and close operation are a combination of the former two. Corrosion is an operation that eliminates the highlighted area of the boundary and shrinks the boundary to the inside. The noise spots in the original image can be reduced after processing. Expansion is the process of merging all the background points in contact with the object to expand the boundary to the outside. It is often used to fill holes in the original image or eliminate small particle noise in the target area.

The principle of open operation is to perform corrosion operation first, expand the background and remove isolated points. Then perform the expansion operation to restore the image area to its original size. This method is often used when removing tiny objects. It can maintain smooth boundaries and not change the area of the object as much as possible. On the contrary, the closed operation is the process of expansion before corrosion. It can fill holes and small cracks in the image and avoid no deformation or position changes in the target area.

10.2.2 Detection of Face Position

The human face contains a wealth of characteristic information. It is easier to judge the learning state of the learners by observing their facial features. Therefore, face detection is the basis for subsequent research. Common detection methods include traditional detection methods, template matching methods, and statistical modeling methods. Table 10.1 compares the principles, advantages and disadvantages of these methods.

10.2.3 Recognition of Key Facial Features

The recognition technology of key parts of the face is through the recognition and analysis of some obvious facial features, such as eyes, nose, eyebrows, mouth, forehead and other parts. In a combined or separate manner, the feature changes of the parts or the distance between the parts are used to identify key facial information and determine the learning status. Table 10.2 lists the facial features of students in different learning states.

10.2.3.1 Learning State Recognition Based on Eye Movement Features

The eye is an important sensory organ of humans. In the detection of the learning state, the changes in the eyes are also the most obvious. The state of the eyes can usually be recorded by the opening and closing state of the eyes, the characteristics of the eye movement and the relative position of the eyes. And then used these to judge the attention situation. Figure 10.3 shows all possible positions of the eyes.

Yi [6] designed a system for extracting implicit information of eye movements to analyze students' learning behaviors. After the facial image sequence is extracted, the iris sequence of location changes representing the eye motion is established. Then use the Hidden Markov Model (HMM) classifier to analyze the students' learning mode, and check their course status in class at any time. Yi [7] detected and modeled the learner's gaze changes by tracking the relative position changes of the corners of the eyes and the iris. Through the eyes, the cognitive behavior of learners can be widely separated as three categories: saccade, search and idleness. Wang [8] performed face region detection based on the AdaBoost method of Haar features. It is used to construct a sample database for convolutional neural network (CNN)

Table 10.1 Common face position detection methods

Category	Method	Principle	Advantages	Disadvantages
Traditional detection methods	Contour feature [34]	Detect face edges and extract face image profile features.	It has a good noise resistance performance.	When the light intensity is high, the anti-interference ability decreases.
	Grayscale feature [35]	Determine whether the image is a human face according to the facial light and dark rules.	The algorithm is simple and easy to implement.	Affected by illumination.
	Structural feature [36]	Face structural features are used to determine the presence of human faces.	Suitable for face front detection.	The detection effect of face deflection is poor.
	Color feature [37]	The skin color is proposed from the color image to further obtain the face range.	Insensitive to changes in the face posture.	The false detection rate is high.
	Movement feature [38]	Detect human faces in videos through changes in facial expressions and muscles.	Dynamic detection can be performed.	The effect is poor for objects whose position does not change for a long time.
Template matching methods	Fixed template matching [39]	A standard face template is constructed by a certain proportion and matched with the input face point by point.	The calculation is simple and fast.	The general accuracy is relatively low.
	Variable template matching [40]	The template parameters are adjustable, and the presence of the face in the graph is judged by the energy function.	Not easily affected by the appearance of the face.	The amount of data is large and the real-time performance is poor.

(continued)

experiments, and to train a classification model of the human eye state. Duan [9] recognized the key parts of the eye and calculated the aspect ratio of the eye. After obtaining the degree of opening and closing of the eyes, the classroom learning status can be distinguished. Zheng [10] proposed an attention detection method based on RNN-EMA eye movement analysis to extract eye movement features in real time.

Table 10.1 (continued)

Category	Method	Principle	Advantages	Disadvantages
Statistical modeling methods	Subspace detection [41]	The dimensionality of the face image is reduced to find the difference between the face and the non-face image in thelow-dimensional space.	The face detection accuracy is high, and the robustness is good.	The algorithm is more complex and has a long operation time.
	Artificial neural network [42]	The network is trained with the features of face sub-regions as input.	There is no need to manually select image features in advance.	Large data volume and time-consuming.
	Support vector machine [43]	Find the hyperplane that maximizes the positive and negative sample boundaries in the sample space.	Good recognition effect for high dimensions and small samples.	Sensitive to the missing data.
	AdaBoost iterative algorithm [44]	Multiple different weak classifiers are trained on the same training set.	High accuracy and fast detection speed.	The number of weak classifiers is not easy to set.

Table 10.2 Key features of the students' learning status

Status	Eyes	Sight	Mouth	Head	Eyebrows	Forehead
Focus	Eyes wide open	Fixed sight	Mouth closed	Less head movement	Raised eyebrows	Frown
General	No obvious features	Slight shaking of sight	No obvious features	No obvious features	No obvious features	No obvious features
Doubt	Decreased blink frequency	Fixed vision fixed	Mouth curled, mouth sinking	Head tilt	Raised eyebrows	Forehead lines
Fatigue	Eyes closed for a long time	No obvious features	Yawn, mouth open	Get down and nod frequently	No obvious features	Sinking forehead

The cyclic neural network is used to analyze the eye movement characteristics of the sequence, and the learning state is divided into reading, searching, and distraction. The detection accuracy is improved by 5.3% compared with similar algorithms.

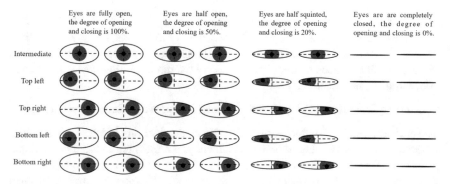

Fig. 10.3 Diagram of opening and closing of different positions of eyes

10.2.3.2   Learning Status Recognition Based on Multiple Facial Features

Facial multi-feature fusion is performed by combining many single characteristic points for observation and analysis. Through its common changes and distance conditions, the learning state can be judged and recognized, and the detection error caused by a single feature can be minimized.

1. Learning State Recognition Based on Facial Combination Features

When the learning state changes, small changes occur in various parts of the face, and these small changes are related to each other. Thus, by detecting multiple feature points at the same time, the learning state of the learner can be judged more effectively. Common facial feature points are shown in Fig. 10.4.

Tseng [11] measured the distance changes of various key parts such as eyes, nose, eyebrows and mouth, and trained a classifier to judge the changes in the students' learning status. Sun et al. [12] used closed eyes feature, yawn feature, closed mouth feature, nodding doze feature, viewing angle change feature and the proportions of forward-leaning characteristics to divide students' learning state into three states of focus, general and confusion. Zhang [13] determined the characteristics of the eyes and mouth by analyzing the degree of eye-opening and the curvature of the mouth. And put forward a deep perception classification method of online learning behavior based on CNN-SVM. Vettivel et al. [14] extracted precise facial features of the eyes, eyebrows, nose and ears. The auxiliary sensors collected heart rate and brain

Fig. 10.4 Common facial feature points

wave data to train classification models by extracting feature feedback. Gong [15] calculated the eye aspect ratio, PERCLOS value, blinking frequency, mouth width ratio, and mouth arc value as the feature input vector. The support vector machine (SVM) classifier is used to identify and classify the three learning states of students' concentration, doubt and fatigue.

2. Learning State Recognition Based on Facial Features and Expression Changes

The emotional state of online learners directly affects learning efficiency. Therefore, in remote network learning, researchers should pay more attention to the emotional problems of students. The wide application of facial expression recognition technology not only indirectly helps learners improve the efficiency of learning, but also makes up for the lack of emotion in distance education, and makes the education mode more intelligent and humanized.

Li [16] based on the detection of face, eye and mouth positioning, and analyzed the facial feature changes of network learners, moreover defined the expressions of three learning states of concentration, fatigue and normal. Comprehensive decision-making methods combined with expert experience are used to formulate fuzzy rule bases that meet the research needs. Dewan [17] analyzed the learner's facial expressions as emotional characteristics, thereby changing teaching strategies. Gupta [18] analyzed the facial expressions of students to judge their emotional state in the learning process, and divided emotions into four types: high positive emotion, low positive emotion, high negative emotion, and low negative emotion to help teachers improve their teaching strategies. Pei [19] used a multi-task Deep Convolutional Network (DNN) to detect facial landmarks, and designed a hybrid DNN to extract the features of micro-expressions, and improved the extracted features by removing redundancy and dimensionality reduction. Tang [20] elevated on the CNN model. By removing the fully connected layer, the speed of facial expression recognition in the classroom is improved. Provide teachers with feedback on the real-time status of students, with high detection accuracy and robustness.

3. Learning State Recognition Based on Facial and Head Feature Fusion

Changes in learning status are often accompanied by changes in head deflection and posture. Figure 10.5 shows a common head posture movement direction diagram, combined with head features that can provide more data for detecting the learning state.

Thomas [21] collected data on students' facial expressions, head posture and eye gaze points in the classroom. Training machine learning achieves automatic classification, so as to measure or analyze student curriculum engagement. Feng [22] used a low-cost camera, a low-resolution eye monitor and a mouse to collect learner information about head posture, and facial emotional features and eye movement message to assess their attention. Xiong [23] captured images with a camera, and analyzed the eye closure characteristics, head deflection characteristics and line of sight characteristics of the students in each frame of the image. Thereby, it can effectively detect distracted behaviors such as drowsiness and vision deviation from the teaching area in online learning. Bosch [24] analyzed students' upper body movement, head posture, facial

Fig. 10.5 Common head posture changes

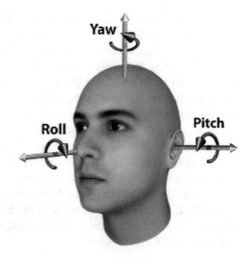

texture, facial movements, common features, time dynamics and other information. Simultaneously, a machine learning model composed of a SVM network and a deep neural network can automatically detect facial features and distract. Tao [25] designed a classroom concentration evaluation method that combined the facial expressions and head posture of students in classroom. According to classroom expressions and head pitch and deflection angles, the concentration is divided into levels and weights are assigned.

10.2.3.3   Learning Status Recognition Based on Fusion Other Features

In addition to the methods mentioned above, the researcher also combines the motion sensors, eye trackers, Electroencephalogram (EEG) and other electronic equipment shown in Fig. 10.6 to collect information from the face, head, eyes, brain waves, etc., and comprehensively evaluate the status of the learner through the fusion of the above data.

Yu [26] combined computer vision and brain wave detection methods, and used a wearable Mindware detection device to collect brain wave data from learners, and

Fig. 10.6 Common electronic collection devices

explored the relationship between concentration value, meditation value, blink intensity and attention. Lu [27] collected head posture, facial expression and eye movement data during online learning through the Kinect sensor and Tobii eye tracker. The PERCLOS, blink frequency, yawning frequency, nod frequency, average eye jump amplitude and horizontal displacement ratio are extracted to monitor the students' learning status in real time. Cheng [28] used frontal lobe sensors, earlobe sensors and data processing chips to detect brain waves, and measured and recorded participants' attention values in real time. Through the visual sensor for visual detection, capture and identify the visual attention of students. In order to confirm whether the learner is viewing the screen. Janez [29] obtained students' gaze points, facial features and body attributes through the Kinect sensors, and used machine learning algorithms to train students' level classifiers in different states. So as to automatically estimate students' status in the classroom. Lee [30] used three electrodes to obtain the EEG of subjects who watched the lecture through multimedia under different conditions and assessed their attention status.

10.3 Current Problem

At present, there are mainly the following problems in online learning attention detection research:

(1) The detection technology has limitations. Attention detection based on single facial features can only make simple judgments such as attentiveness or inattention, understanding or incomprehension. It cannot analyze students' classroom situations in detail. Although the multi-feature recognition technology greatly improves the disadvantages of the former. This method still has few recognizable states to accurately identify various subtle situations and dynamic images. In spite of the detection method based on the instrument or sensor can achieve a higher accuracy rate, it increases the detection cost to a large extent. Therefore, it does not have the universality of large-area application.

(2) The image resolution affects. The research uses image processing technology, which is greatly affected by environmental factors. When the face offset angle is too large, there is occlusion, and the light environment is poor, the effect of face detection is not ideal. At the same time, when the learner is facing the screen and the point of sight is also on the screen, it is difficult to detect the state of daze and distraction.

(3) There are fewer public datasets. The current mainstream datasets cannot be directly applied to attention detection, and researchers often need to collect educational data on themselves. Different datasets are not uniform in the standards of image acquisition and label annotation, and multiple datasets have errors in the same angle labeling. Obviously, it is hard to evaluate the model methods of different datasets. Meanwhile, datasets need to process huge data and analysis takes a long time.

(4)   The evaluation system is incomplete. Students of different ages, due to their different cognitive levels and individualized development, their learning situation and learning methods are also different. Thus researchers are easily affected by subjective attention. So, it is necessary to establish a variety of evaluation systems from many aspects of cognitive level and behavioral methods, and match appropriate testing standards to the teaching characteristics of each subject.

(5)   Ethics and thinking. Acquisition of students' classroom conditions via camera may lead to leakage of basic information. It also virtually increases the learning pressure and psychological pressure of students. How to deal with such ethical and moral problems, let students conduct online learning in a more natural state has also become another challenge.

10.4   Development Trend

On the basis of the above-mentioned existing problems and challenges, summarize the development trend of attention detection in recent years:

(1)   Application of interactive interface. With the gradual development of human–computer interaction, this method is slowly being used in attention detection scenes. But with the deepening of technical research, people are no longer satisfied with simple human–computer interaction. Enabling machines to intelligently understand user needs is increasingly gaining attention from developers.

(2)   Improve the efficiency of artificial intelligence algorithms. In the face of the huge data in attention detection, technical engineers are constantly improving the operational efficiency of electronic chips and the real-time computation of artificial intelligence algorithms to meet the real-time interaction of the attention detection system.

(3)   Classification is more humane. The system research can only detect the attention of the learners while ignoring the deeper information of their emotions and points of interest in the course. The identification of this information is gradually incorporated into the research scope of scientific researchers in order to better serve the learners.

(4)   Resolution of the bottleneck of image processing technology. Restricted by the image resolution, it is difficult to detect clear and accurate tiny facial features such as iris location and pupil profile in a specific environment. Consequently, attention detection research for low-resolution images has become a difficult problem to be solved urgently.

10.5 Conclusions

Artificial intelligence technology has received extensive attention in various fields, and the application of AI technology in network learning has become a development trend in recent years. This paper briefly summarizes the related research on attention detection technology based on AI methods in online learning in the recent five years. The implementation method of this technology and the detection performance in Internet learning are analyzed and evaluated. Meanwhile, it points out the problems that need to be solved urgently and analyzes the trend and characteristics of the future development of the technology.

Acknowledgements This paper is supported by Youth Research Project of Tianjin Normal University (52XQ2101).

References

1. The 47th "Statistical Report on Internet Development in China". News World **2021**(03), 96
2. R. Shang, Today's online learning methods and its impact on college students. Think Tank Era **03**, 179–180 (2019)
3. C. Wang, Institutions of Higher Learning Online Learning Platform Design and Implementation. University of Electronic Science and Technology of China (2013)
4. L. Guo, Study on Learners' Online Learning Ability and Its Influencing Factors in Online Live Teaching. Central China Normal University (2019)
5. L. Sun, Y. Ma, A summary of the research on the application of deep learning in education. China Inform. Technol. Educ. **17**, 98–101 (2019)
6. J. Yi, B. Sheng, R. Shen, L. Weiyao, E. Wu, Real time learning evaluation based on gaze tracking. In: IEEE 2015 14th International Conference on Computer-Aided Design and Computer Graphics, pp. 157–164 (2015)
7. J. Yi, Research and Application of Learning Status Evaluation Based on Eye Movements. Shanghai Jiao Tong University (2016)
8. Q. Wang, Research and Implementation of the Key Technology of Students Fatigue State Detection Based on CNN. Central China Normal University (2016)
9. J. Duan, Evaluation and Evaluation System of Students' Attentiveness Based on Machine Vision. Zhejiang Gongshang University (2018)
10. Q. Zheng. Study on Learning State Based on Facial Features[D]. Changchun University of Technology, 2020.
11. C.H. Tseng, Y.H. Chen, A camera-based attention level assessment tool designed for classroom usage. J. Supercomput. **74**(11), 1–14 (2017)
12. C. Sun, Research on Recognition of Learning Condition and Learning Emotion in Network Teaching. Jilin University (2018)
13. J. Zhang, Research and Application of Deep Learning of Online Learning Behavior Based on Face Recognition Technology. Nanjing Normal University (2018)
14. N. Vettivel, N. Jeyaratnam, V. Ravindran, S. Sumathipala, System for detecting student attention pertaining and alerting. In: 2018 3rd International Conference on Information Technology Research, 1–6 (2018)
15. J. Gong, Design of Student Learning State Detection System Based on Facial Features. Chengdu University of Technology (2019)

16. W. Li, Study on Learning Concentration Recognition Method for Distance Education. Hangzhou Dianzi University (2018)
17. M. Ali Akber Dewan, F. Lin, D. Wen, M. Murshed, Z. Uddin, A deep learning approach to detecting engagement of online learners. IEEE International Conference on Internet of People, 1895–1902 (2018)
18. S.K. Gupta, T.S. Ashwin, R.M.R. Guddeti, Students' affective content analysis in smartclassroom environment using deep learning techniques. Multimed Tools Appl. **78**(18), 25321–25348 (2019)
19. J. Pei, P. Shan, A micro-expression recognition algorithm for students in classroom learning based on convolutional neural network. Traitement du Signal **36**(6) (2019)
20. J. Tang, X. Zhou, J. Zheng, Design of intelligent classroom facial recognition based on deep learning. J. Phys. Conf. Ser. 1168 (2019)
21. C. Thomas, J. Dinesh Babu, Predicting student engagement in classrooms using facial behavioral cues. Proceedings of the 1st ACM SIGCHI international workshop on multimodal interaction for education, pp. 33–40 (2017)
22. T. Feng, J. Yue, X. Wan, K.-M. Chao, Q. Zheng, Learning unit state recognition based on multi-channel data fusion. Comput. Vis. Pattern Recog. (2018)
23. B. Xiong, H. Zhou, J. Huang, Y. Ruan, L. Zhou, A method of attention detection integrated with eye movement detection. Softw Guide **17**(07), 31–36 (2018)
24. N. Bosch, S. D'Mello, Automatic detection of mind wandering from video in the lab and in the classroom. IEEE Trans. Affect. Comput. (2019)
25. T. Yi, Analysis and Evaluation of Classroom Concentration based on Facial Expression and Head Pose Recognition. Yunnan Normal University (2020)
26. R. Yu, Application Research of Attention Detection Technology Based on Brain Wave and Computer Vision in E-Learning. Kunming University of Science and Technology (2015)
27. X. Lu, A Tool for Student State Detection in Online Learning: Design and Implementation. Huazhong University of Science and Technology (2016)
28. P.-Y. Cheng, Y.-C. Chien, Y.-M. Huang, The design and implementation of a real-time attention recognition/feedback system in online learning course. In: The Sixth International Conference of Educational Innovation through Technology, 214–217 (2017)
29. Z. Janez, A. Košir, Predicting students' attention in the classroom from Kinect facial and body features. EURASIP J. Image Video Process **1**, 1–12 (2017)
30. H. Lee, Y. Kim, C. Park, Classification of human attention to multimedia lecture. In: 2018 International Conference on Information Networking (ICOIN). IEEE, pp. 914–916 (2018)
31. C. Braccini, Image Analysis and Processing. Springer (1995)
32. A. Khellaf, A. Beghdadi, H. Dupoiset, Entropic contrast enhancement. IEEE Trans. Med. Imag. **10**(4), 589–592 (1991)
33. H. Park, R.T. Chin, Decopmosition of arbitrarily shaped morphological structuring elements. IEEE Trans. PAMI **17**(1), 2–15 (1995)
34. K.C. Yow, R. Cipolla, Feature-based human face detection. Image Vis. Comput. **15**(9), 713–735 (1997)
35. Y. Dai, Y. Nakano, Face-texture model based on SGLD and its application in face detection in a color scene. Pattern Recogn. **29**(6), 1007–1017 (1996)
36. D. Reisfeld, H. Wolfson, Y. Yeshurun, Context-free attentional operators: The generalized symmetry transform. Int. J. Comput. Vision **14**(2), 119–130 (1995)
37. H. Wu, Q. Chen, M. Yachida, Face detection from color images using a fuzzy pattern matching method. IEEE Trans. Pattern Anal. Mach. Intell. **21**(6), 557–563 (1999)
38. K. Sobottka, I. Pitas, Segmentation and tracking of faces in color images. In: Proceedings of the Second International Conference on Automatic Face and Gesture Recognition. IEEE, pp. 236–241 (1996)
39. T.K. Leung, M.C. Burl, P. Perona, Finding faces in cluttered scenes using random labeled graph matching. Comput. Vis. (1995)
40. A.L. Yuille, P.W. Hallinan, D.S. Cohen, Feature extraction from faces using deformable templates. Int. J. Comput. Vision **8**(2), 99–111 (1992)

41. M.A. Turk, A.P. Pentland, Face recognition using eigenfaces. In: Proceedings CVPR'91 IEEE Computer Society Conference on Computer Vision and Pattern Recognition. IEEE, pp. 586–591 (1991)
42. H.A. Rowley, S. Baluja, T. Kanade, Human face detection in visual scenes. Adv. Neural Inform. Process. Syst. 875–881 (1996)
43. E. Osuna, R. Freund, F. Girosit, Training support vector machines: an application to face detection. In: Proceedings of IEEE computer society conference on computer vision and pattern recognition. IEEE, pp. 130–136 (1997)
44. S.Z. Li, Z.Q. Zhang, Floatboost learning and statistical face detection. IEEE Trans. Pattern Anal. Mach. Intell. **26**(9), 1112–1123 (2004)

Chapter 11
Analysis of Teaching Introspection Text Based on Semantic Similarity

Xinyuan Zhang, Chen Zhao, and Wei Wang

Abstract With the accelerated innovation and development of artificial intelligence (AI), more AI technologies have entered the classroom to assist teaching. In this paper, we use semantic similarity to evaluate and analyze teaching introspection texts. According to the known teaching introspection content indicators, the weight of the divided words is computed by using TF-IDF, and the words with larger weight values are selected as the characteristic words that can identify the text. Next, we analyzed the semantic relationships between words based on the HowNet knowledge base, computed the sememes similarity, and then obtained the similarity between the texts. Finally, the evaluation of the introspection text is completed through similarity matching. The evaluation and analysis of teaching introspection texts are conducive to improving teaching efficiency. Besides, the level of teachers' professional skills and the mastery of students' knowledge points in classroom are also effectively investigated and quantified, to improve the quality of education and teaching.

Keywords Teaching introspection · Semantic similarity · Sememes similarity · Text evaluation

11.1 Introduction

In May 2019, the UNESCO released the "Beijing Consensus-Artificial Intelligence and Education" document with the theme of "Leading and Leaping, Planning Education in the Artificial Intelligence Era" [1], which aims to promote artificial intelligence and education systems deeply integrate, innovate learning, teaching and education methods, and build a flexible and high-quality education system.

Traditional teaching introspection behaviors in classroom are mostly evaluated by teachers. A large number of manual evaluations of teaching introspection will not only bring a lot of work pressure to teachers, but also lack a basis of professional evaluation and low efficiency. Based on this situation, this paper uses the

X. Zhang · C. Zhao · W. Wang (✉)
College of Artificial Intelligence, Tianjin Normal University, Tianjin 300387, China
e-mail: weiwang@tjnu.edu.cn

method of semantic similarity computation to classify the teaching introspection text written by teachers, and compare the text manually classified by experts, which can automatically and intelligently evaluate and analyze the introspection text. Similarity computation is one of the common methods in text evaluation and analysis. In 1998, Dekang Li first proposed a broadly meaningful definition of similarity [2]. He believed that similarity is related to the commonalities between things. When the similarity between two things is greater, there are more commonalities. On the contrary, the difference between things is greater. However, the traditional text similarity measurement does not take account of the semantic relationship between words, which leads to the low accuracy of text classification assessment. Dong Zhendong et al. used the concept of words as the object of description. According to the attributes of the word concept, the word similarity is computed. Tang Xinyu [3] reduced the dimensionality by computing the semantic similarity between the feature words and improved the accuracy of text classification. Deep learning is a multi-level representation learning method that has powerful feature extraction capabilities for things, and also has a good performance in text classification. For example, in 2013, Mikolov proposed a recurrent neural network (RNN) based on time series to solve the text classification problem; Li Mei et al. [4] proposed a convolutional neural network (CNN) based on the attention mechanism combined with long and short-term memory networks (LSTM) neural network prediction model, which combines coarse and fine-grained features, can extract the subtle features of short texts, and then realize text classification.

Although the neural network's text classification model has strong feature extraction capabilities, it needs to collect a large amount of text predictions for training, which requires a lot of time. For long text, the effect of feature extraction using neural network is often unsatisfactory. As the number of texts collected in this experiment is small, and the teaching introspection texts are longer in content and complex in structure. TF-IDF can effectively filter out text keywords and reduce redundancy; the computation method of HowNet semantic similarity can obtain the semantic distance [5] according to the semantic relationship between words, and compute the semantic similarity. In this way, we can get the similarity of the teaching introspection text and realize the analysis and evaluation of the text.

According to the large amount of text and rich semantics, this paper uses HowNet semantic similarity to evaluate and analyze the introspection text, and proves its effectiveness. The rest of this paper is organized as follows. In Sect. 2, it mainly introduces the text preprocessing process and the principle of HowNet semantic similarity computation method. In Sect. 3, the selection of feature words and the computation of semantic similarity of words are enumerated by weights. Finally, the results of systematic text classification and manual classification are compared with experimental data, which proves the feasibility of the research. Conclusion and discussion is in Sect. 4.

11.2   Text Evaluation Process

As a kind of supervised learning, text classification evaluation is one of the key technologies in natural language processing. Introspection text evaluation is generally composed of three parts: text preprocessing, feature word selection and similarity computation. In the part of text preprocessing, we mainly introduce the Chinese word segmentation based on Jieba and stopwords removal.

11.2.1   Chinese Word Segmentation

Chinese word segmentation can be roughly divided into three methods: string matching based, understanding based and statistics based [6]. In this paper, we use the most widely used Chinese word segmentation tool Jieba, its basic principles: (1) Efficient word map scanning based on Trie tree structure. With its own dictionary, it contains more than 340,000 words as well as frequency and word type. Using the prefixes of these words together to form a Trie tree, the combination of words and phrases in all possible situations in a sentence to be processed is quickly searched in the dictionary to generate a directed acyclic graph (DAG), as shown in Fig. 11.1.

The above figure is a directed acyclic graph generated by the example sentence "今天的天气真暖和". Make "今" as the starting position of the sentence, with the help of *{idx:[x_i]}*, *idx* represents the starting position, the position x_i of each Chinese character in the sentence represents the end position of the vocabulary. Set {0:[1, 2, 3, 4, 5, 6, 7]} as a simple DAG, and its location dictionary DAG is shown:

{0[0, 1], 1 : [1], 2 : [2], 3 : [3, 4], 4 : [4], 5 : [5], 6 : [6, 7], 7 : [7]}

These number combinations indicate the position index corresponding to each word in the sentence and possible word combinations, such as{6:[6, 7]}: It means that there are two possible combinations of words that can be found in the dictionary with the word "暖" corresponding to the sentence: "暖" and "暖和". (2) Based on dynamic programming, the maximum probability path is found and the maximum tangent combination of word frequency is found. According to the results of multiple combinations of words in the DAG, each word is regarded as a node of the DAG.

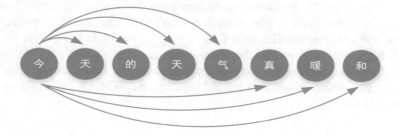

Fig. 11.1 Directed Acyclic Graph of words

From back to front, whenever a node is reached, the path between the two points can be obtained. So by traversing all the paths and finding the shortest path in the DAG, the maximum probability path can be obtained. Wei Renyu [7] gave a detailed introduction on the maximum probability path finding. With the help of *{idx:[xᵢ]}* to traverse each Chinese character in the sentence from back to front, the formula for computing the maximum probability of *idx* based on word frequency is as follows:

$$P(idx) = \max\left(\ln\left(\frac{count(word)}{\sum_{i=0}^{dict.txt} count(i)}\right) + P(x_i + 1)\right) \tag{11.1}$$

where, *count (word)* denotes the frequency of all possible combinations of words in the dictionary. $P(x_i + 1)$ is the maximum path probability where the location node $x_i + 1$ is the starting position. Jieba word segmentation supports three word segmentation modes: exact mode, full mode and search engine mode. For unregistered words, the Hidden Markov Model (HMM) [8] can be used to accurately segment the words. When segmenting texts, different segmentation modes are often adopted for different segmentation requirements. In addition, there are some special words or proper nouns; Jieba word segmentation supports customized dictionaries. By building a customized dictionary by oneself, the accuracy of word segmentation can be improved. The customized dictionary is composed of words and word frequency: {word, word frequency}.

> Example: "江宁市市长江大桥将出席长江大桥开通仪式。".
> No dictionary: "江宁/市市/长江大桥/将/出席/长江大桥/开通/仪式/。".
> Customized dictionary: {"江宁", 200 "江大桥", 500}.
> Loading dictionary: "江宁市/市长/江大桥/将/出席/长江大桥/开通/仪式/。

11.2.2 Remove Stopwords

After word segmentation, there are some words or symbols that have little effect on the meaning of text information, but they appear more frequently in the text, and their contribution to the text similarity measurement can be ignored, such as "的", "了", "?", "*" and so on. These words or symbols are collectively called stop words. In text processing, these words are often considered interference, so they should be filtered out as much as possible. The method of filtering stop words is to establish a stop word list that contains various functional words and symbols with little meaning. Then, by judging whether the words are included in the list, and filtered out. Thereby reduced the amount of computation and improved the efficiency and accuracy of computation.

11.2.3 TF-IDF

One of the most effective ways to compute word weights is TF-IDF, a word frequency weighting method [9, 10], proposed by Salton in 1988. It is often used in information retrieval and data mining. The main idea is that: if a word appears more often in text, the TF value will be larger, and the IDF value will be larger when there are fewer occurrences in other text. It indicates that the better discriminatory performance of this word category, the more important it is. Among them, TF represents the frequency of occurrence of a certain word in the text. Supposing the introspection text set is D, which contains n documents respectively $d_1, d_2, ..., d_n$ and the word is w, then the mathematical expression of word frequency computation of word w with respect to text d is shown in Formula 11.2:

$$TF(w, d) = \alpha_{w,d} = \frac{n_{w,d}}{\sum_{u \in d} n_{u,d}} \tag{11.2}$$

where, $n_{w,d}$ is the number of times the word w appears in the text d, and $n_{u,d}$ denotes the total times the word appears in the text d. IDF is a measure to describe the universality of words in a text set. IDF is a measure of the universality of vocabulary in a text set. It means that the more documents with a word w in the document set, the lower the category discrimination ability and the smaller the IDF. Supposing that n_w denotes the number of texts in which the word w appears in the introspection document D, the mathematical expression of IDF is shown in Formula 11.3:

$$IDF(w, D) = \beta_{w,D} = \log \frac{n}{n_w + 1}, \forall w \in D \tag{11.3}$$

where, $w \in D$ denotes that the word w occurs in a certain text of the document D. However, in order to avoid a certain word w that does not exist in any text of the document D, there is a computation error, and 1 is often added to the denominator. With the above two formulas, we can get the word w about the TF-IDF definition of document D, as shown in Formula 11.4:

$$TF - IDF(w, d) = TF \times IDF = \alpha_{w,d} \cdot \beta_{w,D} \tag{11.4}$$

It can be seen from Formula 11.4. When a word appears more frequently in the text, and it appears less frequently in the entire document set, then the word has a higher weight value, indicating that the word can reflect the characteristic information of the text well, and the more important it is.

11.2.4 HowNet Semantic Similarity

HowNet is a common-sense knowledge base that regards Chinese characters, words and English words as the description object, and reveals the attribute relationships between concepts as the basic content. HowNet semantics is mainly composed of two concepts: "Concept" and "Sememe". "Concept" is a description of the semantics of words, but some words have more than one meaning, which can be presented through "Sememe", which is the smallest unit of "Concept" [11]. In this paper, we use the latest WHOLE.DAT file in the sememes dictionary, which contains a total of 57,153 content word concepts and 1,618 sememes. The following are some examples of language descriptions cited in dictionary files, such as:

(1)   introspection V think |思考
(2)   behavior N fact|事情, act|行动
(3)   Tianjin N place |地方, city |市, Proper Name |专, (China |中国)
(4)   limit N attribute |属性, boundary |界限, extreme |极, & entity |实体

For word " Tianjin ", it is defined as the three sememes of "地方", "市" and "专, (China |中国)". A total of 2,600 sememes are used in the existed HowNet, which can be divided into the following 10 categories, as shown in Table 11.1:

HowNet also defines some symbols, such as "#", "%", "$", etc. According to the combination of these symbols and the sememes, the semantics can be described in more detail. The description rules of content words in HowNet are complex and changeable. They are described by the relationship between the sememes. The conceptual descriptions of specific content words mainly include: the first basic sememes description, the other basic sememes description, the relation sememes description and the relational symbols description [12]. HowNet describes the relationship between 8 kinds of sememes, the most important of which is the subordinate relationship. According to this relationship, the basic sememes constitute a tree-like structure of the sememes hierarchy, as shown in Fig. 11.2:

Table 11.1 Ten types of sememes	(1)	Event|事件	(6)	qValue|数量值
	(2)	entity|实体	(7)	Secondary Feature|次要特征
	(3)	aValue |属性值	(8)	Syntax|语法
	(4)	Attribute|属性值	(9)	Event Role|动态角色
	(5)	quantity|数量	(10)	Event Feature|动态属性

Fig. 11.2 Sememes tree
hierarchy

```
—  entity│实体
    ├  thing│万物
  …  ├  physical│物质
      …  ├  animate│生物
          …  ├  AnimalHuman│动物
              …  ├  human│人
                  │      └  humanized│拟人
                  └      animal│兽
                         ├  beast│走兽

              …
```

The complex relationship descriptions between sememes form an intricate network tree hierarchy, which is the basis of similarity computation. The computation of the sememes similarity is affected by the distance between sememes, the level of nodes, and the density of nodes, etc.[13]. The sememes similarity is inversely proportional to the distance between sememes and the level of nodes, and directly proportional to the density of nodes. If the path and length of nodes is same, when the level of the node is higher, the similarity is smaller, and the distance between sememes is closer, and the similarity is greater. Besides, the nodes density is greater, the finer the classification and the greater the similarity. According to the characteristics of semantic expression description, in 2002, Liu Qun et al. [14] proposed to transform the relationship of the distance between the sememes in nodes into the similarity between the sememes. The computation is shown in Formula 11.5:

$$sim(p_1, p_2) = \frac{\alpha}{dis(p_1, p_2) + \alpha} \tag{11.5}$$

where, $dis(p_1, p_2)$ denotes the shortest path distance of the two sememes of p_1 and p_2 in the hierarchical structure, and α is an adjustable parameter, which means the sememes distance when the similarity is about 0.5. When computing the similarity of text words, words often contain multiple concepts. Suppose two words W_1 and W_2 contain n concepts, namely $S_{11}, S_{12},…, S_{1n}$ and $S_{21}, S_{22},…, S_{2n}$. Then the similarity of the word W_1 and the word W_2 takes the maximum value of the similarity of all concepts, and its computation is shown in Formula 11.6:

$$sim(W_1, W_2) = \max_{i=1…n; j=1…m} \left(sim(S_{1i}, S_{2j}) \right) \tag{11.6}$$

In HowNet, the similarity computation of the content word is obtained by integrating four-part sememes description similarity of the content word. The first basic sememes similarity is computed by Formula 11.5 to obtain $sim1(S_1, S_2)$; The other basic similarity is matched by the redundant content word sememes each other, according to the method of first basic sememes, select the largest group with the computed similarity of all possible pairs, and repeat, until all pairs of similarity is obtained and then weighted and averaged to obtain the similarity sim2(S_1,S_2). The relation sememes description similarity sim3(S_1,S_2) is obtained by combining the same semantics in the same group. The relationship symbol description similarity sim4(S_1,S_2) is computed according to the sememes similarity of the same relationship. And then with the help of the set parameter factor β, the concept similarity computation is obtained as shown in Formula 11.7:

$$sim(S_1, S_2) = \sum_{i=1}^{4} \beta_i \prod_{j=1}^{i} sim_j(S_1, S_2) \tag{11.7}$$

The four adjustable parameters in the formula satisfy $\beta_1 + \beta_2 + \beta_3 + \beta_4 = 1$ and $\beta_1 > \beta_2 > \beta_3 > \beta_4$. Different parameter factors can reflect the degree of influence of each concept description part on the similarity computation. After many experiments, the values of the adjustment parameters are: $\alpha = 1.6$, $\beta_1 = 0.5$, $\beta_2 = 0.2$, $\beta_3 = 0.17$, $\beta_4 = 0.13$. Therefore, the semantic similarity computation based on HowNet ultimately comes down to the sememes similarity computation, the text is composed of multiple paragraph sentences, sentences are weighted by the most basic word similarity, thus finally realize the similarity computation of the text.

The following is an introduction to the main process of text semantic similarity computation through pseudo code.

Algorithm 1   compute TF-IDF

Input：collected introspection texts are segmented by Jieba, removed stopwords, obtained feature word

Output：word frequency(TF) corresponding to each word

 1:**for** word[i] ∈words **do**

 2:         **if** word[i] such that wordi ∈d **then**

 3:                   count_wordi←count_wordi +1

 4:         **end if**

 5:         count_words+=count_word[i]

 6:         word_tf=count_wordi / count_words

 7:**end for**

 8:**for** word[i] ∈D **do**

 9:          **for** wordi ∈D **do**

10:                   **if**   wordi ∈d **then**

11:                   n_wordi ←n_wordi +1

12:                   **else** n_wordi=0

13:                   **end if**

14:                   n_wordi,d ←n_wordi,d +1

15:          word_idf=log(n_D / (n_word , d+1))

16:**end for**

17:tf-idf=word_tf * word_idf

Algorithm 2   compute similarity

Input：text words

Output：text similarity value

 1：S ← words

 2：**for** i=1 to 4 , j<i, i++ **do**

 3：   According to HowNet Knowledge Base, compute the similarity of each part;

 4：   sim1(S_1,S_2)←the first basic sememes similarity;

 5：   sim2(S_1,S_2)←the other basic sememes similarity;

 6：   sim3(S_1,S_2)←the relation sememes similarity;

 7：   sim4(S_1,S_2)←the relational symbols similarity;

 8：   compute and obtained the semantic similarity sim(S_1,S_2)

 9： **end for**

Comparing the similarity value computed by the sample with the average similarity between each category, define the category with the largest value as the most approximate category of the sample, thus complete the sample classification and realize the text measurement analysis.

11.3 Experimental Results

In order to satisfy the effect of real and effective data set, we select the teaching introspection text of the middle school mathematics curriculum written by Tianjin pre-service or frontline teachers as the research object of this topic. In this paper, we take teaching courses, content introduction and the situation of students as indicators in teaching introspection. Next, TF-IDF is used to compute the weight of text keywords, and the top K keywords are selected as text feature words according to the weight value. To verify the feasibility of this method, three random texts from the introspection text are selected, and the top 10 keyword examples are computed by TF-IDF, as shown in Table 11.2.

According to manual evaluation, the text information identified by the keywords computed by TF-IDF is almost the same as the actual text content, which demonstrates that TF-IDF has good representativeness and accuracy in filtering text keywords. According to WHOLE.DAT file, we obtained the sememes description of the top k text feature words. The distance between sememes is computed according to the sememe tree hierarchy. The basic sememe similarity is computed by Formula 11.5, and then the word semantic similarity is obtained by Formula 11.7. What's more, when a word contains multiple concepts, the similarity between each concept can be computed by Formula 11.6, and the maximum value is taken as the similarity between the two words. In order to prove the feasibility of the algorithm, some feature words from the above three texts are selected, and word semantic similarity values were computed. Here, the number 1 denotes the closest semantic relationship between words. The experiment results are shown in Fig. 11.3.

As can be seen from the histogram graph above, the HowNet Semantic Similarity algorithm shows reliability in terms of word similarity measurement. Long text is composed of multiple paragraph sentences. The similarity of the introspection text is actually obtained by the weighted average of the similarity of the composed sentences. However the sentence similarity is obtained by weighting the most basic

Table 11.2 Examples of experimental results of text word weight computation

Text 1 keywords	TF-IDF	Text 2 keywords	TF-IDF	Text 3 keywords	TF-IDF
Definition	0.65398	Function	0.72238	Rate of change	0.75047
Ratio	0.39287	Zero point	0.68153	Derivative	0.69023
Problem	0.33458	Equation	0.47296	Teaching	0.45915
Origin	0.32303	Student	0.45025	Concept	0.40328
Right triangle	0.21448	Literacy	0.44984	Situation	0.38207
Unit	0.20886	Mathematics	0.37860	Definition	0.27883
Coordinates	0.19845	Image	0.23183	Student	0.22338
Teaching	0.19230	Teaching	0.23137	Problem	0.21507
Student	0.18711	Intuitive	0.22262	Mathematics	0.20490
Example	0.17152	Process	0.19329	Teaching mode	0.13579

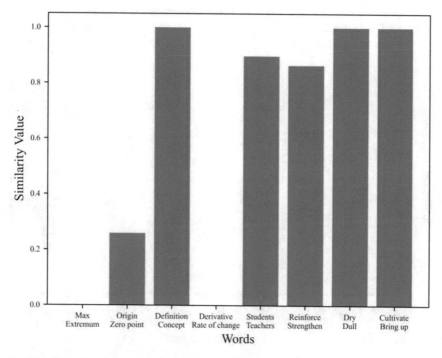

Fig. 11.3 Example computation of semantic similarity of text words

word similarity. Finally, the similarity computation of the text is realized. In order to verify the effectiveness of semantic similarity in the evaluation and measurement of introspection texts, we collected 20 teaching introspections written by frontline teachers. By inviting introspection experts and professors to participate in manual text judgment, the collected teaching introspection texts were classified according to different levels, which is divided into four levels, namely, Class A (excellent), Class B (good).Class C (qualified) and Class D (poor).Then we use the algorithm of this paper to evaluate the 20 texts, and obtain the evaluation and analysis results. As shown in Fig. 11.4, it is a line graph of the comparison between manual classification and semantic classification.

From the evaluation and comparison line graph in Fig. 11.4, it can be concluded that the teaching introspection text evaluation system based on semantic similarity can conduct effective introspection text analysis and evaluation, and the total text classification accuracy rate reaches more than 80%. Although compared with the manual evaluation of professional introspection experts, there is a certain deviation. But on the whole, its impact is relatively small. It has important research value for the improvement of the efficiency of teachers' teaching work, the improvement of teachers' professional skills and the improvement of teaching behavior.

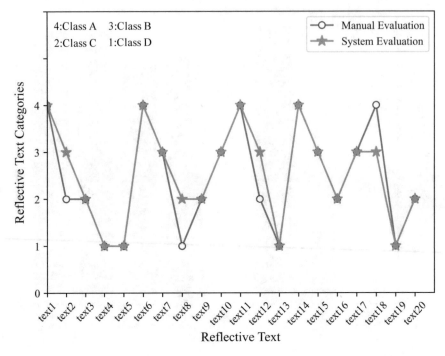

Fig. 11.4 Comparison of two evaluation methods

11.4   Conclusion

With the deep integration of artificial intelligence technology and education, more and more classroom teaching behaviors will be analyzed with the aid of information technology. However, how to effectively use these technologies to analyze these behaviors and assist teaching is a challenge faced by scientific and technological researchers.

In order to effectively reduce the redundant information vocabulary of the text, this paper uses TF-IDF with the help of teaching reflection content indicators to calculate and filter the vocabulary with a large weight contribution as the text feature words. In addition, according to the principle of HowNet semantic similarity, we analyzed the relationship between the "concept" and the "meaning original" of words, calculated word similarity, and realized effective text similarity measurement, which can be matched the text that can be judged manually by experts more accurately, and then completed the evaluation and analysis of the text of teaching introspection. Therefore, on the basis of effectively reducing the teaching working time of teachers, guide teachers to carefully reflect on their own teaching behaviors and improve the level of teaching professional skills.

Due to the limited number of reflective text corpora provided by the research, and after manual processing, standard and reliable data texts are even rarer. In addition,

HowNet semantic similarity calculation method is based on the knowledge base, and some words are not included in the dictionary, which makes this teaching introspection text analysis research still have many shortcomings. For the improvement of calculation accuracy, further research is needed to invest more energy and time to improve.

Acknowledgements The work was supported by the Natural Science Foundation of China (61731006, 61971310).

References

1. L. Chen, P. Chen, Z. Lin, Artificial intelligence in education: a review. IEEE Access **8**, 75264–75278 (2020). https://doi.org/10.1109/ACCESS.2020.2988510
2. Y. Hedley, M. Younas, A. James, The categorisation of hidden Web databases through concept specificity and coverage, in *19th International Conference on Advanced Information Networking and Applications (AINA'05)*, vol 1 (AINA papers) (2005), pp. 671–676
3. T. Xinyu et al., Research on feature dimensionality reduction method based on HowNet semantic similarity computation. Sci. Technol. Eng. **21**, 3442–3446 (2006)
4. Li., Mei, N. Dejun, G. Jiacheng, CNN-LSTM model based on attention mechanism and its application. Comput. Eng. Appl. **55**(13), 20–27 (2019)
5. H. Nie, J. Zhou, H. Wang, M. Li, Word similarity computing based on HowNet and synonymy thesaurus, in *IIntelligent Systems and Applications. IntelliSys 2019. Advances in Intelligent Systems and Computing,* ed. by Y. Bi, R. Bhatia, S. Kapoor, vol. 1038 (Springer, Cham, 2019)
6. F. Li, Overview of Chinese word segmentation technology. Modern Comput. (Professional Edition) **34**(2018):17–20. CNKI:SUN:XDJS.0.2018-34-005
7. W. Renyu, Research on chinese word segmentation technology. Inf. Comput. (Theoretical Edition) **32**(10), 26–29 (2020). CNKI:SUN:XXDL.0.2020-10-010
8. T. Lin, G. Chonghui, C. Jingfeng, Review of chinese word segmentation studies. Data Anal. Knowl. Discov. **4**(2/3), 1–17 (2020)
9. P. Bafna, D. Pramod, A. Vaidya, Document clustering: TF-IDF approach, in *2016 International Conference on Electrical, Electronics, and Optimization Techniques (ICEEOT)* (2016), pp. 61–66. https://doi.org/10.1109/ICEEOT.2016.7754750
10. C. Liu, Y. Sheng, Z. Wei, Y. Yang, Research of text classification based on improved TF-IDF algorithm, in *2018 IEEE International Conference of Intelligent Robotic and Control Engineering (IRCE)* (2018), pp. 218–222. https://doi.org/10.1109/IRCE.2018.8492945
11. Y. Zhang, L. Gong, Y. Wang (2005) Chinese word sense disambiguation using HowNet, in *Advances in Natural Computation. ICNC 2005. Lecture Notes in Computer Science*, vol. 3610 (Springer, Berlin, Heidelberg, 2005). https://doi.org/10.1007/11539087_123
12. Q.-L. Liu, X.-F. Gu, J.-P. Li, Researches of Chinese sentence similarity based on HowNet, in *The 2010 International Conference on Apperceiving Computing and Intelligence Analysis Proceeding* (2010), pp. 26–29. https://doi.org/10.1109/ICACIA.2010.5709843
13. J. Bai, Y. Bu, An improved algorithm for semantic similarity based on HowNet, in *2018 2nd International Conference on Data Science and Business Analytics (ICDSBA)* (2018), pp. 65–70. https://doi.org/10.1109/ICDSBA.2018.00020
14. L. Qun, L. Sujian, Computation of word semantic similarity based on HowNet. Chin. Comput. Linguist. (2002)

Chapter 12
A Summary of Text Classification Technology and Its Application in Teacher Language Classification

Feng Tang, Tingting Han, and Libao Wu

Abstract With the rapid development of the Internet, the text data on the Internet has also increased. Under this trend, text classification has become a hot research issue, and has been applied in many fields, such as education. In education, teachers' teaching language is an important means of transferring knowledge to students. Teacher language classification is of great significance to teaching evaluation and can effectively improve the teaching quality and skills of teachers. This paper mainly studied the text classification technology and introduced several representative deep learning-based network structures. In addition, the application in teachers' language classification was introduced. Finally, the future research prospects were put forward.

Keywords Deep learning · Text classification · Neural network · Teacher language

12.1 Introduction

In recent years, with the rapid development of the Internet, massive amounts of data is generated every day, and these data mainly exists in the form of text. How to deal with these data has attracted the attention of many researchers. Retrieving and extracting valuable information from these text data is of great significance, and the development of text mining technology is particularly important. Text classification is an important branch in text mining, and it is a classic problem in natural language processing (NLP). Currently it has been applied in many fields. Education is one of the most important fields, which is the country's top plan for cultivating talents. Now, countries all over the world are emphasizing the construction of a new education system that includes intelligent and interactive learning. In addition, promoting the

F. Tang · T. Han (✉)
Tianjin Key Laboratory of Wireless Mobile Communications and Power Transmission, Tianjin Normal University, Tianjin 300387, China
e-mail: hanting608@163.com

L. Wu
Faculty of Education, Tianjin Normal University, Tianjin 300387, China

informatization of education should mainly focus on the promotion of educational reforms and the improvement of education quality by new technologies.

As an important base for teaching and learning research, the classroom is the main activity place for education and teaching. Discovering teaching problems in real classroom is the primary basis of current education research. The traditional classroom teaching behavior is mainly analyzed manually. Moreover, the analysis results are inevitably subjective. With the rapid development of new technologies such as artificial intelligence, the leading role of education informatization in education modernization will become more prominent. Using artificial intelligence technology to analyze classroom teaching behavior will be more convenient. Promoting the further integration of information technology and teaching, and strengthening the application of artificial intelligence in education will have a profound impact.

In this paper, we mainly studied text classification technology, introduced several representative network models based on deep learning. In addition, we introduced the application of artificial intelligence technology in teachers' language classification. Finally, the prospects for future research directions were put forward.

12.2 Text Classification Technology

Text classification is an efficient information retrieval and data mining technology. It plays a very important role in the management of text data. It has therefore become an important task in NLP. Many applications are based on this, such as emotions analysis, topic analysis, question answering system, machine translation, etc. [1]. There are many methods for text classification, including early rule-based methods, traditional machine learning methods, and current deep learning methods. Early classification methods based on rule systems are easy to understand, but they rely too much on the knowledge of experts, leading to higher system construction costs and poor portability [2]. Later, as machine learning technology gradually matured, some classic text classification algorithms appeared, such as Decision Tree (DT) [3], Naive Bayesian Classifier (NBC) [4], Support Vector Machine (SVM) [5], K-Nearest Neighbor (KNN) [6], etc. These methods partially solve the problems of early classification methods based on rule systems. However, in these methods, manual feature extraction is usually required. In addition, text data also has high dimensionality and sparseness, which limits its further development.

To solve these problems, researchers began to try to use deep learning techniques for text classification. With the introduction of word vector models such as word2vec [7], GloVe [8] and BERT [9], deep learning has made great achievements in text processing, and various text classification methods based on deep neural networks are proposed. These methods include the use of Convolutional Neural Network (CNN), Recurrent Neural Network (RNN), and attention mechanism. Compared with traditional text classification methods, they undoubtedly have better performance. Their training time is short, and the classification effect is improved.

12.2.1 Text Classification Method Based on CNN

CNN is a deep feedforward neural network. It was originally built for image processing. It has achieved remarkable results in the fields of classification and image recognition, and has since been effectively used for text classification. The basic structure of CNN mainly includes input layer, convolutional layer, pooling layer, fully connected layer and output layer.

Kim [10] proposed a method for text classification using CNN, which used multiple convolution kernels of different sizes to extract key information in sentences, to better capture local correlations and obtain better classification results. Figure 12.1 shows the structure of the CNN text classification model.

The input layer used a dual-channel model architecture. One used the fixed word vector trained by word2vec, and the other was fine-tuned according to each task during the model training process. The convolutional layer used a set of convolution kernels of different sizes to perform front-to-back convolution operations on the text to get multiple features. Then the pooling layer operated on the vector extracted by each convolution kernel, and each convolution kernel corresponded to a number. The fully connected layer connected these convolution kernels to obtain a word vector representing a sentence. Finally, the probability of the text in each category was calculated through the softmax layer, and the final classification result was obtained. The author conducted comparative experiments on seven data sets, and proved the effectiveness of single-layer CNN in text classification tasks. At the same time, it also showed that word vectors derived from unsupervised learning were very meaningful for many NLP tasks.

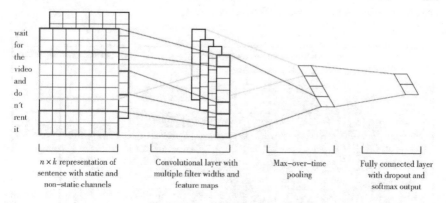

| wait
for
the
video
and
do
n´t
rent
it			
$n \times k$ representation of sentence with static and non−static channels	Convolutional layer with multiple filter widths and feature maps	Max−over−time pooling	Fully connected layer with dropout and softmax output

Fig. 12.1 The structure diagram of CNN text classification model [10]

12.2.2 Text Classification Method Based on RNN

RNN uses variable-length sequence data as data input, and its neurons have a self-feedback function. It is a neural network model with short-term memory capabilities. In text classification task, the Long Short Term Memory Network (LSTM) [11] is actually used more often. It is a special RNN, which has its unique advantages in long-distance information-dependent learning. LSTM operates the addition and deletion of information in the cell state through the "gate" structure. And in this way, the hidden state of each layer is updated.

Lai et al. [11] introduced a recurrent convolutional neural network for text classification without artificially designed features. First, when learning the expression of words, the two-way loop structure was used to obtain text information, which can reduce noise more than traditional window-based neural networks, and it can preserve the word order in a large range when learning text expression. Secondly, the maximum pooling layer was used to obtain the main components of the text, and automatically determined which feature played a more important role in the text classification process. Figure 12.2 shows the network structure of the model.

The model used a bidirectional RNN to learn the left context representation c_l and the right context representation c_r of the current word w_i, and then connected with the representation of the current word itself to form the input x_i of the convolutional layer. After the convolutional layer, the representation of all words was obtained. After the maximum pooling layer and the fully connected layer, the representation of the text was obtained. Finally the softmax layer was used for classification. The author conducted experiments on four commonly used data sets. Experimental results showed that this method outperformed the most advanced methods on several data sets, especially on document-level data sets.

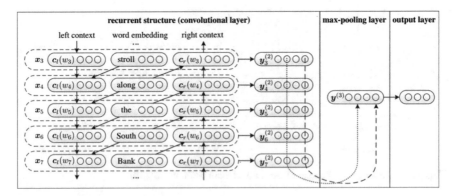

Fig. 12.2 The structure of a recurrent convolutional neural network [11]

12.2.3   Attention Mechanism

Both CNN and RNN can be used in text classification to achieve significant results, but the disadvantage is that the interpretability is not good. The attention mechanism can give a good contribution to the result of each word, which has become the standard configuration of the Seq2Seq [12] model. In fact, text classification can also be understood as a special Seq2Seq model. Therefore, the introduction of attention mechanism can improve the interpretability of the deep learning text classification model to a certain extent.

Yang et al. [13] proposed a hierarchical attention network for document classification. This model has two notable features. First, it has a hierarchical structure that can reflect the hierarchical structure of the document. Secondly, it applies two different attention mechanisms at the word and sentence levels, allowing it to participate differently in increasingly important content when constructing document representations. The model structure is shown in Fig. 12.3.

The model consisted of several parts: word encoder, word-level attention layer, sentence encoder and sentence-level attention layer. The network can be seen as two parts, the first part was the word attention part, and the other part was the sentence attention part. The entire network divided a sentence into several parts. For each part, a bidirectional RNN combined with an attention mechanism was used to map small sentences into a vector. For a set of sequence vectors obtained by mapping, a layer of bidirectional RNN combined with attention mechanism was used to classify the text. Finally, the softmax classifier was used to classify the entire text. The author conducted experiments on Yelp reviews, IMDB reviews, Yahoo answers, and Amazon reviews. The experimental results showed that the method of this article had a good improvement compared with other methods.

12.3   Application in Teacher Language

Classroom teaching is an educational activity in which teachers and students take the dialogue as the main body and the language as the main means of communication [14]. The classroom teaching language has an extremely close relationship with students' learning effects. The research on the characteristics of teachers' language structure is of great significance for improving students' learning effects, enhancing the quality of classroom teaching, and promoting the professional development of teachers.

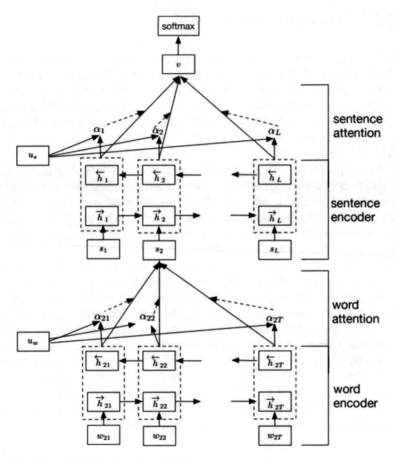

Fig. 12.3 Hierarchical attention network [13]

12.3.1 Teacher Language Classification Categories

Teachers' excellent language expression can turn abstract into concrete, profound into simple, and corruption into magic. Thereby optimizing classroom teaching that can improve teaching quality. According to different classification criteria, teachers' language can be divided into the following categories.

(1) Linguistics: It is divided into affirmative language, promise language, imperative language, inquiry language, expression language, and declaration language [15].
(2) Student sensory and subject characteristics: It is divided into auditory teaching language and visual teaching language, and visual teaching language is further divided into graphic language and symbolic language [16].

(3) Teaching progress: It is divided into introduction, question, evaluation, narration, and summary [17].
(4) Flanders Interactive Analysis System (FIAS): It is divided into feedback language, motivational language, pro-inspiring language, questioning language, declarative language, command language and teacher-student repetition language [18].

12.3.2 Application in Teacher Language Based on Text Classification Technology

Li [19] took the positive emotional behavior recognition of teachers and students as an example. Combined with specific example videos, voice recognition technology was used for sentiment analysis. She demonstrated the practical application of artificial intelligence technology in education scenarios.

The overall processing flow is shown as follows. First, sample the voice data from the video. In order to perform accurate statistical analysis on the voice, the voice was sliced. Set the slicing time to be performed every 30 s to balance the accuracy and complexity of the analysis. Then the speech was converted into text, and word2vec was used to convert it into vector data. The text fragments that were obtained by the emotion recognition model trained on open data set were used for classroom emotion analysis. The analysis flow chart is shown in Fig. 12.4.

For sequence data such as text, this research designed a two-class cyclic neural network. The neural network will give corresponding scores based on the positive and negative emotional output, ranging from 0 to 1. An evaluation score greater than 0 indicated a positive mood, and a score less than 0 indicated a negative mood.

Sun et al. [20] used natural language understanding technology to evaluate relationships and analyze teaching events and sequences to assist human in classroom teaching analysis.

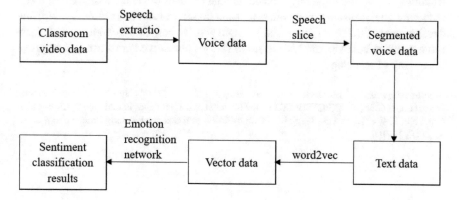

Fig. 12.4 Flow chart of sentiment analysis based on voice data [19]

First, they divided the teaching events into labels and text annotations. 80 lesson cases were selected from the total sample, and a text file with more than 480,000 words and more than 20,000 sentences was generated through video and sound extraction and voice-to-text methods. Then the labels and text annotations of these text files were manually performed. The labeled data would be used for training.

Secondly, they used the deep learning model word2vec to train the weight matrix of the word vector, and input it into the embedding layer of the recurrent neural network for model training. Each layer of the network used the average hidden state to output the classification result. Finally, through the correct rate of the training set and the test set, it was judged whether the model training was successful. According to the results of event classification, combined with the start and end time points of the divided events, a teaching event type and time distribution diagram for each lesson example was generated. Then it was used to analyze teaching behavior.

12.4 Conclusion

This article mainly studied the text classification technology based on deep learning, and introduced several representative network models. In addition, the application of text classification technology in the field of education was introduced. Deep learning provides a new solution for text classification. Compared with traditional text classification methods, deep learning can learn feature representations directly from the input, avoiding complex manual feature engineering, simplifying text preprocessing, and obtaining better classification performance. With the development of technology, it will have better performance.

At the same time, teaching is a highly specialized behavioral activity that requires professional evaluation based on scientific evaluation methods. If it is only a traditional one-sided observation, it will only lead to one-sided evaluation, and it is impossible to have an objective understanding of the curriculum. Although the current technology cannot completely replace manual observation and classification, it can reduce manual pressure to a certain extent and improve evaluation efficiency. With the development of the times, there will be more ways to combine technology and classroom teaching behavior analysis to solve various unresolved problems and improve the quality of teaching.

Acknowledgements This work was supported by the Tianjin Science and Technology Planning Project under Grant No. 20JCYBJC00300, the National Natural Science Foundation of China under Grant No. 11404240, and the Tianjin Philosophy and Social Science Planning Project under Grant No. TJJX17-016.

References

1. Y. Danfeng, K. Nan, G. Chao, C. Jianfei, D. Yiqi, Multi-label text classification model based on semantic embedding. J. China Univ. Posts Telecommun. **26**(01), 99–108 (2019)
2. H. Li, Z. Zaoxian, X. Fengtao, W. Jianzhai, T. Lin, Research progress of text classification technology based on deep learning. Comput. Eng. **47**(02), 1–11 (2021)
3. L. Hang, K. Yamanishi, Text classification using ESC-based stochastic decision lists. Inf. Process. Manage. **38**(3), 343–361 (2002)
4. S.B. Kim, K.S. Han, H.C. Rim et al., Some effective techniques for naive bayes text classification. IEEE Trans. Knowl. Data Eng. **18**, 1457–1466 (2006)
5. T. Joachims, Text categorization with support vector machines: learning with many relevant features, in *Proc. Conference on Machine Learning* (Springer, Berlin, Heidelberg, 1998)
6. W. Yu, Z.O. Wang, A fast KNN algorithm for text categorization, in *Machine Learning and Cybernetics, 2007 International Conference on* (IEEE, 2007)
7. T. Mikolov, G. Corrado, C. Kai, et al., Efficient estimation of word representations in vector space, in *Proceedings of the International Conference on Learning Representations (ICLR 2013)* (2013)
8. J. Pennington, R. Socher, C. Manning, Glove: global vectors for word representation, in *Conference on Empirical Methods in Natural Language Processing* (2014)
9. J. Devlin, M.W. Chang, K. Lee, et al., Bert: pre-training of deep bidirectional transformers for language understanding. arXiv preprint arXiv:1810.04805, (2018)
10. Y. Kim, Convolutional neural networks for sentence classification. Eprint Arxiv (2014)
11. S. Lai, L. Xu, K. Liu, et al., Recurrent convolutional neural networks for text classification, in *Twenty-Ninth AAAI Conference on Artificial Intelligence* (2015)
12. I. Sutskever, O. Vinyals, Q.V. Le, Sequence to sequence learning with neural networks. Adv. Neural Inform. Process. Syst. 3104–3112 (2014)
13. Z. Yang, D. Yang, C. Dyer, et al., Hierarchical attention networks for document classification, in *Proceedings of the 2016 Conference of the North American Chapter of the Association for Computational Linguistics: Human Language Technologies* (2016)
14. Q. Wei, Z. Jie, An empirical study on the speech behavior of teachers and students in classroom teaching. J. Northeast Normal Univ. **05**, 133–138 (2006)
15. Y. Lijun, L. Yan, S. Haixia, A comparative study on the classroom teaching language of new and old junior middle school mathematics teachers. J. Math. Educ. **24**(04), 40–43 (2015)
16. L. Dongxue, *A Comparative Study on the Teaching Language of Middle School Mathematics Novice Teachers and Expert Teachers* (Jiangxi Normal University, 2017)
17. W. Guojun, Research on optimizing the teaching language of high school mathematics classroom. Math. Teach. Newsl. **27**, 29–30 (2016)
18. Y. Lijun, S. Haixia, Research on the teaching language of algebra based on the background of video analysis——Take two lessons of "Multiplication and Division of Fractions" as an example. J. Math. Educ. **20**(01), 42–44 (2011)
19. L. Shengnan, *Research on the Construction of the Analysis Framework of Classroom Teaching Behavior Based on Artificial Intelligence Technology* (Beijing University of Posts and Telecommunications, 2019)
20. S. Zhong, L. Kaiyue, L. Liming, C. Meiling, X. Lin, S. Zhiping, Analysis of Classroom Teaching Based on Artificial Intelligence. China Audio-Vis. Educ. **4**(10), 15–23 (2020)

Chapter 13
Construction of Teacher-Student Interaction Evaluation Index System for High School Mathematics Concept Assimilation Learning Based on Artificial Intelligence

Yiming Zhen, Sumeng Shi, Wei Wang, and Guangming Wang

Abstract Teacher-student interaction is one of the most critical teaching behaviors in high school mathematics classrooms. As one of the main parts of mathematics teaching, concepts are the core of mathematics knowledge. Moreover, concept assimilation is the essential learning approach for senior students to acquire mathematics concepts. Therefore, this study constructed the Teacher-Student Interaction Evaluation Index System for High School Mathematics Concept Assimilation Learning. Combining both qualitative and quantitative perspectives, this study first constructed the evaluation system from the theoretical perspective using the Delphi method. Then, the video analysis was used to verify the evaluation system by conducting a qualitative analysis of high-quality teaching videos from the practical perspective with the help of artificial intelligence. Teacher-Student Interaction Evaluation Index System for High School Mathematics Concept Assimilation Learning constructed in this study included four first-level indicators: teacher-student interaction in the concept recognition stage, teacher-student interaction in the concept processing stage, teacher-student interaction in the concept reinforcement stage, and teacher-student interaction in the concept application stage, and eight second-level indicators: mutual communication, mobilizing learning initiative, explanation and exploration, inspired focus, example analysis, inspiration and concentration, task solving, and encouragement and feedback. This study could provide quantitative evaluation tools and theoretical models for teacher-student interaction in concept assimilation learning, and enrich teachers' understanding of concept teaching theory and teacher-student interaction.

Keywords Concept assimilation · Teacher-student interaction · Evaluation model · Artificial intelligence · Facial recognition · Speech recognition · Qualitative analysis

Y. Zhen · G. Wang (✉)
Faculty of Education, Tianjin Normal University, Tianjin 300387, China
e-mail: bd690310@163.com

S. Shi · W. Wang
College of Artificial Intelligence, Tianjin Normal University, Tianjin 300387, China

13.1 Introduction

Teacher-student interaction is conducive to the construction of a dynamic learning atmosphere. It is the main way for teachers to communicate with students' emotions and thinking, and it is also a highly critical behavior in the mathematics classroom. As one of the main subjects of mathematics teaching and learning, concept lessons are the core of the acquisition of basic mathematical knowledge and skills, and concept assimilation is the main way of learning for senior students to acquire mathematical concepts [5], while the teaching practices in the authentic classroom could determine the effectiveness of mathematics education to a certain extent.

With the keen interest in the quality of education, teacher-student interaction continues to receive attention as a key element in educational practice. Related studies have shown that teacher-student interaction is correlated with students' academic achievement (e.g., [6, 9, 28]) and that it may have a direct or indirect effect on teaching effectiveness [13]. In order to optimize teaching effectiveness, most studies have been conducted to qualitatively analyze teacher-student interaction strategies in the classroom (e.g., [11, 18, 34]). Moreover, some studies have conducted empirical studies on teacher-student interaction to evaluate the quality of teacher-student interaction (e.g., [19, 21, 23, 30]). With the deepening of research, some classroom assessment systems are gradually being widely used (e.g., [12, 14, 27]). However, many evaluation systems are mainly oriented towards the assessment of ubiquitous classrooms and set teacher-student interaction as a dimension in their structural framework. As a result, they suffer from limitations such as lack of subject and age specificity, ambiguous application contexts, and lack of indicator weights. In this context, most of the current evaluation criteria for mathematics classroom teaching follow a pan-disciplinary approach, with attention to subject content to be improved. Research is relatively limited when it comes to how to evaluate teacher-student interaction in high school mathematics concept learning. Therefore, future research should not only emphasize the value of teacher-student interaction but also present how to evaluate interaction in authentic classrooms for practitioners in the mathematics concept learning.

13.2 Literature Review

13.2.1 Assimilation Learning

Ausbel [2] argued that the key factor influencing the learning process is the learner's prior cognition. He asserted that meaningful learning occurs based on the student's prior knowledge base, so that new knowledge is linked to what is already in the learner's cognitive structure. The process of integrating new content with existing cognitive structures can be referred to as assimilation [26], and the cognitive or mental structures generated by the assimilation process are schema [33].

Prior knowledge has a significant impact on students' conceptual learning [22]. From the perspective of educational psychology, most studies on mathematical concepts are based on schema theory, which considers that the ways of concept acquisition include concept formation and concept assimilation, which are two basic modes of teaching mathematical concepts and are important ways for students to learn mathematical concepts [5]. Moreover, concept assimilation is the main way of acquiring concepts for science learning in higher grades [25]. Therefore, integrating the above perspectives, this study defines concept assimilation as a way of learning in mathematical concept learning in which students use their existing knowledge and experience to explore the essential properties of new concepts by establishing connections between old and new concepts and incorporating them into their own cognitive system, which mainly includes four stages: recognition, processing, reinforcement, and application (see Table 13.1).

Current research related to conceptual assimilation is scarce, and the studies that have been conducted mainly focus on instructional practices. For example, based on a controlled experiment with middle school students, Al Tamimi [1] found that assimilation-based instructional strategies were more effective in promoting students' cognitive achievement than traditional approaches. Furthermore, based on assimilation frameworks, Netti et al. [24] conducted a qualitative study with 7th graders to explore students' forms of mathematical communication during problem solving. Conversely, Saleh [32] revealed that there was no statistical difference in student achievement in the Ausubel model and other learning models. Overall, few studies have focused on the evaluation of conceptual assimilation processes, especially in high school.

Table 13.1 The connotation of each stage of mathematics concept assimilation

Stages of concept assimilation	Connotation
Concept recognition stage	Teachers guide students to recall their prior cognitive experiences so that they can identify the properties of the old concept and thus prepare for the introduction of the new concept
Concept processing stage	Teachers guide students to process and reorganize their existing conceptual learning experiences, analyze the common properties of old and new concepts and the connections between concepts, and abstract new concepts so that they can be incorporated into students' existing knowledge system
Concept reinforcement stage	Teachers use examples (concept prototypes or counterexamples), etc. to guide students to identify and discriminate related concepts, and use the new concepts to make judgments and reasoning to reinforce the connotation of their essential properties
Concept application stage	Teachers set learning tasks, students independently apply the new concepts to reason, argue or do arithmetic to further clarify the connotation, extension and application value of the new concepts, and gain a solid and deep understanding of the new concepts

13.2.2   Evaluation of Teacher-Student Interaction

Evaluation has diagnostic and decision-making functions, while the evaluation of teacher-student interaction is an assessment of teaching effectiveness and quality, which could help teachers review the teaching process and optimize instruction. As one of the essential indicators of teaching quality, evaluation tools for teacher-student interaction have received increasing attention from researchers.

The Flanders Interaction Analysis System (FIAS) [12] is an early and representative teacher-student interaction assessment system that is still widely used today (e.g., [15, 20]). FIAS focused on verbal interactions between teachers and students in the classroom, and in its application, the evaluator needs to code through qualitative analysis and derive results through methods such as matrix analysis. However, FIAS did not reflect the value of nonverbal interactions, and the quality of a lesson is not measured only by verbal interactions between teachers and students, interactions between teachers and students in terms of emotions and thinking can also provide positive meaning to students' learning.

The Classroom Assessment Scoring System (CLASS) [27] is a widely used classroom interaction assessment tool that can effectively measure teacher-student interaction in classroom settings and focuses on both verbal and nonverbal behaviors in teacher-student interactions. To be specific, Secondary CLASS was divided into three dimensions: Emotional Support, Instructional Support, and Classroom Organization, and each dimension was subdivided into different indicators according to students' age characteristics and educational goals, which reflected the three aspects of teacher-student interaction: emotional interaction, behavioral interaction, and cognitive interaction. The dimensional division of CLASS was relatively comprehensive and can provide theoretical support for this study, but it had limitations such as not being discipline-specific, lacking indicator weights, and ambiguous application contexts.

Based on the Mathematical Knowledge for Teaching framework [3, 16] developed the Mathematical Quality of Instruction (MQI), which applies to the assessment of mathematics classroom instruction in grades K-9. The MQI was dedicated to evaluating three interactions in mathematics teaching and learning practices: teacher-student, teacher-content, and student-content [8]. Based on the three interactions, it constructed four dimensions about mathematics teaching and learning, including Richness of the Mathematics, Working with Students and Mathematics, Errors and Imprecision, Student Participation in Meaning-Making and Reasoning. The MQI had distinctive characteristics of mathematics disciplines, and the evaluation model was constructed from a three-dimensional perspective of "teacher-content-student", emphasizing students' understanding of mathematical concepts, which can provide a reference for this study. In addition, it has been shown that the MQI correlates well with the CLASS [7], but as a general evaluation tool for mathematics teaching activities, the MQI is not limited to specific course types.

Overall, the evaluation of teacher-student interaction has received relatively extensive attention, and most of the relevant teacher-student interaction evaluation tools present a focus on the interaction style and content of interaction. However, the current assessment tools still have limitations such as unclear disciplinary characteristics, lack of indicator weights, and unclear application contexts.

13.2.3 Research Questions

In the research of concept assimilation, although the related theoretical exploration has gradually deepened, few studies have focused on the evaluation of concept assimilation processes. In addition, some current teacher-student interaction assessment tools still have limitations such as lack of indicator weights, unclear disciplinary characteristics, and unclear application contexts. High school is a critical time for concept learning, and concept assimilation is the primary way that senior grade students acquire mathematical concepts. Therefore, this study tries to explore the question: What is the Teacher-Student Interaction Evaluation Index System for High School Mathematics Concept Assimilation Learning?

13.3 Methods

13.3.1 Instrument

In the construction of the first-level indicators, the study divided teacher-student interaction into four stages according to the characteristics of concept assimilation learning in mathematics: teacher-student interaction in the concept identification stage, teacher-student interaction in the concept processing stage, teacher-student interaction in the concept reinforcement stage, and teacher-student interaction in the concept application stage.

In the process of constructing second-level indicators, CLASS [27] divided teacher-student interaction into three dimensions: emotional support, organizational support, and instructional support, reflecting its attention to the emotional, behavioral, and cognitive aspects of teacher-student interaction. This study adopted CLASS's perspective and directed the teacher-student interaction process to cognitive, behavioral, and emotional aspects. Since the first-level indicators pointed to the different stages of conceptual assimilation learning, which reflected the cognitive interaction in the process of teacher-student interaction, the second-level indicators were divided into behavioral and affective interactions by combining the learning characteristics of each stage of conceptual assimilation, including mutual communication, emotional state, explanation and exploration, learning attention, example analysis, classroom atmosphere, task solving, and encouragement and feedback (see Fig. 13.1).

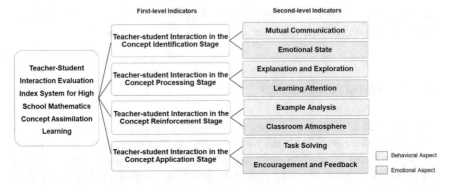

Fig. 13.1 The preliminary edition of teacher-student interaction evaluation index system for high school mathematics concept assimilation Learning

13.3.2   Procedure and Data Analysis

This study adopted a bottom-up logic to construct the evaluation system, i.e., first constructing the evaluation system based on existing research and expert opinions, and then qualitatively analyzing the video lessons with the help of artificial intelligence to construct the evaluation system from both theoretical and practical perspectives, which makes the evaluation system more objective and reasonable. The construction of the evaluation system includes the following four phases.

Phase 1: Revision of the evaluation system

Firstly, using the Delphi method, experts were consulted through the questionnaire to consult the structural framework of the evaluation index system and the connotation of the indicators to ensure the validity of the evaluation system. Then, the mean (M), standard deviation (SD), and coefficient of variation (CV) of the questionnaire data were calculated by the independent rating of the evaluation system by the experts. Specifically, the higher the mean value of an indicator and the smaller the standard deviation, the more concentrated the opinion of experts is and the more important the indicator is; the dispersion of experts' opinions is evaluated by the CV, where $CV = SD/M$, the smaller the CV, the higher the degree of agreement among experts.

Phase 2: Validation of the evaluation system

This study used the video analysis method to perform a qualitative analysis of excellent teaching videos with the help of artificial intelligence, so as to verify the practical value of the evaluation system.

Speech recognition is a relatively mature technology in the field of artificial intelligence, which can process the frequency, amplitude, loudness, and content of the sound signal, thereby assisting in the analysis of the characteristics of speech. For example, James et al. [17] assessed classroom climate by analyzing teacher-student voice frequency, while [31] analyzed student–student interaction patterns by transcribing teacher-student voice content. Moreover, expression recognition is more often used in the affective analysis. For example, Bosch [4] analyzed students' facial features and encode them in order to determine their affective state.

With reference to the above research, the machine learning approach was adopted in this research, speech recognition, speech emotion recognition, and facial recognition algorithms were used to qualitatively analyze the video samples using Python and TensorFlow. To be specific, speech recognition pointed to the behavioral aspect in the second-level indicator, while speech emotion recognition and facial recognition pointed to the emotional aspect in the second-level indicator.

For the second-level indicators of the behavioral aspect, understanding the connotations of speech is the key to analyzing interaction. Therefore, this study focused on analyzing the conversational content of videos by transcribing the speech text. Specifically, this study first used artificial intelligence to output the verbal content of teacher-student interactions and then encoded it manually, thus reducing time consumption and improving the efficiency of encoding.

For the second-level indicators of the emotional aspect, a combination of speech emotion recognition and facial recognition was used for validation. Mel-Frequency Cepstrum is a kind of spectrum that represents short-term audio signals, as a visual presentation of speech emotion recognition results, it is a speech spectrum graph that simulates the characteristics of the human ear to receive sound frequencies, its horizontal coordinates represent time, vertical coordinates represent frequency, and the values of coordinate points represent the energy of speech data, its graph can visually represent the change of speech signal intensity in different frequency bands with time. Since the second-level indicators of the emotional aspect were all positive emotion descriptions of teacher-student interactions, expression recognition, on the other hand, focused on identifying positive emotions of teachers and students.

Convolutional Neural Networks (CNN) is widely used in image discrimination field and is one of the representative algorithms of deep learning. Deep learning-based image discrimination models can learn object features from large-scale image data, and then automatically classify or recognize objects in images. Based on CNN, this study used the Extended Cohn-Kanada (CK+) as the main dataset and the self-built dataset as the supplement and obtained the training set containing 13,370 images and the validation set containing 1191 images to develop the facial recognition system by machine learning. After 10 iterations, the expression recognition accuracy of the validation set was obtained as 94.96% (see Fig. 13.2), indicating that the facial recognition results have high reliability.

For the output of speech text, the study used the Long Form ASR product from iFLYTEK, based on a deep full-sequence convolutional neural network, which is capable of converting long segments (within 5 h) of audio data into text data, thus enabling efficient output of dialogue text from video samples.

The dataset of speech emotion recognition was adopted from CASIA Chinese emotion corpus, and the 1200 items of the corpus were classified into six categories: angry, happy, fear, neutral, sad, and surprise, and according to the emotional characteristics of instruction, angry and happy were classified as a positive emotion, neutral and sad were classified as neutral emotion, and fear and surprise were classified as

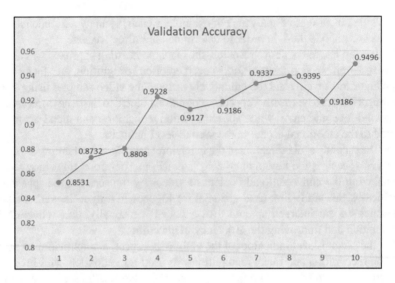

Fig. 13.2 Accuracy of facial recognition

negative emotions. After 100 iterations, the accuracy of speech emotion recognition was obtained as 70.83% (see Fig. 13.3), indicating that the speech emotion recognition results have high reliability.

Phase 3: Calculation of the indicator weight

First, the Delphi method was used to obtain experts' ratings of the relative importance of each indicator (experts who participated in the first round of this study were invited for consistency of the study). Then, Analytic Hierarchy Process was used to transform

Fig. 13.3 Accuracy of speech emotion recognition

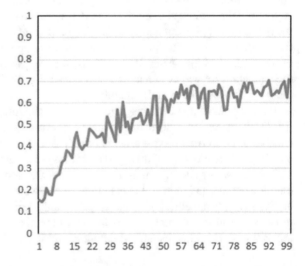

the data into judgment matrixes and a consistency test was performed using yaahp to calculate Consistency Ratio (CR), and when CR less than 0.1, the consistency of the judgment matrix is generally considered acceptable, and thus the indicator weights can be calculated. Finally, the average value of all expert data was calculated to obtain the final indicator weight results.

Phase 4: Testing of the evaluation system

To test the reliability of the evaluation system, first, six graduate students in mathematics education were invited to rate three videos of high school mathematics conceptual courses at different teaching levels using the Teacher-Student Interaction Evaluation Index System for High School Mathematics Concept Assimilation Learning. SPSS was then used to perform ANOVA, calculate Kendall's concordance coefficient (W) and calculate rater agreement as a test of reliability. The formula for W is

$$W = 12 \left[\sum R_i^2 - \frac{\left(\sum R_i \right)^2}{N} \right] / [K^2(N^3 - N)]$$

where K is the number of evaluators, N is the number of evaluated objects, and R_i is the sum of the level of the ith evaluated object.

To test the validity of the evaluation system, first, five experts in the field of mathematics education were invited to judge the correlation between the actual evaluation level and the expected evaluation level of each indicator, filling in the corresponding grade according to the scale (1: no correlation; 2: weak correlation; 3: strong correlation; 4: very strong correlation).

First, the content validity index (CVI) was calculated, then the chance agreement was corrected by calculating the adjusted kappa (K^*), and finally, the scale-level content validity index $(S\text{-}CVI)$ was calculated, and these values were combined to determine the validity of the evaluation system.

The formula for $I\text{-}CVI$ is $I\text{-}CVI = A/n$, where n is the total number of experts, A is the number of experts with a rating of 3 or 4, $K^* = \frac{I-CVI-P_c}{1-P_c}$, and $P_c = \left[\frac{n!}{A!(n-A)!} \right] \times 0.5^n$. For the measurement of K^*, a K^* of 0.40 to 0.59 represents fair validity, a K^* of 0.60 to 0.74 represents good validity, and a K^* greater than 0.74 represents excellent validity [29].

$S\text{-}CVI$ includes the $S\text{-}CVI$ Universal Agreement $(S\text{-}CVI/UA)$ and the $S\text{-}CVI$ Average $(S\text{-}CVI/Ave)$. To be specific, the formula for $S\text{-}CVI/UA$ is $S\text{-}CVI/UA = B/m$, where B is the number of indicators with a rating of 3 or 4, m is the total number of indicators, and when $S\text{-}CVI/UA$ is greater than or equal to 0.8, indicating the validity of the index is good [10]. $S\text{-}CVI/Ave$ is the average of $I\text{-}CVI$ of all indicators, and when $S\text{-}CVI/Ave$ is greater than or equal to 0.90, indicating the validity of the index is good [35].

13.4   Results

13.4.1   Phase 1: Revision of the Evaluation System

The initially constructed evaluation system contained four first-level indicators as well as eight second-level indicators. To ensure the content validity of the evaluation system, questionnaires were distributed to 12 experts in the field of mathematics education for revision, with a recovery rate of 100% and an efficiency rate of 100%.

As can be seen from Table 13.2, the mode of expert opinions was concentrated in 4 and 5, the total mean of expert opinions was 4.32, and the total standard deviation was 0.79, indicating that the expert opinions were relatively concentrated and the arrangement of indicators was reasonable to a certain extent. The total coefficient of variation was less than 1, indicating that the experts' opinions were consistent.

With regard to the revision of the evaluation system, the first-level indicators were agreed by all experts, and the revised opinions of the second-level indicators mainly focused on the emotional aspect. From experts' opinions, affective indicators should be important throughout the classroom, at all stages, and do not have relative importance. In response to such opinions, the second-level indicators were revised to include the evaluation of the "emotional atmosphere of teacher-student interaction"

Table 13.2   Initial revision of the evaluation system

Expert	T_1	T_2	T_3	T_4	T_5	T_6	T_7	T_8
1	3	3	3	3	3	3	3	3
2	5	5	5	5	5	5	5	5
3	4	4	4	4	5	5	5	5
4	4	4	4	4	4	4	5	5
5	5	4	4	4	5	5	5	5
6	3	3	3	3	3	3	3	3
7	4	4	3	4	4	4	3	4
8	5	5	5	5	5	5	5	5
9	4	4	4	5	5	5	5	5
10	5	5	5	5	5	5	5	5
11	5	5	5	5	5	5	5	5
12	4	4	4	4	4	4	4	5
Mode	5	4	4	5	5	5	5	5
M	4.25	4.17	4.08	4.25	4.42	4.42	4.42	4.58
SD	0.75	0.72	0.79	0.75	0.79	0.79	0.90	0.79
$\overline{SD}$ 0.79			$\overline{M}$ 4.32			$\overline{CV}(SD/M)$ 0.18		

5: Strongly reasonable; 4: Basically reasonable; 3: Reasonable; 2: Not reasonable; 1: Strongly unreasonable

Table 13.3 Revision of the evaluation system

First-level indicator	Revision	Second-level indicator	Revision
Teacher-student Interaction in the concept identification stage	–	Mutual Communication	–
		Emotional State	Mobilizing Learning Initiative
Teacher-student Interaction in the Concept Processing Stage	–	Explanation and Exploration	–
		Learning attention	Inspired focus
Teacher-student Interaction in the concept reinforcement stage	–	Example analysis	–
		Classroom atmosphere	Inspiration and concentration
Teacher-student interaction in the concept application stage	–	Task solving	–
		Encouragement and feedback	–

according to the psychological characteristics of conceptual assimilation learning. The revised evaluation system is shown in Tables 13.3, 13.4, and Fig. 13.4.

13.4.2   Phase 2: Validation of the Evaluation System

In a total of 40 high school mathematics concept lessons based on conceptual assimilation learning teaching, videos were selected from the 2019 "One Teacher, One Excellent Lesson, One Lesson, One Famous Teacher" activity in China as the object of this study. The recognition results are as follows:

(1)   **Second-level indicators for behavioral aspect**

The 40 audio sessions were transcribed into texts using artificial intelligence, and then the texts were manually coded for statistics. For the manual coding step, first, each text was divided into four stages of conceptual assimilation learning based on the corresponding time between text and video. Then, four levels were created using NVivo, corresponding to four second-level indicators. Finally, manual coding was performed. As can be seen from Table 13.5, in actual teaching, the number of codes for each second-level indicator is greater than 90%, indicating that the second-level indicators are in line with the teaching practice and have high reliability.

(2)   **Second-level indicators for emotional aspect**

In the validation of the emotional aspect, the combination of facial recognition and speech emotion recognition was illustrated to validate the evaluation system. Due to the limitations of video recording, it was difficult to identify the expressions of all students, while the positive expressions of the teacher can reflect the overall

Table 13.4 The connotation of second-level indicators

Second-level indicator	Connotation
Mutual communication	The teacher introduces new concepts by communicating with students, reproducing their relevant knowledge experiences, and guiding them to recall and identify conceptual attributes in their relevant cognitive experiences. Behaviorally, it is mainly manifested as verbal interaction between teachers and students, i.e., continuous dialogic communication between teachers and students
Mobilizing learning initiative	In the process of teacher-student interaction, the teacher makes students appreciate the necessity of studying new concepts, stimulates students' interest in learning, and students show an active desire to learn new concepts in the process of identifying the properties of old concepts. Emotionally, the main manifestation is that the teacher can motivate the students, and the students are in a state of eagerness to try
Explanation and exploration	Through explanation or exploration, the teacher processes and establishes the connection between the new and the old concepts, and gradually guides students to identify the elements of the new concept, thereby abstracting the new concept and incorporating the new concept into its cognitive structure. The behavior is mainly manifested in the teacher's explanation while the students listen, or the teacher and students explore together
Inspired Focus	In the process of teacher-student interaction, students are highly attentive and follow the teacher in the process of processing old concepts, exploring new concepts, and refining and reorganizing their existing cognitive structures. Emotionally, it is mainly manifested in the teacher's enlightenment, explanation or exploration process, the students intently listen and think
Example analysis	Teachers use targeted instructional materials to help students identify the characteristics of new concepts, analyze and reinforce their understanding of them. Behaviorally, it is mainly manifested in the teacher leading students in analysis and inquiry about the properties of concepts through examples, and students thinking and responding under the guidance of the teacher
Inspiration and concentration	In the process of teacher-student interaction, through teacher's demonstration, students strengthen their understanding of new concepts through high-density interaction. Emotionally, it is mainly manifested as teachers inspire students to think and reason, and students are active in thinking and actively participate in interaction
Task solving	The teacher assigns learning tasks related to problem solving to make students apply and consolidate new concepts in the application of concepts, and students think and explore independently according to the requirements of the problem-solving tasks. Behaviorally, it is mainly manifested as students solving problems independently or with small groups, with teacher guidance and communication

(continued)

Table 13.4 (continued)

Second-level indicator	Connotation
Encouragement and feedback	The teacher gives feedback to students based on their responses and encourages them to explore the connotations and extensions of the concepts in depth and to use the new concepts to solve problems. Emotionally, it is mainly manifested as students' self-devotion into problem-solving learning tasks, teachers giving encouragement feedback to students' answers, and students exploring in depth based on the teachers' feedback

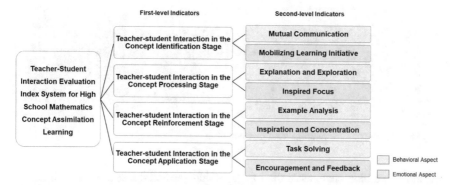

Fig. 13.4 The preliminary edition of Teacher-Student Interaction Evaluation Index System for High School Mathematics Concept Assimilation Learning

Table 13.5 Results of manual coding of second-level indicators for behavioral aspects

Second-level indicator	Number of codes
Mutual communication	40 (100%)
Explanation and exploration	39 (97.5%)
Example analysis	40 (100%)
Task solving	38 (95%)

atmosphere of the classroom. Thus, this study focused on teachers' facial expressions and manually eliminated students' expression misinterpretations.

A sample of excellent teaching videos (sample 19) was randomly selected, and the teacher's expressions in the sample were identified and their expression change trends were plotted (see Fig. 13.5), where the horizontal coordinate represents the number of frames of the video, "1" in the vertical coordinate represents positive expressions, "0" represents natural expressions, and the density of the image indicates the frequency of the teacher's expression change, and the more dense the image is, the greater the teacher's expression change is.

As can be seen from Fig. 13.5, in the concept recognition stage, teachers need to mobilize students' learning interest through changes in facial features such as eyes and expressions, and need to render the classroom atmosphere, so there were

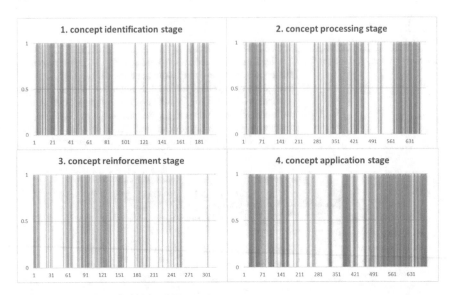

Fig. 13.5 Expression recognition results of sample 19

certain expression changes in the image, which verified the second-level indicator Mobilizing Learning Initiative. In the concept processing stage, teachers need to lead students in a more focused exploration and comprehension than in the first stage, and thus there were more pauses for reflection and verbal communication. This was shown in the image as some blank stages (e.g., frames 70–130 and 210–280 of the concept processing stage in Fig. 13.5), which verified the second-level indicator of Inspired Focus. In the concept reinforcement stage, teachers need to engage in more positive emotional interactions with students to understand their learning status and stimulate their willingness to further exploration, resulting in more intensive images and fewer blank phases, which validated the second-level indicator Inspiration and Concentration. In the concept application stage, teachers need to first encourage students to try to solve the problem on their own, which was mainly presented as student–student interaction or no explicit interaction, thus in the early part of the stage, there were some blank stages in the image. Later in this stage, teachers need to give feedback to students' responses, and teachers and students need to explore the application and expansion of the concept together, so there was more intensive teacher-student emotional interaction, and the images showed a tendency to be more intensive, which verified the second-level indicator Encouragement and Feedback.

In addition, the expressions in the concept recognition stage and concept reinforcement stage changed less frequently than in the concept processing stage and concept application stage. This may be related to the duration of each stage. Specifically, the duration of the concept processing stage and concept application stage of this video sample was longer than the other stages.

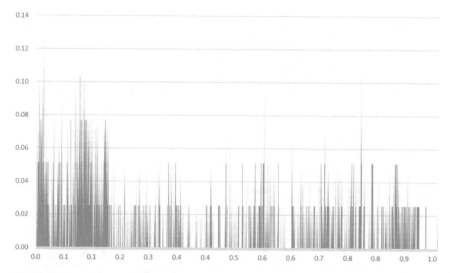

Fig. 13.6 Expression trend of all the video samples

The overall expression trend was obtained by normalizing the 40 video samples according to the video duration (see Fig. 13.6), where the horizontal coordinate represents the normalized time points, the vertical coordinate represents the normalized expression averages, and the coordinate points represent the teacher's expression values, the larger the value, the more positive the expression, and the denser the image, the higher the frequency of the teacher's expression change.

As seen in Fig. 13.6, teachers' expressions changed most frequently at the early stage of concept assimilation learning, indicating that teachers generally used emotional interaction to motivate students at this stage. In the middle stage of concept assimilation learning, the images still showed some expression changes, but they were less frequent than in the early stage. In the later stage of concept assimilation learning, the teacher's expression changed gradually increased in frequency to guide students to apply the new concepts with positive teacher-student interactions. In general, all of the teaching samples emphasized the classroom atmosphere and guided students' active concept assimilation learning through positive expressions.

A sample of teaching videos (sample 15) was randomly selected, and the teacher's speech emotion was recognized by drawing its speech emotion graph (see Fig. 13.7), where the horizontal coordinate of the graph represents the number of frames of the video, "1" in the vertical coordinate represents positive emotion, "0" represents the neutral emotion, "−1" represents the negative emotion, and the density of the image indicates the frequency of the teacher's emotion change, and the denser the image, the greater the teacher's emotion change.

The speech emotions of all video samples were identified in turn and normalized to obtain the overall situation of speech emotion recognition (see Fig. 13.8), where the horizontal coordinate represents the normalized time point, the vertical coordinate represents the normalized emotion average value, and the coordinate point represents

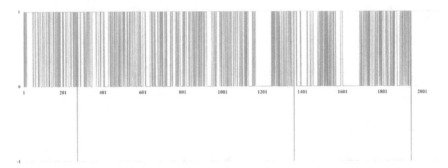

Fig. 13.7 Speech emotion recognition results of sample 15

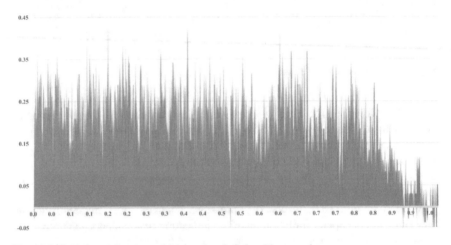

Fig. 13.8 Speech emotion recognition results of all the video samples

the teacher's emotion value, the larger the value, the more positive the emotion, and the denser the image, the higher the frequency of teacher's emotion change.

As seen in Fig. 13.8, positive emotions occupied all stages of concept assimilation learning, especially the first three stages. The fourth stage was mainly concerned with the application of concepts, and mainly reflected the combination of student–student interaction and teacher-student interaction, thus the teacher's and students' speech data will be mixed, and it was difficult to separate them, resulting in greater errors in speech data recognition in this stage compared with other stages, and therefore more negative emotions were recognized. Overall, positive emotions persist throughout the process of concept assimilation learning.

In addition, influenced by different teaching contents, teacher-student character-istics, and teaching environments, there were certain differences in the degree of teacher-student interaction in different teaching videos, which also had some influ-ence on the validation results. In conclusion, the combination of the external features of face and voice, as well as the analysis of the internal meaning of speech content, indicated that the evaluation system constructed in this study has a high consistency with the teaching practice.

13.4.3 Phase 3: Calculation of the Indicator Weight

Taking the data of one expert as an example to illustrate the calculation process. First, convert the data into a judgment matrix, and denote the judgment matrix of the first-level indicator as A_1 and the judgment matrix of the first-level indicator as B_1, B_2, B_3, B_4, which can be seen as follows matrix (13.1) and matrix (13.2). Then, using yaahp software for hierarchical analysis, the maximum characteristic root of the matrix (λ_{max}) was calculated to be 4.0329, and the consistency ratio was 0.0123, which was less than 0.1, indicating that the judgment matrix was valid, thus calculating the indicator weights (see Table 13.6).

$$A_1 = \begin{pmatrix} 1 & 1 & {}^1\!/_5 & {}^1\!/_5 \\ 1 & 1 & {}^1\!/_3 & {}^1\!/_5 \\ 5 & 3 & 1 & 1 \\ 5 & 5 & 1 & 1 \end{pmatrix} \tag{13.1}$$

$$B_1 = \begin{pmatrix} 1 & 3 \\ {}^1\!/_3 & 1 \end{pmatrix}, B_2 = \begin{pmatrix} 1 & 3 \\ {}^1\!/_3 & 1 \end{pmatrix}, B_3 = \begin{pmatrix} 1 & 3 \\ {}^1\!/_3 & 1 \end{pmatrix}, B_4 = \begin{pmatrix} 1 & 4 \\ {}^1\!/_4 & 1 \end{pmatrix} \tag{13.2}$$

Table 13.6 Example of results of indicator weights

Indicator	Indicator weight
S_1 teacher-student interaction in the concept identification stage	0.0864
S_2 teacher-student interaction in the concept processing stage	0.0996
S_3 teacher-student interaction in the concept reinforcement stage	0.382
S_4 Teacher-student Interaction in the concept application stage	0.432
T_1 mutual communication	0.0648
T_2 mobilizing learning initiative	0.0216
T_3 explanation and exploration	0.0747
T_4 inspired focus	0.0249
T_5 example analysis	0.2865
T_6 inspiration and concentration	0.0955
T_7 task solving	0.3456
T_8 encouragement and feedback	0.0864

Table 13.7 Results of maximum characteristic roots of matrix and consistency ratio

Expert	λ_{max}	Consistency ratio
1	4.0329	0.0123
2	4.1726	0.0647
3	4.0000	0.0000
4	4.0605	0.0227
5	4.0207	0.0078
6	4.2124	0.0796
7	4.2632	0.0986
8	4.0000	0.0000
9*	–	0.2571
10	4.1923	0.0720
11	4.0439	0.0164
12*	–	0.6701

According to the above steps, the index weight data of 12 experts were processed separately (see Table 13.7). The consistency ratios of the 9th and 12th experts were greater than 0.1, indicating that their data did not pass the consistency test, so these data were excluded. The consistency ratios of the other 10 data were calculated to be less than 0.1, indicating that a total of 10 experts' opinions on index weights were valid, and the arithmetic mean of the index weights of the 10 experts was further calculated to obtain the index weights of the evaluation system (see Table 13.8).

Based on the above process, the Teacher-Student Interaction Evaluation Index System for High School Mathematics Concept Assimilation Learning was obtained as $I = 0.105T_1 + 0.093T_2 + 0.183T_3 + 0.154T_4 + 0.126T_5 + 0.088T_6 + 0.138T_7 + 0.113T_8$ (I represents the total score of teacher-student interaction, and $T_1 \sim T_8$ represent the scores of each second-level indicator in turn, see Fig. 13.9).

13.4.4 Phase 4: Testing of the Evaluation System

13.4.4.1 Reliability of the Evaluation System

Collecting the scoring data of the six evaluators applying the evaluation system to the teaching videos with different teaching levels (see Table 13.9), it can be found that there was consistency in the ratings of the six evaluators, all of whom agreed that the level of teacher-student interaction from sample 1 to sample 3 decreased in order, which was consistent with the teaching level of the video sample.

The ANOVA was used to further test the consistency of the evaluation results and the results showed that no significant differences were found in the overall mean of the evaluation data (F = 0.642, $p = 0673 > 0.05$). Kendall's concordance coefficient (W) was calculated to be 0.861 and the chi-square (χ^2) was 10.332. According to

Table 13.8 Results of indicator weights

Expert	S_1	S_2	S_3	S_4	T_1	T_2	T_3	T_4	T_5	T_6	T_7	T_8
1	0.0864	0.0996	0.3820	0.4320	0.0648	0.0216	0.0747	0.0249	0.2865	0.0955	0.3456	0.0864
2	0.1123	0.1449	0.1697	0.5731	0.0983	0.0140	0.0290	0.1159	0.0283	0.1414	0.2866	0.2866
3	0.2500	0.2500	0.2500	0.2500	0.1250	0.1250	0.1250	0.1250	0.1250	0.1250	0.1250	0.1250
4	0.3477	0.4870	0.0827	0.0827	0.2897	0.0579	0.4058	0.0812	0.0689	0.0138	0.0689	0.0138
5	0.3845	0.3845	0.1433	0.0878	0.0961	0.2883	0.0769	0.3076	0.0717	0.0717	0.0293	0.0585
6	0.2030	0.5309	0.1405	0.1256	0.1015	0.1015	0.1327	0.3981	0.0703	0.0703	0.0942	0.0314
7	0.0421	0.6277	0.1073	0.2230	0.0351	0.0070	0.4707	0.1569	0.0179	0.0894	0.0557	0.1672
8	0.3000	0.3000	0.3000	0.1000	0.0750	0.2250	0.1500	0.1500	0.2250	0.0750	0.0333	0.0667
10	0.1069	0.1488	0.1796	0.5647	0.0534	0.0534	0.0372	0.1116	0.0449	0.1347	0.2823	0.2823
11	0.1535	0.3889	0.3889	0.0687	0.1151	0.0384	0.3241	0.0648	0.3241	0.0648	0.0601	0.0086
Mean	0.199	0.336	0.214	0.251	0.105	0.093	0.183	0.154	0.126	0.088	0.138	0.113

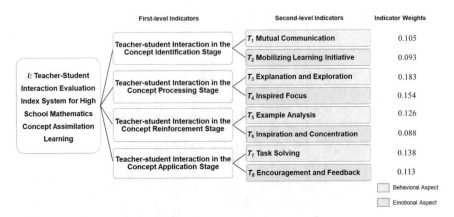

Fig. 13.9 Indicator weights of the evaluation system

Table 13.9 Evaluation results

Evaluator	Sample 1	Sample 2	Sample 3
1	88.75	82.08	84.10
2	94.77	91.81	87.21
3	94.55	86.91	80.68
4	93.47	82.80	79.20
5	92.97	83.78	75.60
6	92.60	84.45	78.95
Mean	92.85	85.30	80.96

the formula $\chi^2 = K(N-1)W$ (K is the number of evaluators and N is the number of evaluation subjects), when the degree of freedom is 3, the critical value of χ^2 is $\chi^2 > \chi^2_{(P=0.025)} = 9.35$, i.e., the consistency of the scores reached 97.5%, indicating that the evaluation system has high reliability.

13.4.4.2 Validity of the Evaluation System

This study invited five experts in the field of mathematics education to test the validity of the evaluation system. The evaluation results (see Table 13.10) showed that the K^* for each indicator was greater than 0.74, and further calculation of the S-CVI revealed that the S-CVI/UA was 0.9 and the S-CVI/Ave was 0.9. The above analysis showed that the Teacher-Student Interaction Evaluation Index System for High School Mathematics Concept Assimilation Learning had good validity.

Table 13.10 Evaluation results of $K*$

Item	Number of experts with a rating of 3 or 4	I-CVI	Pc	$K*$
T_1	4	0.800	0.15625	0.763
T_2	5	1.000	0.03125	1.000
T_3	5	1.000	0.03125	1.000
T_4	5	1.000	0.03125	1.000
T_5	5	1.000	0.03125	1.000
T_6	4	0.800	0.15625	0.763
T_7	4	0.800	0.15625	0.763
T_8	4	0.800	0.15625	0.763

13.5   Conclusion and Discussion

13.5.1   Conclusion

The present study was designed to construct the evaluation model for assimilation learning in high school mathematics courses with the help of artificial intelligence. This study has shown that Teacher-Student Interaction Evaluation Index System for High School Mathematics Concept Assimilation Learning included four first-level indicators: teacher-student interaction in the concept recognition stage, teacher-student interaction in the concept processing stage, teacher-student interaction in the concept reinforcement stage, and teacher-student interaction in the concept application stage, and eight second-level indicators. The specific model can be written as $I = 0.105T_1 + 0.093T_2 + 0.183T_3 + 0.154T_4 + 0.126T_5 + 0.088T_6 + 0.138T_7 + 0.113T_8$ (I represents the total score of teacher-student interaction, and $T_1 \sim T_8$ represent the scores of each second-level indicator in turn, i.e., mutual communication, mobilizing learning initiative, explanation and exploration, inspired focus, example analysis, inspiration and concentration, task solving, and encouragement and feedback, see Fig. 13.9 above).

Through the reliability and validity tests, the consistency of experts' scores was obtained to reach 97.5%, and the validity index was in the excellent range, indicating that the evaluation system had good reliability and validity and can be used as an assessment tool for teacher-student interaction in concept assimilation learning.

13.5.2   Discussion

13.5.2.1   Further Explanation of the Evaluation System

Teacher-Student Interaction Evaluation Index System for High School Mathematics Concept Assimilation Learning is a tool for evaluating the level of teacher-student interaction in high school mathematics concept courses that use the concept assimilation learning approach. In the application process, the evaluator needs to score the second-level indicators separately on a percentage scale according to the actual situation of teacher-student interaction, with reference to the division of the four learning stages and the connotation of each indicator.

The main steps of applying the Teacher-Student Interaction Evaluation Index System for High School Mathematics Concept Assimilation Learning are: first, read the evaluation system and understand the connotation of each indicator. Secondly, with reference to the evaluator's own teaching experience, curriculum standards, and teaching materials, the evaluator should form a deep understanding of the teaching content to be evaluated, so that they can accurately distinguish the four stages of concept assimilation learning in the evaluation process, and thus implement the evaluation of the second-level indicators corresponding to the four stages. Then, corresponding to the connotation of each indicator, the evaluator needs to score the process of teacher-student interaction on a percentage scale. Last but not least, the score of each indicator should be multiplied by the indicator weights, and the weight scores of all indicators should be summed up to get the total score of teacher-student interaction.

13.5.2.2 Limitations

Compared with previous studies, this study has made new attempts in the validation of the index system, mainly by integrating artificial intelligence into the qualitative analysis of the video and reflecting certain innovations in the reliability and validity tests of the evaluation system, but this study also has some limitations:

Firstly, the theoretical basis of qualitative analysis of artificial intelligence needs to be optimized. The construction of educational evaluation models should be built on a certain theoretical foundation. But at present, the integration of artificial intelligence and qualitative analysis of educational evaluation lacks theoretical research. In the process of qualitative analysis, this study identified and developed algorithms based on the purpose of the study. However, the formulation of the algorithms lacks theoretical support, which provides a new direction for future research, and theoretical research on the integration of artificial intelligence and education are urgently needed.

Moreover, the sample size of the validation videos is relatively small. In the validation phase of the evaluation system, this study analyzed 40 high-quality teaching videos qualitatively so as to verify the practical value of the evaluation system. However, due to the limitation of resources, the sample size of the study is small, and further study should continue to expand the sample size so as to increase the reliability.

Last but not least, the quality of the validation videos still needs to be improved. Due to the limitations of video quality, teaching themes, and teachers' teaching characteristics, although the videos selected for this study are representative in the geographical range, teachers' teaching level, video shooting conditions, picture quality, etc., all affect the validation of the evaluation system to some extent, and further research should continue to collect and shoot high-quality teaching videos to strengthen the reliability of qualitative analysis.

Acknowledgements The work was supported by the National Social Science Foundation of 2017 Education Key Project "Research on Teachers Core Literacy and Ability Construction" (AFA170008), TJNU "Artificial Intelligence +Education" United Foundation, and Key Cultivation Project of Tianjin Teaching Achievement Award: Research and Development of Mathematics Learning Assessment Tool and Its Practical Application (PYJJ-036).

References

1. A.-R. Al Tamimi, The effect of using Ausubel's assimilation theory and the metacognitive strategy (KWL) in teaching probabilities and statistics unit for first grade middle school students' achievement and mathematical communication. Eur. Sci. **13**(1), 276–303 (2017)
2. D. Ausbel, *Educational Psychology: A Cognitive Approach* (Holt, Rinehart and Winston, New York, 1968)
3. D.L. Ball, L. Sleep, T.A. Boerst, H. Bass, Combining the development of practice and the practice of development in teacher education. Elementary School J. **109**(5), 458–474 (2009)
4. N. Bosch, S.K. D'mello, J. Ocumpaugh, R.S. Baker, V. Shute, Using video to automatically detect learner affect in computer-enabled classrooms. ACM Trans. Interact. Intell. Syst. **6**(2), 1–26 (2016)
5. Y. Cao, S. Zhang, *Mathematics Pedagogy* (Beijing Normal University Press, Beijing, 2010). ((in Chinese))
6. A.P. Cardoso, M. Ferreira, J.L. Abrantes, C. Seabra, C. Costa, Personal and pedagogical interaction factors as determinants of academic achievement. Procedia Soc. Behav. Sci. **29**, 1596–1605 (2011)
7. C.Y. Charalambous, E. Litke, Studying instructional quality by using a content-specific lens: the case of the Mathematical Quality of Instruction framework. ZDM Mathematics Education **50**(3), 445–460 (2018)
8. D.K. Cohen, S.W. Raudenbush, D.L. Ball, Resources, instruction, and research. Educ. Eval. Policy Anal. **25**(2), 119–142 (2003)
9. C. Costa, A.P. Cardoso, M.P. Lima, M. Ferreira, J.L. Abrantes, Pedagogical interaction and learning performance as determinants of academic achievement. Procedia Soc. Behav. Sci. **171**, 874–881 (2015)
10. L.L. Davis, Instrument review: getting the most from a panel of experts. Appl. Nurs. Res. **5**(4), 194–197 (1992)
11. A. Eckert, P. Nilsson, Introducing a symbolic interactionist approach on teaching mathematics: the case of revoicing as an interactional strategy in the teaching of probability. J. Math. Teacher Educ. **20**(1), 31–48 (2017)
12. N.A. Flanders, Intent, action and feedback: a preparation for teaching. J. Teacher Educ. **14**(3), 251–260 (1963)
13. A. Flieller, A. Jarlégan, Y. Tazouti, Who benefits from dyadic teacher–student interactions in whole-class settings? J. Educ. Res. **109**(3), 311–324 (2016)
14. T.L. Good, J.E. Brophy, Changing teacher and student behavior: an empirical investigation. J. Educ. Psychol. **66**(3), 390–405 (1974)
15. H. Hasanat, R.A.A. Omar, S. Al-Jazi, A study of the extent and nature of classroom verbal interaction in tenth-grade, Arabic language class in Jordan using Flanders interaction analysis category system (FIACS). Int. J. Learn. Dev. **7**(4), 68–86 (2017)

16. J. Hiebert, J.W. Stigler, A proposal for improving classroom teaching: lessons from the TIMSS video study. Element. School J. **101**(1), 3–20 (2000)
17. A. James, M. Kashyap, Y.H.V. Chua, T. Maszczyk, A.M. Núñez, R. Bull, J. Dauwels, Inferring the climate in classrooms from audio and video recordings: a machine learning approach. Paper presented at the 2018 IEEE International Conference on Teaching, Assessment, and Learning for Engineering (TALE) (2018)
18. W. Lee, S. Ng, Reducing student reticence through teacher interaction strategy. ELT J. **64**(3), 302–313 (2009)
19. G. Li, Z. Sun, Y. Jee, The more technology the better? A comparison of teacher-student interaction in high and low technology use elementary EFL classrooms in China. System **84**, 24–40 (2019)
20. F. Mahmoodi, E. Fathi Azar, R. Esfandiari, The evolution of the quality of teaching of high school teachers in Tabriz using flanders' interaction analysis system. Teach. Learn. Res. **7**(1), 23–40 (2009)
21. D.P. Martin, S.E. Rimm-Kaufman, Do student self-efficacy and teacher-student interaction quality contribute to emotional and social engagement in fifth grade math? J. School Psychol. **53**(5), 359–373 (2015)
22. M.K. McAdaragh, The effect of background experience and an advance organizer on the attainment of certain science concepts. Doctoral dissertation. Retrieved from Proquest Digital Dissertations (8116295) (1981)
23. J.E. Netten, W.H. Spain, Student-teacher interaction patterns in the French immersion classroom: implications for levels of achievement in French language proficiency. Can. Modern Lang. Rev. **45**(3), 485–501 (1989)
24. S. Netti, K. Khairul, P. Amelia, Student's mathematical communication skill based on the assimilation and accommodation framework. Int. J. Trends Math. Educ. Res. **2**(3), 133–137 (2019)
25. J.C. Otero, Assimilation problems in traditional representations of scientific knowledge. Eur. J. Sci. Educ. **7**(4), 361–369 (1985)
26. J. Piaget, Schemes of action and language learning, in *Language and Learning: The Debate Between Jean Piaget and Noam Chomsky*, ed. by M. Piattelli-Palmarini (Harvard University Press, Cambridge, 1980)
27. R.C. Pianta, K.M. La Paro, B.K. Hamre, *Classroom Assessment Scoring SystemTM: Manual K-3* (Paul H Brookes Publishing, Baltimore, MD, US, 2008)
28. S. Podschuweit, S. Bernholt, M. Brückmann, Classroom learning and achievement: how the complexity of classroom interaction impacts students' learning. Res. Sci. Technol. Educ. **34**(2), 142–163 (2016)
29. D.F. Polit, C.T. Beck, S.V. Owen, Is the CVI an acceptable indicator of content validity? Appraisal and recommendations. Res. Nursing Health **30**(4), 459–467 (2007)
30. S.E. Rimm-Kaufman, A.E. Baroody, R.A. Larsen, T.W. Curby, T. Abry, To what extent do teacher–student interaction quality and student gender contribute to fifth graders' engagement in mathematics learning? J. Educ. Psychol. **107**(1), 170–185 (2015)
31. A.-L. Rostvall, T. West, Theoretical and methodological perspectives on designing video studies of interaction. Int. J. Qual. Methods **4**(4), 87–108 (2005)
32. A.M. Saleh, The effect of using the educational models of Gagne and Ausubel on achievement and learning retention in first grade secondary students in biology in the province of Abyan. Unpublished Master's thesis. University of Aden, Aden, Yemen (2006)
33. R.R. Skemp, *The Psychology of Learning Mathematics: Expanded American Edition*, 1st edn. (Routledge, New York, 1982)
34. N. Suryati, Classroom interaction strategies employed by English teachers at lower secondary schools. TEFLIN J. **26**(2), 247–264 (2015)
35. C.F. Waltz, O.L. Strickland, E.R. Lenz, *Measurement in Nursing and Health Research* (Springer publishing company, New York, 2010)

Chapter 14
An Overview of Data Mining Techniques for Student Performance Prediction

Xiu Zhang and Xin Zhang

Abstract In order to better understand and optimize the learning process and learning environment, educational data mining technology is becoming more and more important in processing a large number of educational data. Through the analysis of large amounts of educational data, students' academic performance is predicted, identifying a "high risk" of dropping out and predicting their future achievement, e.g., on final exams. The predicted results can provide early warning for students' own learning, and provide suggestions for educators to allocate educational resources more reasonably and improve the teaching mode. The purpose of this chapter is to comprehensively introduce the more advanced supervised machine learning technology, different educational resource dataset, and the latest research results.

Keywords Educational data mining · Machine learning · Student performance prediction · Survey

14.1 Introduction

With the development of the network technology, a large amount of data information have been collected which cover a wide range of fields, such as business data, education data, agriculture data, military data and so on. In order to explore the meaning behind the data, the data mining technology has received more and more attention from all over the world. In the field of education, especially, it has become the research hotspot to predict the student performance using data mining technology [1, 2].

In the educational data mining (EDM) work, the result of student achievement evaluation is often one of the important indicators to evaluate students' development potential, development level and performance. Entity and efficient educators often collect all aspects of information from students through research and other methods,

X. Zhang · X. Zhang (✉)
Tianjin Key Laboratory of Wireless Mobile Communications and Power Transmission, Tianjin Normal University, Tianjin, China
e-mail: ecemark@tjnu.edu.cn

© The Author(s), under exclusive license to Springer Nature Singapore Pte Ltd. 2021
W. Wang et al. (eds.), *Artificial Intelligence in Education and Teaching Assessment*,
https://doi.org/10.1007/978-981-16-6502-8_14

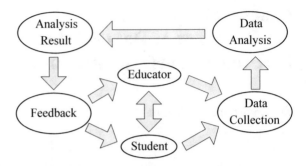

Fig. 14.1 The relationship between the students, educators and EDM

and organize them into relevant documents. With these documents as the data support [3], so as to dig deeply the value behind these data, for the teaching administrators to provide a basis, humanized, directional guidance. Teaching quality is an important factor to measure the grade of a school, while students' academic level is the main index to evaluate teachers' teaching effect and students' learning quality [4, 5].

The work of student's performance prediction using data mining technology has extensive instruction for educational work as shown in Fig. 14.1 [6, 7]. For students, it can help them to understand their learning efficiency and learning progress, so as to know more about their learning abilities. For teachers, it can help them to master the progress of teaching, and adjust their teaching schedule according to the predicted results. For educational administrator, it can provide decision support, improve the management system, and allocate educational resources scientifically.

The subjects most closely associated with EDM are computer science, education, and statistics. The workflow of educational data mining includes data collection, data preprocessing, data analysis and prediction as shown in Fig. 14.2. Data collection includes questionnaire survey, online course data acquisition, offline examination information collection and so on. The purpose of data preprocessing mainly focused on the following aspects: (i) Remove useless information from the data; (ii) Transform unstructured data into structured data; (iii) Split and merge the attributes. The most important step in EDM is data analysis. The technologies include statistic analysis such as descriptive statistics analysis and inferential statistics analysis, cluster analysis such as K-means cluster method, performance prediction approaches such as similarity-based methods, model-based methods and probabilistic method [1–5].

The chapter is organized as follows. Section 14.2 provides an overview of the dataset. Section 14.3 describes data mining technology. Section 14.4 summarizes the research results. Section 14.5 gives the conclusion.

Fig. 14.2 Flow chart of EDM

Table 14.1 Dataset information freely available

Authors	Number of instances	Number of attributes	Associated tasks	Country	Date
Hussain [1]	300	22	Classification	India	2018
Hussain [2]	666	11	Classification	India	2018
Gunduz and Fokoue [3]	5820	33	Classification, Clustering	Turkey	2013
Vurkac [4]	10,800	20	Classification	America	2011
Vahdat et al. [5, 6]	230,318	13	Classification, Clustering, Regression	Italy	2015
Petkovic et al. [7]	74	102	Classification	America	2017
Kuzilek et al. [8]	32,593	12	Classification	Czech	2017

14.2   Overview of the Dataset

At present, because of the rise of online education, a large amount of education data has been produced. The collection of educational data includes the traditional questionnaire survey, the information stored in the educational administration system of each school, the data collection set by the teaching unit according to the actual situation, and the data collection in the online education system.

In this part, we list several publicly available data sets since 2010 that are available for download online as shown in Table 14.1.

14.3   Data Mining Method in Performance Predication

14.3.1   Data Mining Tools

In this part, we will give an overview of several commonly used data mining tools all over the world.

(1)   Rapid Miner [9]

Rapid Miner is an environment for machine learning and data mining experiments which is applied in research and practical data mining tasks. This tool is developed in Java programming language and provides high-level analysis through a template-based framework.

It has rich data mining analysis and algorithm functions. The biggest advantage of the tool is that it doesn't require the user to write code. It already has many templates and other tools that make it easy to analyze the data.

(2)   KNIME [10]

KNIME is a user-friendly, understandable and comprehensive open source for data integration, processing, analysis and exploration platform. It has a graphical user interface to help users easily connect nodes for data processing.

It is easy to integrate with third-party Big Data frameworks, such as Apache Hadoop and Spark, through the Big Data Extension. It is Compatible with multiple data formats, including plain text, database, document, image, network, and even Hadoop-based data formats. Meanwhile, it is compatible with multiple data analysis tools and languages including R and Python language support for scripts, so that the experts can use powerful visualization function to provide an easy-to-use graphical interface, which can show the analysis results to users through vivid graphics.

(3)   Smartbi [11]

Smartbi Mining is a professional data Mining platform that provides predictive capabilities to businesses. This platform is integrated with rich algorithms and supports 5 categories of mature machine learning algorithms including classification, regression, clustering, prediction, correlation algorithms. In addition to providing the main algorithm and visual modeling functions, SmartBi Mining also provides essential data preprocessing functions. In general, this platform is easy to learn and use.

(4)   TANAGRA [12]

TANAGRA is a data mining software for academic and research purposes. The software has exploratory data analysis, statistical analysis, machine learning. TANAGRA contains some supervised learning, but also includes other paradigms such as clustering, factor analysis, parametric and nonparametric statistics, relevant rules, feature selection, and building algorithms.

(5)   Orange [13]

Orange is a suite of component-based data mining and machine learning software written in Python. It is an open source for data visualization and analysis. Data mining can be done through visual programming or Python scripts. It can be visualized using scenarios, bar charts, trees, networks, and heat maps.

(6)   Weka [14]

Weka (Waikato Environment for Knowledge Analysis) is the best known open source machine learning and data mining software. It can invoke the analysis component including data preparation, classification, regression, clustering, association rules mining, and visualization through Java programming and the command line.

(7)   Scikit-learn [15]

Scikit-Learn is a simple and efficient data mining and data analysis tool. It's a machine learning library in Python, built on top of Numpy, Scipy, and Matplotlib, and it's also open source. Its characteristics include classification, regression, clustering, dimensionality reduction, model selection and preprocessing.

14.3.2   Performance Prediction Approaches

In the educational data mining, classification and regression are commonly used to predict the student's performance. In the following, the main methods are briefly introduced and discussed.

(1)   Decision Tree (DT) [16]

Decision tree is a basic classification and regression method, which makes decisions based on tree structure and can be considered as the set of if–then rules. Generally, a decision tree contains a root node, several internal nodes and several leaf nodes. The root node contains all the sample points, the internal node serves as the partition node (attribute test), and the leaf node corresponds to the decision result. The advantages of the algorithm are low computational complexity, easy to understand the output results, insensitivity to the absence of intermediate values, and the ability to process irrelevant feature data. The downside is that it can cause overmatching problems.

For the decision tree construction based on ID3 algorithm, the criterion of feature selection is information gain. ID3 algorithm originated from concept learning system (CLS). C4.5 algorithm is a kind of classification decision tree algorithm, whose core algorithm is ID3 algorithm. C4.5 algorithm uses information gain rate to select feature, which overcomes the shortcoming of choosing feature with more values when using information gain to select feature. However, the disadvantage is that in the process of constructing the tree, the data set needs to be scanned and sorted for many times, which leads to the low efficiency of the algorithm. C4.5 algorithm was developed in Java in Weka as J48.

(2)   Naïve Bayes (NB) [17]

Naive Bayes model (NBM) originated from classical mathematical theory, which has a solid mathematical foundation and stable classification efficiency. At the same time, the NBC model requires few parameters to estimate and is not sensitive to missing data, and the algorithm is relatively simple. In theory, the NBC model has the smallest error rate compared with other classification methods. However, in fact, this is not always the case, because the NBC model assumes that the attributes are independent of each other, which is often not valid in practical application, which has a certain impact on the correct classification of the NBC model. When the number of generics is large or the correlation between attributes is large, the classification efficiency of NBC model is inferior to that of decision tree model. When the attribute correlation is small, the performance of NBC model is the best.

(3)   Support vector machines (SVM) [18]

SVM is a kind of supervised learning method, which is widely used in statistical classification and regression analysis. The support vector machine maps the vector into a higher dimensional space and establishes a hyperplane with maximum spacing in this space. Two parallel hyperplanes are built on both sides of the hyperplanes separating the data. Separating hyperplanes maximizes the distance between two parallel hyperplanes. The larger the distance or gap between the pseudo-definite parallel hyperplanes, the smaller the total error of the classifier.

The advantages of the SVM are low generalization error rate and low computational overhead. The disadvantage is sensitive to parameter adjustment and kernel function selection.

(4)   K-Nearest Neighbor (KNN) [19]

KNN classification algorithm is a relatively mature method in theory and one of the simplest machine learning algorithms. The idea of this method is that if most of the K most similar samples in the feature space of a sample belong to a certain category, then the sample also belongs to this category.

The advantages of KNN are high accuracy, insensitivity to outliers and assumption of no data input. The disadvantages are high computational complexity, and high space complexity.

(5)   Random Forest (RF) [29]

Random forest is composed of many decision trees, and there is no correlation between different decision trees. When we carry out the classification task, new input samples come in, and each decision tree in the forest will be judged and classified separately. Each decision tree will get its own classification result. Which one of the classification results of the decision tree has the most classification will be regarded as the final result by the random forest.

The advantages of RF are that it can use very high dimensional data, and don't have to reduce dimensions and do feature selection. The disadvantage of RF has been shown to overfit for some noisy classification or regression problems.

(6)   Artificial Neural Network (ANN) [31]

ANN can simulate the activity of neurons by mathematical model, which is an information processing system based on the structure and function of the Neural Network of the brain. The multi-layer forward neuron network (also called multi-layer perceptron, MLP) proposed by Minsley and Papert is the most commonly used network structure at present.

Compared with traditional data processing methods, neural network technology has obvious advantages in processing fuzzy data, random data and nonlinear data, and is especially suitable for systems with large scale, complex structure and unclear information.

(7)   Classification and Regression Tree (CART) [20]

CART algorithm is a binary recursive segmentation technology. The current sample is divided into two sub-samples, so that each non-leaf node generated has two branches. Therefore, the decision tree generated by CART algorithm is a binary tree with simple structure.

14.4   Results and Discussions

In order to study the influence of different attributes on students' performance and to mine the meaning behind the data, different researchers have studied different attributes and analyzed their importance in students' performance prediction as shown in Table 14.2.

Before the classification algorithms applied to analyze the data, the feature selection approach was used to select 12 highly influential attributes from 24 attributes [1]. The results showed that it can greatly improve the accuracy of predictions. The researchers [7] collected the data about student team project activities. It can predict the student teams' performance.

The researcher [21] studied the effect of student background and social activities on the student's performance. It came to a conclusion that the student background and social activities had significant to the student's performance prediction in the binary classification. Different from other researches on academic prediction after the end of the course, the researchers [22, 23] studied the prediction of students' academic performance while the course is in progress, so as to give early warning to students and provide suggestions to teachers. In addition, Kahraman et al [24] developed an Intuitive Knowledge Classifier to analyze the web-based adaptive learning environment. It can greatly improve the accuracy of the classification. The authors [25–27] use data collected in a traditional teaching setting to learn how to predict students' academic performance in early stage. Among these, the authors [27] considered the role of students' self-assessment in the performance prediction.

The above researches focused on analyzing the effect of the student information on the performance prediction. Khan et al. [28] studied the impact of teaching on the student's performance. It indicated that teaching had a positive impact on the

Table 14.2 Attributes affect the performance

Authors	Attributes affect the performance
Kiu [21]	Student background, student social activities and student coursework result
Hu et al. [22]	Time-dependent variables
Huang et al. [23]	Student's cumulative GPA, grades earned in four pre-requisite courses and scores on three dynamics mid-term exams
Hussain et al. [1]	The 12 high influential attributes were selected among 24 attributes
Petkovic et al. [7]	Team Activity Measures
Kahraman et al. [24]	Web-based adaptive learning environments in different domains
Carter et al. [25]	Affirms the importance of social interaction in the learning process
Yu et al. [27]	Self-evaluation comments can play an important role in improving the accuracy of early-stage predictions
Khan et al. [28]	Teaching
Liu et al. [33]	Historical learning records, learning target and prerequisite graph

student's performance. The researchers [30] developed a performance prediction models with less information for predicting at-risk students. The results indicate that the subject which relied on knowledge of other subjects in the program generally performed better than those which relied less on previous subjects. Lee et al. [32] investigated the course dropout in a mobile learning environment. The researchers in [33] proposed a Cognitive Structure Enhanced framework for Adaptive Learning which combined knowledge levels of learners or knowledge structure of learning. The framework can dynamically provide the suggestions and guidance for the next learning during the whole learning process.

At present, there are many data mining techniques that can be used to predict students' academic performance. We list and summarize the classification rates of the current commonly used algorithms as shown in Table 14.3. There are other algorithms can be used to predict the students' performance. For example, Bendangnuksung et al. [31] proposed the Deep Neural Network (DNN) model to analyze the students' performance. The results indicated that DNN outperformed other algorithms (DT, NB, ANN) in accuracy.

As shown in Table 14.3, the same algorithm has different classification accuracy in different dataset. However, most of the algorithms have high accuracy for binary classification type. As shown in Fig. 14.3, the classification accuracy for multi-class classification problem is relatively low.

It can be seen from Fig. 14.3 that RF and ANN attains better performance compared with NB, DT and SVM. The minimum values of classification accuracy of the five methods have small gap compared with the maximum classification accuracy values.

Table 14.3 Classification accuracy

Authors	Type of classification	EDM accuracy (%)						
		NB	DT	RF	ANN	CART	SVM	KNN
Kiu [21]	Binary	88.9	92.4	89.4	86.3	–	–	–
	5-level	71	79.1	74.9	68.7	–	–	–
Hu et al. [22]	Binary	–	93.4	–	–	95	–	–
Huang et al. [23]	Binary	–	–	–	88.5	–	86.5	–
Hussain et al. [1]	5-level	65.3	73	99	–	–	–	–
Hussain et al. [2]	4-level	57.8	64.7	–	90.8	–	–	–
Petkovic et al. [7]	Binary	–	–	70	–	–	–	–
Kahraman et al. [24]	4-level	73.8	–	–	–	–	–	85
Bucos et al. [25]	Binary	–	82	84	–	–	84	–
Yu et al. [27]	Binary	–	–	–	–	–	74	–
Ahmed et al. [29]	Binary	–	–	83.6	–	–	–	–
Chanlekha et al. [30]	9-level	57.5	65	62.5	62.5	–	57.5	–
Bendangnuksung et al. [31]	5-level	80	82.2	–	80	–	–	–

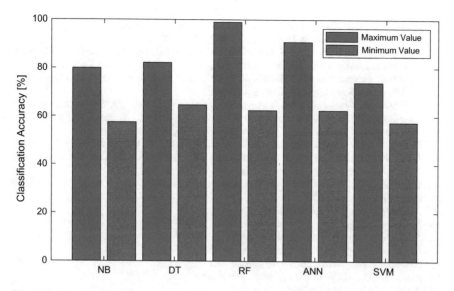

Fig. 14.3 The classification accuracy of different algorithms for multi-class classification problems

14.5 Summary

The rapid development of data mining technology has promoted the extensive application of educational data analysis. By mining the effective information behind the educational data and predicting the academic performance of students, it can not only help students understand their own learning state, but also help educators to specify corresponding strategies to improve the efficiency of education.

In the future, with the continuous progress of science and technology, online education will become more and more popular. A large number of online education data will provide more materials for data mining, and how to make better use of online and offline education data will provide better guidance for education.

References

1. S. Hussain, N.A. Dahan, F.M. Baalwi, N. Ribata, Educational data mining and analysis of students' academic performance using WEKA. Indonesian J. Electr. Eng. Comput. Sci. **9**(31), 447–459 (2018)
2. S. Hussain, R. Atallah, A. Kamsin, J. Hazarika, Classification, clustering and association rule mining in educational datasets using data mining tools: a case study, in *Cybernetics and Algorithms in Intelligent Systems. CSOC2018 2018. Advances in Intelligent Systems and Computing, AISC 765*, ed. by R. Silhavy (Springer, 2019), pp. 196–211
3. G. Gunduz, E. Fokoue, *UCI Machine Learning Repository* (University of California, School of Information and Computer Science, Irvine, CA, 2013)

4. M. Vurkac, Clave-direction analysis: a new arena for educational and creative applications of music technology. J. Music, Technol. Educ. **4**(1), 27–46 (2011)
5. M. Vahdat, L. Oneto, A. Ghio, G. Donzellini, D. Anguita, M. Funk, M. Rauterberg, A learning analytics methodology to profile students behavior and explore interactions with a digital electronics simulator, in *EC-TEL 2014. LNCS, 8719*, ed. by S. de Freitas, C. Rensing, T. Ley, P.J. Munoz-Merino (Springer, 2014), pp. 596–597
6. M. Vahdat, A. Ghio, L. Oneto, D. Anguita, M. Funk, M. Rauterberg, Advances in learning analytics and educational data mining, in: *European Symposium on Artificial Neural Networks, Computational Intelligence and Machine Learning, Bruges* (2015)
7. D. Petkovic, M. Sosnick-Pérez, K. Okada, R. Todtenhoefer, S. Huang, N. Miglani, A. Vigil, *Using the Random Forest Classifier to Assess and Predict Student Learning of Software Engineering Teamwork, Frontiers in Education (FIE)* (Erie, PA, 2016)
8. J. Kuzilek et al., Open university learning analytics dataset. Sci. Data **4**, 170171 (2017). https://doi.org/10.1038/sdata.2017.171
9. Available in https://rapidminer.com/
10. Available in https://www.knime.com/
11. Available in https://www.smartbi.com.cn/
12. Available in https://eric.msh-lse.fr/wricco/tanagra/
13. Available in https://orangedatamining.com/
14. Available in https://www.cs.waikato.ac.nz/ml/weka/
15. Available in https://scikit-learn.org/stable/
16. Available in https://www.investopedia.com/terms/d/decision-tree.asp
17. O. Okun, Feature Select. Ensemble Methods Bioinform. 13–31 (2011)
18. P. Andrzej, J. Luo, The more you learn, the less you store: memory-controlled incremental SVM for visual place recognition. Image Vis. Comput. **28**(7), 1080–1097 (2010)
19. P. Leif, K-nearest neighbor. Scholarpedia **4**, 2 (2009)
20. M. Krzywinski, N. Altman, Classification and regression trees. Nat. Methods **14**, 757–758 (2017)
21. C. C. Kiu, data mining analysis on student's academic performance through exploration of student's background and social activities, in *2018 Fourth International Conference on Advances in Computing, Communication & Automation (ICACCA)* (2018)
22. Y. Hu, C. Lo, S. Shih, Developing early warning systems to predict students' online learning performance. Comput. Hum. Behav. **36**, 469–478 (2014)
23. S. Huang, N. Fang, Predicting student academic performance in an engineering dynamics course: a comparison of four types of predictive mathematical models. Comput. Educ. **61**, 133–145 (2013)
24. H.T. Kahraman, S. Sagiroglu, I. Colak, The development of intuitive knowledge classifier and the modeling of domain dependent data. Knowl.-Based Syst. **37**, 283–295 (2013)
25. M. Bucos, B. Druagulescu, Predicting student success using data generated in traditional educational environments. TEM J. **7**(3), 617–625 (2018)
26. A.S. Carter, C.D. Hundhausen, O. Adesope, Blending measures of programming and social behavior into predictive models of student achievement in early computing courses. ACM Trans. Comput. Educ. **17**, 3 (2017)
27. L.C. Yu, C.W. Lee, H. I. Pan, C. Y. Chou, P.Y. Chao, Z.H. Chen, S.F. Tseng, C.L. Chan, K.R. Lai, Improving early prediction of academic failure using sentiment analysis on self-evaluated comments. J. Comput. Assist. Learn. (2018)
28. A. Khan, S.K. Ghosh, Data mining based analysis to explore the effect of teaching on student performance. Educ. Inf. Technol. **23**, 1677–1697 (2018)
29. N.S. Ahmed, M.H. Sadiq, Clarify of the random forest algorithm in an educational field, in *2018 international conference on advanced science and engineering (ICOASE)* (IEEE, 2018), pp. 179–184
30. H. Chanlekha, J. Niramitranon, Student performance prediction model for early-identification of at-risk students in traditional classroom settings, in *Proceedings of the 10th International Conference on Management of Digital Ecosystems—MEDES '18* (ACM, 2018), pp. 239–245

31. P.P. Bendangnuksung, Students' performance prediction using deep neural network. Int. J. Appl. Eng. Res. **13**(2), 1171–1176 (2018)
32. Y. Lee, D. Shin, H. Loh, J. Lee, P. Chae, J. Cho, S. Park, J. Lee, J. Baek, B. Kim, Y. Choi, Deep attentive study session dropout prediction in mobile learning environment, in *12th International Conference on Computer Supported Education* (2020)
33. Q. Liu, S. Tong, C. Liu, H. Zhao, E. Chen, H. Ma, S. Wang, Exploiting cognitive structure for adaptive learning, in *The 25th ACM SIGKDD Conference on Knowledge Discovery & Data Mining (KDD'19)* (2019)

Chapter 15
Eye Tracking and Its Applications in the Field of Intelligent Education

Linlin Li, Ying Tong, and Libo Qiao

Abstract Relying on artificial intelligence, eye-tracking technology continues to develop and mature. It helps analyse students' visual attention and mental cognition by recording their eye movement data, which can provide support for research on intelligent education. This paper mainly analyses and summarizes commonly used eye movement metrics, principles of eye-tracking technology, and applications of eye-tracking research in the field of intelligent education. The purpose is to enrich the research methods and application scope of eye tracking in intelligent education and to promote further development of eye tracking and artificial intelligence.

Keywords Eye tracking · Artificial intelligence · Online learning · Intelligent education · Learning analytics

15.1 Introduction

In the last decade, along with the popularity of Internet and the rising demand of human beings for intelligence, applications of artificial intelligence in education has become more diversified, gradually forming a system of intelligent education [1].

Eye movements reflect human visual processing, reveal mental characteristics, and play an important role in information extraction, processing and integration [2, 3]. Recently, with the rapid development of low-cost hardware, digital image processing technology and artificial intelligence, various eye-tracking methods have been proposed and improved.

As an intersection of artificial intelligence, education and psychology, eye-tracking technology has been applied to pedagogical research for about forty years, and it was mainly used to study the psychological mechanism of reading in the

L. Li · Y. Tong (✉)
Tianjin Key Laboratory of Wireless Mobile Communications and Power Transmission, Tianjin Normal University, Tianjin 300387, China
e-mail: tongying2334@163.com

L. Qiao
Department of Psychology, Tianjin Normal University, Tianjin 300387, China

early stages [4]. With the development of artificial intelligence, applications of eye-tracking research in instructional resource design, teaching method improvement, learning process analytics, student performance prediction continue to increase.

15.2 Eye Movement Metrics

Through statistical analysis of eye-tracking data, different indicators can be obtained, which allow for a deeper understanding of learner's cognition. Before eye tracking is applied to intelligent educational research, researchers need to know what eye movement metrics are commonly used and what they mean.

After a comprehensive analysis of eye-tracking measures commonly used in recent studies, it was found that these metrics can be classified into four types according to measurement dimension: temporal dimension, spatial dimension, numerical dimension and others [5].

Temporal dimension involves some temporal indicators, such as total fixation duration, average fixation duration, first fixation duration, which are more commonly used. Spatial dimension involves position, distance and direction, such as fixation position, saccade amplitude and gaze plot, etc. Due to the predominantly qualitative approach and more time-consuming nature, these types of indicators are relatively less used. Numerical dimension metrics are generally used to reveal the importance of visual material. These common metrics are summarized as Table 15.1 [6–8].

In sum, each eye movement metric has its scope of application. Using only an eye movement indicator may miss some valuable information and make it difficult to reflect problem comprehensively. Therefore, when conducting eye-movement research on intelligent education, researchers should use multiple eye-movement indicators flexibly according to their experimental needs [8].

15.3 Principles and Methods of Eye Tracking

Over a century, human beings have continuously explored and improved on how to achieve eye tracking, and eye-tracking technology has undergone the evolution of observation method, mechanical recording method, reflective recording method, scleral search coil method, iris-scleral heterochromatic limbus method, electro-oculography (EOG) and others [9]. These methods directly contact eyes with some actuators, electrodes or coils, which causes discomfort or even injury to them.

Nowadays, research on eye movements has evolved from early methods for determining the amplitude of eye movements to methods for estimating the location of gaze points [10]. With the development of cameras and image processing hardware, video-oculography (VOG) methods have been proposed and matured. This method acquires eye images through cameras. It is used without the need to fit a device to subject's eye, making the process of gaze tracking natural and comfortable.

Table 15.1 Common eye-tracking metrics

Dimension	Metrics	Definition	Meaning
Temporal	First fixation duration	Duration at the first point in an AOI	Initial attention tendencies
	Gaze duration	Total fixation duration within a word or an AOI	Attention allocation
	Revisited fixation duration	Total duration of all fixations back to an AOI	Information reprocessing
	Total fixation duration	Total time of all fixations on an AOI or stimulus	Total cognitive resource input, and cognitive load
	Average fixation duration	Average time of fixation on each AOI	Average cognitive resource input
Spatial	Fixation position	Position of a fixation	Visual attention
	Saccade amplitude	Distance from one fixation to the next	Reading efficiency and perceptual breadth
	Gaze plot	Diagram showing location, order, and time spent looking at the stimulus	Temporal and spatial characteristics of eye movements and process of interest change
	Heat map	Diagram showing how looking is distributed over the stimulus	Focus of visual attention for dozens or even hundreds of participants at a time
Numerical	Total fixation count	Total number of fixations on an AOI or stimulus	Total cognitive resource input, cognitive load and interest
	Average fixation count	Average number of fixations in each AOI	Average cognitive resource input, cognitive load
	Revisit count	Number of fixations back to what has been looked at	Cognitive coherence and information reprocessing degree
	Saccade count	Total number of saccades in an AOI	Attention shifting, information integration
Others	Pupil size	Pupil diameter and its variation values	Cognitive processing effort degree and cognitive load
	Blank rate	Frequency of blinking	Cognitive control

The method has a two-step process: image pre-processing and gaze estimation. Image pre-processing performs filtering, denoising, face detection and eye positioning operations. Depending on the gaze mapping model used for gaze estimation, VOG methods are divided into four categories:

1. 2D Regression-Based. This method assumes a fixed matching relationship between eye map features and gaze points [9]. Through image processing techniques, some significant eye features are extracted, such as pupil centre and

corneal reflection. Then, a mapping relationship is established between these eye parametric features and two-dimensional coordinates of calibration points, which is used to obtain the next real-time eye positions.

2. 3D Model-Based. Based on eye structure and principles of optical imaging, a three-dimensional eye model is established to mimic the structure and function of human visual system. The gaze direction is solved in a three-dimensional geometric relationship, with the intersection of gaze direction and screen as gaze point [11]. This method requires a series of parameter calibrations, including camera calibration, geometric calibration and user calibration [12], to derive eye model parameters and help calculate the orientation of optical and visual axes. Depending on hardware required for the system, it can be classified as single-camera methods, multi-camera methods and depth camera methods [13].

3. Appearance-Based. Numerous face images in different environments need to be acquired. Input eye diagrams to the model and calculate changes of gaze point based on changes in shape and texture properties of eye and positions of pupil relative to canthus [9]. This method establishes the mapping relationship between eye diagrams and gaze points through machine learning, including multilayer network, Gaussian process, deep learning, etc.

4. Shape-Based. This method uses a deformable template for detecting the eye region, where eye contours is represented by two closed parabolas and iris is represented using a circle [13]. The aim is to determine the similarity between the template of a selected region and images of that region.

The advantages and disadvantages of these methods are shown in Table 15.2.

15.4 Applications of Eye-Tracking Technology in Intelligent Education

Recently, with the continuous development of image processing, artificial intelligence and related algorithms, researchers have conducted in-depth research on applications of gaze tracking in the field of intelligent education. According to their research purpose, applications can be divided into four categories: (1) instructional resource design; (2) teaching method improvement; (3) learning process analytics; (4) student performance prediction.

15.4.1 Instructional Resource Design

Intelligent education plays an irreplaceable role in breaking through time and space constraints of teaching, integrating high-quality educational resources and promoting the balanced development of education across regions.

Table 15.2 The advantages and disadvantages of eye-tracking approaches

Category	Advantages	Disadvantages
2D regression-based	It can be achieved using a single camera and a few near-infrared LEDs, with simple system configuration and no additional calibration operations required	Susceptible to head movement, and it requires users to use a device such as a chin rest to keep their head stationary
3D model-based	It overcomes the effects of changes in head position and posture and improves the accuracy of gaze tracking	High hardware requirements, typically requiring multiple cameras and light sources. Most require complex calibration of screen, camera, infrared light source and user position
Appearance-based	It has low hardware requirements and is suitable for implementation on platforms without high-resolution cameras or additional light sources	Accuracy is low in the case of head movement and light changes. To obtain high robustness, a large amount of training data is required
Shape-based	It allows estimation of the line of sight on low-resolution images	Occlusion of eye area and changes in head posture and eye shape can result in reduced accuracy and high computational complexity in gaze detection

Instructional resources are an important carrier of teaching information. Suarez [14] used eye-tracking and EEG techniques to measure participants' pupillary responses and brain frequencies while performing tasks to explore the effects of instructional design and emotional state on academic performance. Results showed that instructional design had a significant effect on student academic performance.

Instructional resources can be divided into dynamic and static resources, and the design of their elements can have a significant impact on the effectiveness of teaching and learning. The use of eye-tracking technology to record learners' visual responses to different design schemes helps to scientifically design these elements.

15.4.1.1   Static Resource Design

Static teaching resource design includes text design, image design, colour design, resource presentation design, etc. Liu [15] used eye movement metrics such as gaze duration, heat map to characterize learners' visual attention, comparing and analysing differences in learning effects when different text and pictures design strategies were used. Combining eye movement and brain signals, Cao [16] conducted experiments from three perspectives: colour coding design, colour cue design, and colour signal design to explore the influence of colour representation in teaching scenes on learning attention.

Li [17] applied eye-tracking technology to the optimisation of online course presentations. A quantitative model of cognitive load of online course resources is proposed; optimization methods of online course resources and the impact of optimized courses on student cognitive load are explored.

15.4.1.2 Dynamic Resource Design

Dynamic resource design mainly includes subtitle layout, playback speed and teacher presentation of instructional videos. Sun [18] used an eye tracker to record learners' eye movements when they watched MOOC video interfaces with different subtitle layouts and analysed their visual behaviour and attention distribution. Duan et al. [19] investigate the effect of playback speed of animated learning materials on attention shifting and learning outcomes with the help of eye-tracking. Ma et al. [20] had subjects watch instructional videos at different speeds but for the same total duration, and explored whether the increased number of learning sessions associated with fast playback would result in better learning outcomes and learning satisfaction than with normal speed.

In traditional education, teachers face students and guide them through eye contact. However, teacher presentation in online education is an issue that needs to be studied. Gog et al. [21] designed video materials with and without teachers and analysed learners' eye movement while watching videos. The study found that teacher presentation can attract learners' attention and improve learning outcomes. Wang et al. [22] explored the influence of teachers' gaze guidance and postural guidance on learners' eye movement and learning effects. The research results show that videos with gaze guidance or postural guidance were more effective.

15.4.2 Teaching Method Improvement

With the development of big data, terminal technology and artificial intelligence, new instructional methods have been proposed, such as intelligent tutor system, pedagogical agent, adaptive learning and game-based learning. The use of eye-tracking technology helps to make these approaches possible and facilitate their development.

15.4.2.1 Intelligent Tutor System

Intelligent tutor system refers to the use of artificial intelligence technology to guide learners to acquire knowledge and skills without guidance of human teachers. It provides instant guidance, accurate learning diagnosis and intelligent intervention to increase learning efficiency.

D'Mello et al. [23] developed Gaze tutor, an intelligent teaching system for learners' gaze, which first uses an eye-tracking device to dynamically monitor learners' gaze patterns and identify whether learners are in "boredom", "disengage-ment" or "zoning out." The tutor then uses an intelligent teaching agent to guide learners into an active state. Empirical studies have shown that the tutor is effective in directing learners' attention to key areas of system interfaces and increasing their deeper thinking about important issues, but effects vary between learners.

Intelligent tutor system makes instructional decisions for students based on their models, which are generally invisible to them. However, studies have shown that opening models to students allows them to see how the system perceives them, which is beneficial to learning.

Mathews et al. [24] developed an intelligent tutor system called EER-Tutor, which detects learner models through eye-tracking and later visualises learner models so that students can see their models. The system helps developers to design better and more accessible models and find out which models are suitable for specific students.

15.4.2.2   Pedagogical Agent

Some educational researchers have incorporated virtual visual images (i.e. Pedagog-ical agent) into teaching systems to guide and feedback learning, to collaborate and interact with learners and to convey non-verbal information through gestures and facial expressions, which helps to create an interesting learning environment [25].

Accurate identification of affective and cognitive states is the basis for interaction between online learners and pedagogical agents. To solve the problem that teaching agents don't recognize the states adequately, Zhan [26] combined eye-tracking with expression recognition to simultaneously detect learners' visual fields, emotions and cognitive states. It improved the recognition accuracy of remote learners' states and provided new ideas and methods for the study of interaction mechanisms between intelligent teaching agents and remote learners.

Since the emergence of pedagogical agents, there have been inconsistent findings on whether they facilitate learning. Through tracking learners' eye movement when using agents, their effectiveness can be evaluated. Prendinger et al. [27] evaluated the effect of life-like interface agents on user cognition by eye tracking, and found that agent's body movements were more effective in directing their attention than text and speech, but it also slightly affected their concentration level, sometimes distracting them to pay attention to agent's actions. Using eye-movement techniques, Kang [28] investigated the influence of learners' agent image preference, knowledge experience and learning material complexity on learning outcomes. It was found that learners devoted more attention to the deeper processing of learning material when agent image matched their preference.

There are still some controversies about the effect of pedagogical agents on learning, for example, effects differ for learners of different ages and cognitive styles. Therefore, the effects on learners and how to design agents that work better need to be confirmed by more studies.

15.4.2.3   Adaptive Learning

Adaptive learning helps analyse learners' psychological characteristics based on eye-tracking data, tap their behavior preferences and cognitive styles, and provide learners with personalized learning resources, which has become a new trend of intelligent education.

Pivec et al. [29] proposed an adaptive e-learning framework based on eye tracking and content tracking, called AdELE. The framework captures users' behaviour in real-time, including skimming, reading, searching for information, observing pictures, viewing navigational elements, etc., whereby learners' cognitive styles are analysed. Based on a template, authors provide different content blocks suitable for learners with different knowledge levels (e.g. novice, advanced, expert). Adaption engine helps to dynamically create personalised content from available information blocks and different representation layers.

Schmidt et al. [30] connected an eye-tracking system with a multimedia learning environment, linked gaze data to browser-based learning content, and adjusted learning content and controlled learning process through predefined conditions and user input.

Xue and Zeng [31] proposed an application framework for applying eye-tracking data to the design and development process of an adaptive learning system. As shown in Fig. 15.1, it is divided into five modules. Through eye-tracking experiments, differences in eye-movement patterns of learners with different cognitive styles were studied to form a user portrait database, which provided a new approach for adaptive learning systems.

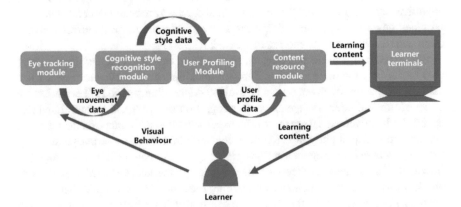

Fig. 15.1 The adaptive learning system framework

15.4.2.4   Game-Based Learning

Game-based learning (GBL) environment is a dynamic, multi-tasking, and highly interactive learning environment. It can improve learners' attentional control, cognitive flexibility and problem-solving skills, which has great potential for intelligent education.

In terms of visual attention, game flow and conceptual achievement, Tsai et al. [32] explored behavioural differences among learners with different conceptual understanding abilities and discovered patterns of their visual behaviour in a GBL environment, providing some insights into learning mechanism of GBL and helping researchers develop more effective games to facilitate learning.

15.4.3   Learning Process Analytics

Collection, processing and application of learning process data help understand learning behaviour and learning state, giving students timely feedback and intervention.

15.4.3.1   Collection and Processing of Learning Process Data

Before applying eye movement data for analysis, we should first collect and process eye movement data from learning processes.

Xu et al. [33] proposed a remote learning monitoring system based on biosignals such as eye movements. The system includes three modules: signal acquisition and transmission, signal processing, and signal feedback, as shown in Fig. 15.2. Dynamically collected biosignals are input to learning terminal through wireless transmission and then transmitted to remote management centre via the Internet. The collected biosignals are compared with classification database to obtain real-time

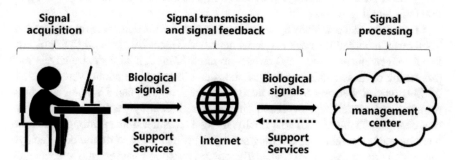

Fig. 15.2 Online learning monitoring system

learning status and provide support services such as timely intelligent intervention and feedback for learners.

15.4.3.2 Learning Behaviour Analytics

Eye-tracking technology can reveal changes in visual focus and depth of information processing during learning, and thus analyse students' learning behaviour.

Tests are indispensable in learning as a way of assessing knowledge levels. Eye behavior analysis during tests can reflect visual attention and cognitive process and has a strong correlation with test scores [34]. Wang [35] used Tobii EyeX to record learner's eye behavior data in online test scenes, to explore their eye movement characteristics and visual attention patterns. It found that question types and test difficulty affect subjects' visual attention.

Coding skills are emerging as one of the important skills for the twenty-first century. To have a deeper understanding of the process of different age groups learning to code, Papavlasopoulou et al. [36] investigated eye movement data of children and adolescents when they learn to program. Lin [37] used an eye-tracker to explore students' cognitive processes while debugging programs and investigated behavioral differences between students with different performance levels. Based on the findings, adapted teaching strategies and materials can be developed for students at different performance levels.

15.4.3.3 Learning State Detection

Due to the lack of face-to-face interaction between teachers and students in an online learning environment, teachers are unaware of their students' state. The existing solutions are questionnaires and interviews, the use of instrumental software and data mining techniques to analyse students' clicking interaction behaviour. However, these methods can't capture true intentions of students. Using eye-tracking technology to capture students' eye movement signals can help provide deeper insights into their learning status.

Lu [38] designed a learning state detection tool for online learning scenarios. Tobii eyeX recorded learner's eye movement and Kinect 2.0 captured their posture, facial movement unit and head deflection angle. Through statistical analysis and processing of these data, their fatigue status and learning behaviour were detected. Yi [39] used a webcam to periodically capture learners' facial images and then detected and modelled their vision change movements by tracking relative position changes of canthus and iris; finally, using a classifier trained through machine learning methods, real-time learning state was estimated based on the detected eye movement sequences. Zheng et al. [40] proposed an RNN-based eye movement analysis algorithm, RNN-EMA, which accomplishes detection of three learning states, reading, searching and distracting, by analysing sequential eye-movement vectors.

Students' attention state is one of the important learning states. Xiong [41] proposed an attention detection method fused with gaze detection, using low-resolution cameras and ordinary PCs to perform face detection, head deflection detection and gaze detection through related algorithms. It can effectively detect learner's lack of concentration, such as sleepiness, looking around, and deviation of vision.

Sharma et al. [42] defined a gaze-based metric called "with-me-ness", which measures the common attention between teacher's dialogue and student's gaze. The research results show that "with-me-ness" can be used as an attention indicator, and there is a positive correlation with students' learning results. On this basis, Srivastava et al. [43] proposed a measure of 'with-me-ness direction' to determine learners' attentional state, covering both temporal and directional aspects of student–teacher joint attention. The sequence of 'with-me-ness' directions and the proportion of time learners spent looking at each direction were analysed to understand their attention patterns when watching video lectures.

15.4.4 Student Performance Prediction

Eye movement measurements can be used to quantify learning performance in an online learning environment, as eye movements measure visual attention, which is the primary focus of learning processes.

Khedher et al. [44] analysed gaze data of learners when interacting with a learning environment based on medical educational games, assessed their learning experience, and explored the impact of eye movements on their performance. Kim and Nembhard [45] explored the effects of time pressure and feedback on academic performance by measuring participants' eye movements to track their attention and information acquisition. Through eye tracking, researchers gain methodological insights on how eye movement metrics can be modelled to predict academic performance. The results could help improve academic performance and class completion rates and facilitate the design of more effective online learning systems.

15.5 Conclusion

Eye-tracking technology records learners' eye movement and reveals their cognitive processing patterns, playing an important role in the field of intelligent education. The demand for smart education, along with decreasing cost of hardware and improvement of image processing algorithms, has led to the increasing use of eye-tracking technology in the field of intelligent education.

Taking the above analysis into account, future research should focus on the following areas:

1. As eye trackers are expensive and difficult to use widely, there is a need to develop devices specifically designed for educational purposes. To be used in real learning environments, eye-tracking devices should be developed that are inexpensive and highly accurate and allow for slight head movement, or even complete movement. Additionally, the integration of eye-tracking technology into electronic devices, such as phones, tablets and laptops, will facilitate the widespread use of eye tracking in educational environments.

2. Learning research based on biological data has great potential for emotion modelling, activity tracking, behavioral trait extracting and adaptive learning. Researchers should conduct a multimodal analysis of learning processes, fusing eye-movement data with other modal data such as EEG, ECG and expression data to comprehensively reflect learners' physiological characteristics, emotional state, cognitive changes, and behavioural motivation.

3. As university students are the main participant group in learning studies using eye-tracking technology and online learning opportunities increase, researchers need to examine the learning processes of different types of learners to improve the generalizability of existing research findings.

4. Learning research is a complex and systematic process, and learning effectiveness depends on the combined interaction of instructional resources content, learners' characteristics and teaching strategies. Therefore, the influence of multiple factors needs to be considered in a more integrated framework.

Acknowledgements This paper is supported by Youth Research Project of Tianjin Normal University (52XQ2101), Teaching Reform Project of Tianjin Normal University (JGYB01220075).

References

1. K. Chen, J. Sha, Y. He, X. Wang, The technological path and practice exploration of reconstructing learning based on artificial intelligence (AI) 2.0: also on the functional upgrade of intelligent tutoring system. J. Distance Educ. **35**(05), 40–53 (2017)
2. Q. Zhang, F. Wu, Biological data representation in learning analytics: prospect of the application of eye movements and multiple modality technology. e-Educ. Res. **37**(09), 76–81+109 (2016)
3. E. Alemdag, K. Cagiltay, A systematic review of eye tracking research on multimedia learning. Comput. Educ. **125**, 413–428 (2018)
4. X. Wang, Research of eye-tracking experiment in multimedia learning. Res. Explo. Lab. **34**(03), 190–193+201 (2015)
5. M.L. Lai, M.J. Tsai, F.Y. Yang et al., A review of using eye-tracking technology in exploring learning from 2000 to 2012. Educ. Res. Rev. **10**, 90–115 (2013)
6. Y. Zheng, Y. Wang, L. Cui, The application of eye tracking technology in multimedia learning: a review of research from 2005 to 2015. e-Educ. Res. **37**(04), 68–76+91 (2016)
7. Z. Yan, X. Guo, R. Wang, The review of eye movement index in the multimedia learning. Mod. Educ. Technol. **28**(05), 33–39 (2018)
8. G. Yan, J. Xiong, C. Zang, L. Yu, L. Cui, X. Bai, Review of eye-movement measures in reading research. Adv. Psychol. Sci. **21**(04), 589–605 (2013)
9. H. Peng, Research and implementation of key technology for eye tracking system, Xidian University, 2020

10. A.T. Duchowski, in *Eye Tracking Methodology: Theory and Practice* (Springer, 2017)
11. J. Zhang, G. Sun, K. Zheng, Review of gaze tracking and its application in intelligent education. J. Comput. Appl. **40**(11), 3346–3356 (2020)
12. Y. Zhang, A Study of Calibration Technology in Gaze Tracking System, Xidian University, 2015
13. A. Kar, P. Corcoran, A review and analysis of eye-gaze estimation systems, algorithms and performance evaluation methods in consumer platforms. IEEE Access **5**, 16495–16519 (2017)
14. K. Suarez, Effects of instructional design and emotional state on performance, Mediated by interest and attention, 2019
15. Q. Liu, Research on video design strategy and learning effect of micro-lecture based on eye-tracker, Nanjing University of Posts and Telecommunications, 2020
16. X. Cao, Research on the influence of colour representations of learning resources screen on learning attention, Tianjin Normal University, 2020
17. Z. Li, Design and research of online course resources optimization based on eye movement technology, East China Normal University, 2020
18. Y. Sun, An eye-tracking study of the effect of MOOC video interface layout on learning effective, Shannxi Normal University, 2016
19. Z. Duan, Z. Yan, Z. Zhou, The effect of animation's presentation speed on multimedia learning: an eye movement study. Psychol. Dev. Educ. **29**(01), 46–53 (2013)
20. A. Ma, Y. Wang, F. Wang, Z. Zhou, Effects of accelerating the playback of micro teaching video on learning performance. Psychol. Dev. Educ. **37**(03), 391–399 (2021)
21. T. Van Gog, I. Verveer, L. Verveer, Learning from video modeling examples: effects of seeing the human model's face. Comput. Educ. **72**, 323–327 (2014)
22. H. Wang, W. Hu, Z. Pi, W. Ge, Y. Xu, X. Fan, Y. Liang, Effects of the instructor's behaviors on learning performance in teaching video lectures. J. Distance Educ. Eye Track. **05**, 103–112 (2018)
23. S. D'Mello, A. Olney, C. Williams et al., Gaze tutor: A gaze-reactive intelligent tutoring system. Int. J. Hum Comput Stud. **70**(5), 377–398 (2012)
24. M. Mathews, A. Mitrovic, B. Lin et al., Do your eyes give it away? Using eye tracking data to understand students' attitudes towards open student model representations. in *International Conference on Intelligent Tutoring Systems* (Springer, Berlin, Heidelberg, 2012), pp. 422–427
25. L. Sun, Z. Liu, M.T. Sun, Real time gaze estimation with a consumer depth camera. Inf. Sci. **320**, 346–360 (2015)
26. Z. Zhan, An emotional and cognitive recognition model for distance learners based on intelligent agent: the coupling of eye tracking and expression recognition techniques. Modern Distance Educ. Res. **05**, 100–105 (2013)
27. H. Prendinger, C. Ma, M. Ishizuka, Eye movements as indices for the utility of life-like interface agents: a pilot study. Interact. Comput. **19**(2), 281–292 (2007)
28. S. Kang, The effect of animated pedagogical agent in multimedia learning: the role of learner characteristic and learning material, Central China Normal University, 2014
29. M. Pivec, C. Trummer, J. Pripfl, Eye-tracking adaptable e-learning and content authoring support. Informatica **30**(1), (2006)
30. H. Schmidt, B. Wassermann, G. Zimmermann, An adaptive and adaptable learning platform with realtime eye-tracking support: lessons learned. in *DeLFI 2014-Die 12 e-Learning Fachtagung Informatik* (2014)
31. Y. Xue, Z. Zeng, Research on the eye movement model of learners with different cognitive styles oriented to adaptive learning. Mod. Educ. Technol. **30**(08), 91–97 (2020)
32. M.J. Tsai, L.J. Huang, H.T. Hou et al., Visual behavior, flow and achievement in game-based learning. Comput. Educ. **98**, 115–129 (2016)
33. L. Xu, X. Ran, M. Chen, The study of monitoring system of distance learning process based on physiological signals. Modern Distance Educ. Res. **05**, 104–112 (2014)
34. S.C. Chen, H.C. She, M.H. Chuang et al., Eye movements predict students' computer-based assessment performance of physics concepts in different presentation modalities. Comput. Educ. **74**, 61–72 (2014)

35. X. Wang, Research on learners' eye-movement behavior in online testing, Zhejiang University of Technology, (2018)
36. S. Papavlasopoulou, K. Sharma, M. Giannakos et al., Using eye-tracking to unveil differences between kids and teens in coding activities. in *Proceedings of the 2017 Conference on Interaction Design and Children* (2017), pp. 171–181
37. Y.T. Lin, C.C. Wu, T.Y. Hou et al., Tracking students' cognitive processes during program debugging—an eye-movement approach. IEEE Trans. Educ. **59**(3), 175–186 (2015)
38. X. Lu, A tool for student state detection in online learning: design and implementation, Huazhong University of Science and Technology, 2016
39. J. Yi, Research and application of learning status evaluation based on eye movements, Shanghai Jiao Tong University, 2016
40. Q. Zhen, H. ZhenG, X. Hou, Detection of the learning state based on neural network. Softw. Eng. **23**(05), 6–8+5 (2020)
41. B. Xiong, Research and application of attention detection method with eye gaze analysis in online learning, Hangzhou Dianzi University, 2018
42. K. Sharma, P. Jermann, P. Dillenbourg, With-me-ness: a gaze-measure for students' attention in MOOCs. in *Proceedings of International Conference of the Learning Sciences 2014* (ISLS, 2014), pp. 1017–1022
43. N. Srivastava, S. Nawaz, J. Newn et al., Are you with me? Measurement of learners' video-watching attention with eye trackingC. in *LAK21: 11th International Learning Analytics and Knowledge Conference* (2021), pp. 88–98
44. A.B. Khedher, I. Jraidi, C. Frasson, Exploring students' eye movements to assess learning performance in a serious gameC. EdMedia+Innovate Learning. Assoc. Adv. Comput. Educ. (AACE) 394–401 (2018)
45. J.E. Kim, D.A. Nembhard, Eye movement as a mediator of the relationships among time pressure, feedback, and learning performance. Int. J. Ind. Ergon. **70**, 116–123 (2019)

Chapter 16
Personalised Material and Course Recommendation System for High School Students

Simbarashe Tembo and Jin Chen

Abstract The use of recommendation systems for personalised education has been a hot topic amongst researchers in the last couple of decades. Their implementation in various learning institutions has been on the steady rise, especially in online learning settings. With advancements in artificial intelligence technologies, research into how to use technology to improve education systems has gained a lot of traction and is changing the way that learning institutions approach learning. In this paper we propose a hybrid recommendation system for personalised learning material recommendation for high school students in order to improves the their performance by tailoring the learning experience, using the individual learner's characteristics like learning style, interests, preferences, prior knowledge, level of expertise and abilities.

Keywords Recommendation systems · Learning styles · Personalised learning

16.1 Introduction

The use of Recommendation Systems (RS) in education has been on an exponential rise in the last two decades. There is a lot of ongoing research into the use of recommendation systems for personalised education, for tasks like learning material recommendation, learning objective recommendation and course selection recommendation etc. This is in order to improve the learning experience for individual students in the various learning institutions, especially in an e-learning (online learning) environment where learning is mostly done online, which makes it easier to implement some of the techniques used in recommendation systems like data mining, web scrapping and deep learning techniques. The transition to e-learning is mostly due the rise in demand for distance online learning, increased ratio of students to instructors, various economic, geographical and demographical factors and the COVID-19 pandemic in 2020 which forced people to work and study from home.

S. Tembo · J. Chen (✉)
Tianjin Key Laboratory of Wireless Mobile Communications and Power Transmission, Tianjin Normal University, Tianjin 300387, China
e-mail: cjwoods@163.com

© The Author(s), under exclusive license to Springer Nature Singapore Pte Ltd. 2021
W. Wang et al. (eds.), *Artificial Intelligence in Education and Teaching Assessment*,
https://doi.org/10.1007/978-981-16-6502-8_16

Most education systems and learning institutions around the world are not tailored for individual or personalised learning, but rather they mostly implement a one size fits all approach to learning. This is where a set standard of a predefined school curriculum (district, state or international) is used for all students. This is all regardless of the students learning preferences, learning style, prior knowledge, ability to retain information, current mental or emotional state and learning disabilities if present. This is especially prominent in the K-12 systems [1]. This kind of approach can lead to certain students at an advanced level to easily get bored and disinterested in learning, while others have an even harder time understanding the most fundamental and basic theories and concepts being taught. In addition to that, students with learning disabilities might never get noticed and receive the special attention they need in order to aid their learning. Personalised learning has been proposed as a solution to some of the disadvantages and challenges of traditional learning. Personalization in education aims to tailor the system to a learner's needs and characteristics such as levels of expertise, prior knowledge, cognitive abilities, skills, interests, preferences and learning styles, so as to improve a learner's overall satisfaction and performance within a given course [2]. By personalising the learning experience for students, learning becomes more student centred, which in turn reduces the work load for the teachers and gives them more time to work with the students in a more interactive and immersive manner.

There is a lot of research into making personalised learning recommendation systems for higher learning institutions and e-learning platforms all around the world, however, research and implementation of personalised learning recommendation systems for high schools is still very limited. Some commonly attributed reasons are mindset of some teachers and parents, logistics of such a transition, involves high-stakes and major change and shift from the normal operations [3].

The last four to five years of the k-12 system of learning (secondary or high school) are the most crucial times in a student's life as they determine the direction for the rest of their learning. The courses one chooses during this time will determine which field and majors they can get into in university, and eventually, the types of jobs that they can get after graduation. With learning becoming life long, it is very important to lay a good foundation for the student to build upon, personalised learning is one such tool that can help stir the individual learner in the best direction. Helping students find the right courses to pick during this time and personalising learning according to their learning style, prior knowledge, interests and abilities through material recommendation, would ensure that the student receives the right guidance they need and that they meet the and surpass the standard requirements through better academic performance. The main aims of our proposed systems are:

(a) Propose a material recommendation system to help supplement the learning materials used in the various high schools according to the students' learning style, prior knowledge, interests and abilities which would keep the student interested and engaged in learning.

(b) Integrate a course recommendation system for courses that might be of interest to the student and also help guide them in selection of careers and fields they can get into according to their current interests, knowledge and skills.

We don't aim to propose a drastic change to the current school curriculum but rather supplement the learning system by improving the student's performance with personalised course and material recommendations, provide a career guidance tool to aid the students with course selection that are in line with their fields of interest, and lastly, provide instructors with tools for monitoring the students' performance and progress, which also acts as an early warning system for a drop in students' performance below a set threshold and detection of any learning disabilities, allowing for timely intervention.

This paper is organised as follows. Section 16.2 reviews the relevant literature on personalised recommendation systems. Section 16.3 discusses the architecture of our proposed model. Section 16.4 discusses some of the challenges, limitations and implications of using such systems, and lastly Sect. 16.5 is conclusion on the main contributions of our work.

16.2 Related Works

16.2.1 Learning Management Systems

Learning Management Systems (LMS) are a computer software or program designed to deliver education courses or training programs in education and training institutions and even companies and businesses. They are used as a collection of all relevant teaching tools in a centralised place. They are primarily web-based, designed for e-learning, but they also offer support for blended or flipped classes. LMS provides an intuitive user interface with support for media access, file and resource management and a social access for messaging and forums for group discussions; they also provide support for easy creation of courses and planning features such as course starting and finish times and assignment due dates; tracking and analysis of student performance. Some of the most widely used LMS are Moodle [4], ATutor [5], Blackboard [6], Dokeos [7], Canvas [8] etc.

16.2.2 Artificial Intelligence

Artificial Intelligence is a branch in computer science that is dedicated to solving cognitive problems commonly associated with human intelligence, such as learning, problem-solving, and pattern recognition [9]. Most recommender systems use Deep Learning (DL) techniques which are Machine learning (ML) techniques. Machine learning is an application of artificial intelligence (AI) that provides systems the ability to automatically learn and improve from experience without being explicitly programmed [10], deep learning allows for the creation of even more complex algorithms for learning complex data. AI has been widely adopted in various fields like medicine, biological research, pharmaceuticals, robotics, financial investment, manufacturing industries, mobile devices, computer technologies, education etc. This is largely due to breakthroughs in machine learning and deep learning algorithms. The use of Artificial Intelligence in Education (AIEd) has been on a steady rise in the last few decades. Advancements and innovations in computer technologies have helped propel the adoption and implementation of these AI techniques in education.

16.2.3 Personalised Recommendation Systems

Personalised recommendation systems are mostly used in e-commerce for product and service recommendations. They are a computer system that relies on interaction between the users and websites or software, can automatically mine, represent and maintain the interest information of individual users by analysing the historical access data of users, user preferences and provide personalized recommendation service for each user according to the acquired interest information [11]. Companies like Amazon, Alibaba and eBay provide personalise recommendations for online shopping, Netflix, Hulu, Spotify and YouTube personalise recommendations for movies and music that people might be interested in; online advertising, news, social networks and other fields all tailor content recommendations based on the users' preferences using recommendation systems.

Most recommendation systems proposed by researchers in recent years include the following 4 types, content-based recommendation systems, collaborative filtering recommendation systems, knowledge-based recommendation systems and hybrid recommendation systems.

Content-based recommendation system(CB): Depend on the users' historical data. The authors of [12] defined it as "Content-based recommendation selects items based on the correlation between the content of the items (products, services or contents) and user profile most time by using physiological models."

Collaborative filtering recommendation system(CF): Deal with recommending items to target users by identifying users with similar interests [11, 13]. They aim to provide recommendation by looking at the correlation between the interests and preferences of similar users. The major downside to this approach is the cold start problem.

Knowledge-based recommendation system: These systems are used to recommend items with more complex data representation. They are used to guide users to make the right decisions when buying items whose item domains tend to be complex in terms of their various properties [13–15]. Knowledge-based systems are able to be used for recommending products, items or services that have various attributes. This also helps overcome the problem of cold start commonly face with CF recommendation systems.

Hybrid *recommendation system:* Are a combination of different recommendation algorithms, mostly content-based and collaborative filtering in order to overcome the limitations of individual recommendation systems [12, 14, 16]. Different researchers have proposed different combinations and have achieved varying levels of efficiency and accuracy.

16.2.4   Learning Styles

Every learner has a different approach to learning due to the individual differences that exist from one person to the next. What governs these subtle differences in learning is commonly known as learning styles. Researchers define learning style in a variety of different ways but can be commonly defined as set of factors, behaviours and attitudes that facilitate individual learning [17]. It is necessary to determine what is most likely to trigger each learner's concentration, how to maintain it, and how to respond to his or her natural processing style to produce long term memory and retention [16]. It is therefore important to create an environment that caters for the different learning styles of students. There are a lot of proposed ways to identify these learning styles, one of the most widely recognised is Felder & Soloman's Index of Learning styles questionnaire ILSQ. ILSQ has 44 MCQs that assess and individual's learning style and preferences in four different dimensions each having two opposing categories [18]. Table 16.1 shows the index of learning styles by Felder and Solomon [19] (Fig. 16.1).

Understanding the learners' learning style and preferences helps build models that are more robust to the individual differences of learners.

Table 16.1   Index of learning styles

Index of Learning Styles (Felder & Soloman)		
Processing	Active	Reflective
	Group work, likes to apply and explain/discuss with others.	Think and process things, work in solitude.
Perception	Sensing	Intuitive
	Prefers facts, detail oriented.	Prefers conceptual and theoretical information.
Reception	Visual	Verbal
	Prefers visuals like pictures, videos, flow charts.	Prefers written and spoken information
Understanding	Sequential	Global
	Prefers linear flow of information in small chunks.	Prefers the big picture approach before getting detailed information.

Fig. 16.1 K-12 Education system overview

16.3 Proposed System

In this section, we present the architecture of our proposed system and use case scenarios. We propose a hybrid recommendation system. This system will have the learner profile module, and material database recommendation system module. A hybrid approach is able leverage the advantages of the individual recommendation systems, while being robust to the disadvantages and limitations that plague individual systems.

We have chosen to implement this system in a hybrid or blended classroom scenario in high schools. High school students are usually at an age where they're mature, self-aware and know or have an idea of what their learning styles, preferences, interests and future prospects might be. Therefore, having such a system for high school students is very beneficial and useful in helping improve academic performance through personalised learning using recommendation systems. Blended classes allow for the use of LMS which can be used to prepare courses, monitor student performance, host learning materials, schedule classes, assignment deadlines and exam dates and so many other organisational tasks, while still keeping the advantages of traditional classes.

16.3.1 Learner Profile Module

The learner profile is built upon the student's enrolment in school and updated when registering for a given course. The main purpose of this module is to collect information of the student and track academic performance which will be used to make personalised recommendations for the for a personalised learning experience. This would be done in three parts.

The first thing is to collect the student's personal information like name. sex, age interests, etc. The students would fill out a basic information page, after which, the student would be given a survey to determine what are their interests, these would contain MCQs with various categories of interests. They would then be asked to rate these interests on a scale of 1–5, 1 being not interested and 5 being very interested. By doing this, we are able to build the basic profile that has the student's interest and basic information that can be used to make the initial recommendations during the initial phase of using the system. This is beneficial in understanding the student and making recommendations based on their interests.

Secondly we would have the student take the ILSQ test, in order to understand the student's learning style. Using this, the recommendation system would be able to recommend materials based on the student's individual learning style. Video and picture-based materials can be recommended to students who are more of visual learners, while written articles, books and audio files recommended to those whose preferred learning style is more verbal. We would further group students with similar learning style together so as to recommend materials based on what other students rank highly.

Lastly, when a student is registering for a particular course, they would be given an assessment test to know their level of expertise, prior knowledge and preferences for that particular course. The student's level of expertise would be categorised into beginner, intermediate or advanced. They would also be grouped together with others of the same level expertise and setting the learning content and pace with all these in mind.

The learner profile would also store the student's progress for each course they are enrolled in which is monitored by the teacher. We would also run a prediction algorithm on the student's academic performance data to predict the student's performance trajectory based on their performance during exams, assignments, quizzes and overall class participation. This prediction can then be used to see if a student's performance is improving or declining, at which point the teacher would intervein and work closely with the particular student to see the best way forward.

16.3.2 Material Database Module

The material database is where all the class material would be stored and organised. Since this would be a high school setup, students have to follow a set curriculum by the school, this means that there would be school provide and recommended martials that the students would initially have in their collection. These materials would serve as a guideline for recommending other materials for students to take a look at based on the various aspects like prior knowledge, level of expertise and interests.

This module would contain 2 parts. The first would be the database of all school provided materials and resources like electronic text books, audio and video lesson files and articles etc. For most part these martials would remain the same with minor updates as the teacher or school sees fit. These materials would serve as a foundation on which other materials can be recommended. The second part would be the recommendation database, this would store all the recommended materials and resources. The recommended materials would be categorised by course, type (videos, books, articles, forum discussions etc.), topics etc. (see Fig. 16.2).

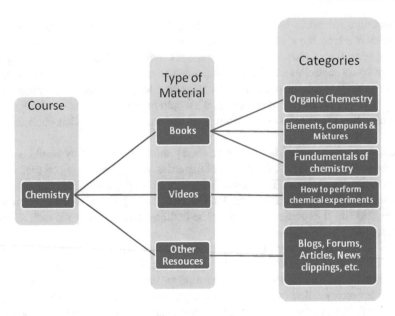

Fig. 16.2 Material database

16.3.3 Recommendation Module

We propose the use of a hybrid recommendation system. The recommendation system would utilise knowledge-based and collaborative filtering techniques. Knowledge based filtering techniques would be used to make recommendations based on the interests, prior knowledge, level of expertise and learning style of the student collected in the learner module. This knowledge about the student would be used to make the first materials recommendations to the student. After the recommendations have been provided, the user would be asked to rate the quality of recommended materials, this and the users log data such as browsing history, how long they spend on a web page, reading a book or watching a video would be used to periodically update the system and improve recommendation accuracy. After this, would then use collaborative filtering to group students with similar learning styles and interests, which would fine tune recommendations by giving recommendations from learners with similar learning styles.

In order to help with course selection for students, we also propose applying the techniques suggested in [13]. This can be done at the end of the school semester as the system would have had enough time to learn about the student's interests and abilities and be able to give recommendations of courses they can take upon enrolment in university. This gives the students an advantage in that they can be able to utilise their free time learning more about the fields via recommendations made by our proposed system. We would also include statistical data about the field including information like employment and entrepreneurship opportunities, related fields and people's real-world account of studying and working in that particular field.

16.4 Discussion

The implementation of recommendation systems in high schools brings a lot of concern like effects of personalisation on the students, data privacy and usability of the system.

One important question to ask is just how would personalisation affect the students; would a student still be able to keep up with the set school curriculum if everything is personalised to his or her individual characteristics? It is therefore very important to continue researching on ways to improve recommendations and monitoring them such that they do not leave the student handicap to an extent that they are unable to keep up with others of the same class, age group or level of expertise at enrolment. We must design such systems with the teachers in order to be able to truly understand how personalisation can be implemented in classrooms without such problems. It is also very important to have teachers monitoring the progress of the students using personalised systems and ensure that they still manage to keep up with the set school curriculum.

Data privacy is another very vital concern and is still a hot field of research by a lot of researchers around the world. Ensuring data safety would increase the student's, teachers, parents and society's confidence in using personalised recommendation systems. We must therefore ensure that proper data management policies are implemented in order to ensure proper storage and transmission of sensitive user data.

Lastly, teachers and technical personnel in schools, should be given proper training on the use of LMS with personalised recommendation systems. In the end, technology is just a tool that if used well would bring vast improvements to the education systems all around the world.

16.5 Conclusion

As technology advances, new ways of learning and teaching emerge and are slowly changing how learning is done from nursery schools to higher learning institutions. The use of technology in learning institutions has paved way for personalised education. The personalisation of learning content for students in high schools allows for students to receive a more guided direction into the fields they'd like to get into in the future based on their personal interests and preferences.

In this paper we proposed a hybrid-based recommendation system that utilises knowledge-based and collaborative filtering techniques to make material recommendations for high school students which in turn would help guide them to course selection. Recommendations are made with the students learning style, interests, prior knowledge, level of expertise and what similar learners find useful in mind.

We aim to use recommendation systems to aid the teachers in personalising education for students in ways that they cannot due to the physical limitation of traditional classes. High school students need to be guided to in the type of courses and materials to use depending on their interests so as to cater to their needs and interests and not according to the teacher's personal opinion which might at times be limited. The final outcome of recommendation systems depends on their implementation, and it is our hope that high schools all around the world would embrace the use of personalised recommendation systems in order to increase student performance and overall satisfaction.

Acknowledgements This work was supported by Youth Research Project of Tianjin Normal University (52XQ2101), Teaching Reform Project of Tianjin Normal University (JGYB01220075).

References

1. Relocate Editorial. K-12 Curriculum and pupil assessment. https://www.relocatemagazine.com/articles/education-k-12-curriculum-the-us-education-system. 2017
2. H. Imran, M. Belghis-Zadeh, T.W. Chang et al., PLORS: a personalized learning object recommender system. Vietnam J. Comput. Sci. **3**, 3–13 (2016)
3. N. Dougherty, How to successfully personalize learning in secondary schools: https://www.edelements.com/blog/how-to-successfully-personalize-learning-in-secondary-schools (2019)
4. Moodle https://moodle.org
5. Atutor https://atutor.github.io
6. Blackboard https://www.blackboard.com
7. Dekeos https://www.dokeos.com
8. Canvas https://learn.canvas.net
9. What is Artificial Intelligence https://aws.amazon.com/machine-learning/what-is-ai/
10. Expert.ai Team, What is machine learning? A definition. https://www.expert.ai/blog/machine-learning-definition/ (2020)
11. G. Baiqiang, Z. Chi, Design of personalized recommendation system for online learning resources based on improved collaborative filtering algorithm (2020)
12. O. Bourkoukou, E.E. Bachari, Toward a hybrid recommender system for e-learning personalization based on data mining techniques (2018)
13. N.D. Lynn, A.W.R. Emanuel, A review on recommender systems for course selection in higher education (2021)
14. J.K. Tarus, Z. Niu, A. Yousif, A hybrid knowledge-based recommender system for e-learning based on ontology and sequential pattern mining. Future Gener. Comput. Syst. (2017)
15. R. Burke, Knowledge-based recommender systems (2020)
16. A.A. Klasnja-Milicevic, B. Vesin, E-Learning personalization based on hybrid recommendation strategy and learning style identification
17. J. Reiff C, Learning styles (what research says to the teacher). National Education Association, (Washington, DC, 1992)
18. R. Felder M., B. Soloman. Index of learning styles questionnaire. https://www.webtools.ncsu.edu/learningstyles/. North Carolina State University 2001. Accessed July 2021
19. Index of learning styles. https://thepeakperformancecenter.com/educational-learning/learning/preferences/learning-styles/felder-silverman/index-of-learning-styles/

Chapter 17
Research on Mathematics Teachers' Professional Growth Factors Based on Keyword Extraction and Sentiment Analysis

Xu Gao, Xiaoming Ding, Wei Wang, Guangming Wang, Yueyuan Kang, and Shaofang Wang

Abstract This paper proposes a method to extract the keywords of interviews test from 22 excellent teachers automatically for the analysis of teachers' professional growth factors. 110 keywords in all were obtained based on the TF-IDF algorithm, which meant the most influencing factors for teachers' professional growth. In order to consider the effect of sentences sentiment, especially the negative sentences, emotional analyses for each keyword were also performed, the results of which make a significant supplement for the final conclusion.

Keywords Teachers' professional growth · TF-IDF · Keyword extraction · Sentiment analysis · Wordcloud

17.1 Introduction

In today's increasingly competitive teaching profession, an ordinary teacher wants to grow into an excellent teacher, in addition to their own efforts can not do without the influence of other teachers, learn the experiences of other great teachers and effective factors that can help you grow. By using keyword extraction and clustering algorithm, this paper analyses the interview texts of excellent teachers, finds out the main factors that affect the growth of teachers, and then instructs young teachers to improve and perfect their professional quality and ability. While TF-IDF Algorithm based on python can analyse the text in batches, accurately segment the words, get the result we want, and analyse the emotion of each key word, showing the negative or positive.

X. Gao · X. Ding (✉) · W. Wang
College of Artificial Intelligence, Tianjin Normal University, Tianjin 300387, China
e-mail: xmding@tjnu.edu.cn

G. Wang · Y. Kang · S. Wang
Faculty of Education, Tianjin Normal University, Tianjin 300387, China

At present, numerous scholars at home and abroad have proposed relatively mature research and processing methods for keyword extraction methods. The core of automatic keyword extraction is the statistics of word frequency, and the method of word frequency statistics was first proposed by Luhn [1], a scientist from IBM Corporation in 1958, and the research on automatic indexing has been started since then. In 2007, American scholars summarized the current automatic summarization algorithm, including word frequency statistics, and gave a detailed introduction to it [2].The automatic keyword extraction system has been continuously improved and gradually penetrated into more fields. In the past 60 years, Witten [3] proposed a new algorithm Kea, which is a way of training and keyword extraction using the naive Bayes algorithm. Turney [4] proposed a GenEx keyword automatic extraction system based on C4.5 algorithm using decision tree training classifier, and conducted feasibility analysis to prove the research prospect and commercial value of this system. Hulth [5] proposed a method for automatically extracting keywords from academic paper abstracts. He adopted a learning algorithm called Rule Induction, using some syntactic analysis to help automatically extract keywords, not just using word frequency statistics. Using NLP technology to distinguish the part of speech of each word, through this method, the effect of automatic extraction is greatly improved. Abulaish, Jahiruddin, and Dey [6] proposed a text mining system based on deep text mining to identify key phrases in unstructured or semi-structured text documents. The system uses parsing technology to identify candidate phrases, and comparative experiments prove that this system is preferable to Kea. Kumar and Srinathan [7] proposed that N-gram filtration uses the LZ78 data compression algorithm to obtain n-grams, filters out units that are not suitable for keywords, and then calculates the weight of candidate words to finally obtain the keywords that we need.

The above algorithms proposed by domestic and foreign scholars is mainly used in the extraction of keywords in papers, consumer reviews in the news network industry, various service industries, and user experience reviews of major websites or apps. Based on the above scholars' research on keyword extraction in all walks of life, this article aims at the interview texts of outstanding mathematics teachers in the education industry, establishes a corresponding corpus, extracts the keywords of each text, and studies the influencing factors on the path of teacher growth.

17.2   TF-IDF Algorithm for Keyword Extraction

Keyword extraction is the base and core technology in natural language processing. It has a wide range of applications in the fields of information retrieval, text classification, text clustering, information matching, topic tracking, automatic summarization, human–computer dialogue, string similarity measurement, etc. However, for different fields, the extraction requirements for keywords are very different. At present, most of them rely on manual labeling methods in different fields. With the increasing amount of data, manual labeling methods are no longer in competent, so relying on computers to automatically extract keywords appears to be incompetent very important. Therefore, this paper proposes a method to extract keywords using the TF-IDF algorithm.

17.2.1 TF-IDF Algorithm

In this article, the keyword extraction of unsupervised learning is adopted: keyword extraction based on the statistical features of the TFIDF algorithm.

In the TF-IDF algorithm, TF is to perform word frequency statistics on the result of jieba word segmentation. IDF (Inverse Document Frequency) inverse document frequency, the IDF of a particular word, can be obtained by dividing the total number of documents by the number of documents containing the word, and then taking the logarithm of the obtained quotient. According to the literature [8], we know that it is mainly used to measure the importance of a word in a text database. The higher the frequency of its appearance in the text, the more significant it is. The specific formula is shown in formula (17.1),

$$TF - IDF_{i,j} \rightarrow TF \times IDF = \frac{n_{i,j}}{\sum_k n_{k,j}} \times \log \frac{|D|}{\{j, t_i \in d_j\}} \qquad (17.1)$$

In the formula, $n_{i,j}$ represents the number of times a word t_i appears in the text j, and represents the sum of the frequencies of all words; $|D|$ represents the number of documents in the text database d, and represents the text database d The number of documents with term t_i in document j contained in.

The higher the importance of a word in the article, the greater its TF-IDF value, so the first few words are the keywords of the article.

17.2.2 Keyword Extraction Based on TF-IDF Algorithm

The specific process of extracting keywords is as follows:

(1) Creating a corpus. The 22 interview documents we need and the location of each are stored in a new corpus.
(2) Text preprocessing.

- Word segmentation. Use Python's built-in stammering thesaurus for word segmentation, but this article studies the extraction of keywords in the teacher industry, so you need to customize a dictionary newdict, add professional vocabulary commonly used in the teacher industry to prevent errors in word segmentation. The format of the words in the custom word segmentation database is for each word to occupy a separate line.

- Stop word filtering. In the word segmentation results, we will find words like me, you, of, good, etc., which will interfere with the extraction results, so we need to filter these useless words in advance before extracting keywords. The stopwords database stopwords.txt can be downloaded directly from "China Knowledge Network". However, in the articles of the education industry, there are some words like education, as well as the names of teachers we interviewed and some place names, which will appear frequently, but they are not the results we want, so we need Customize a stop word database mysyopwords.txt.

(3) Keyword extraction.

- Calculate the TF-IDF value. Calculate with the TF-IDF algorithm to obtain the TF value of each filtered word, and keep the words with a word frequency greater than 1, and then calculate the value of the candidate keyword TF-IDF according to the formula in formula (17.1).
- Extract keywords. Sort the candidate keywords according to the calculated value in the previous step, and extract the top five keywords for each text as the final result.

17.2.3 Classification Based on Similarity

The TF-IDF algorithm cannot automatically remove the same or similar keywords in the final result, so this article has performed further processing on the extraction results after extracting 5 keywords in each article, removing the repeated words, and obtaining 81 keywords. Finally, we classify these 81 keywords. Because using this method will wait for a lot of classifications, and some classifications have no keyword or only a few related words, then these classifications may not be needed, we just put them directly filtered. The principle of classifying keywords is to use cosine similarity, which measures vector similarity by the angle between two vectors [10]. The calculation formula of cosine similarity is as follows (17.2):

$$\cos\theta = \frac{a - b}{|a| \times |b|} = \frac{\sum_{i=1}^{n} A_i \times B_i}{\sqrt{\sum_{i=1}^{n} A_i^2} \times \sqrt{\sum_{i=1}^{n} B_i^2}} \tag{17.2}$$

In the formula, suppose the coordinates of vectors a and b are respectively $A = (A_1, A_2,..., A_n)$, $B = (B_1, B_2,..., B_n)$, and expand to n-dimensional space, we get The above formula.

The 110 vocabularies obtained from 22 articles were tested for similarity, and the same or extremely similar keywords were removed, and 81 keywords were finally obtained. Sort the results of partial keywords according to word frequency, and plot them into the following Table 17.1.

Table 17.1 Partial word frequency statistics

Keyword	Word frequency	Keyword	Word frequency
优秀教师（Excellent teacher）	58	校长（Principal）	36
机会(Opportunity)	25	学校（School）	23
课堂（Classroom）	21	专业（Profession）	21
学生（Student）	20	意识（Awareness）	15
爱心（Love）	14	能力（Ability）	14
卓越（Excellence）	12	师傅（Master）	11
青年教师（Young teacher）	11	知识（Knowledge）	10
品质（Quality）	9	讲课（Lecture）	9
教研员（Faculty and Researcher）	9	观念（Idea）	7
专业知识(Professional knowledge)	9	班主任（Head teacher）	9
钻研（Delve into）	8	教授（Professor）	8
耐心（Patient）	8	成绩（Grade）	7
实践（Practice）	7	课程（Course）	7
绩效（Performance）	7	专业（Profession）	7
管理（Management）	7	比赛（Macth）	6
外部环境（External environment）	6	比赛（competition）	6
责任心（Sense of responsibility）	6	价值观（Values）	6
数学知识（Mathematical knowledge）	6	特级教师（Special teacher）	6
组织管理能力（Organizational management ability）	5	理解数学（Understand mathematics）	5
特级（Premium）	5	反思（Reflection）	5
成就感（Sense of accomplishment）	5	证书（certificate）	5
同学（Classmate）	4	评定（assessment）	4
热情（enthusiasm）	4	教案（Lesson plan）	4
自我意识（self conscious）	4	师德（Teacher ethics）	4
引导（guide）	4	态度（attitude）	4
教数学班（Teaching math class）	4	精神（spirit）	3
个体（individual）	3	勤奋（diligent）	3
创新意识（innovative mind）	3	老教师（Old teacher）	3
教研活动（Teaching and research activities）	3	教书育人（Teach and educate people）	3
数学教师（Math teacher）	3	福利（welfare）	3
积极向上（Motivated）	2	伯乐（Bole）	2
氛围（Atmosphere）	2	环境（surroundings）	2
同行（Accompany）	2	回报（Return）	2
终身学习（life-long learning）	2	师长（Teacher）	2
竞争（life-long learning）	2	勤奋努力（work hard）	2
家庭教育（family Education）	2	交流平台（Platform）	2
职业规划（career planning）	2	能力（ability）	2
教师职业（Teacher occupation）	2	听课（Attend class）	2
科研能力（research ability）	2	大学（the University）	2
课堂教学（Classroom teaching）	2	修养（self-cultivation）	2
早期教育（early education）	2	理念（idea）	2
教育理念（Teacher occupation）	2		

From the table above, we can see that some words such as excellent teachers, principals, schools, classrooms, and students are more important in the growth of teachers. This conclusion also tells teachers who have just entered the teaching profession, do not just immersed in your knowledge of the teaching profession, and must continue to communicate with excellent teachers, old teachers, principals and other experienced people, or communicate more with students, so that you can be more smoothly on the road to becoming an excellent teacher. The detailed flow chart is shown in Fig. 17.1 below:

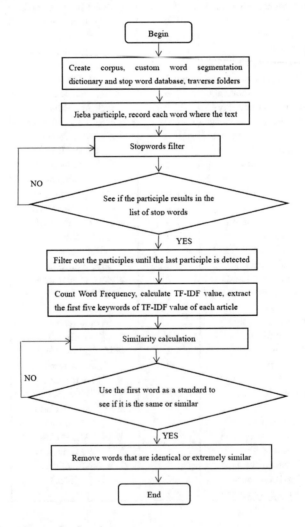

Fig. 17.1 Keyword extraction flowchart

17.3   Sentiment Analysis of Keywords Based on the Situation

In the above research, we only started based on word frequency, and the conclusions drawn in this way are not accurate enough. It is impossible to determine whether a word with a large number of occurrences must have a positive effect or a negative effect on the growth of teachers. Therefore, in this chapter, we conduct further analysis on the keywords obtained in Chap. 2.

17.3.1   Sentiment Analysis

In the sentiment analysis of keywords, we use Baidu's intelligent cloud platform to perform sentiment analysis on the keywords we have summarized, and process each interview document separately to obtain the results.

(1)   Baidu API call. Log On to Baidu's smart cloud website to create the APP, get token, and the parameters used to call the sentiment analysis API, get your own APP, API, and SECRET.
(2)   Emotional analysis.
(3)   Extract 81 keywords after similarity classification.

- Reading the text and making the text divided into clauses and words, than statistical the word frequency.
- The obtained keywords are analyzed by the interface method provided by Baidu. Input the key words extracted in Chap. 2, track the sentences where the keywords are, and analyze whether the keywords are positive or negative according to the semantics. The final output is three groups of values: word frequency, total value of positive emotion and total value of negative emotion. The average value of positive emotion and average value of negative emotion are between 0 and 1.
- Count the average value of positive emotion and the average value of negative emotion of the keywords.

17.3.2   Statistics and Analysis

The experimental results show that the average positive emotions ranked in the top are: positive, teacher profession, spirit, old teacher, enthusiasm, etc. This shows that an excellent teacher needs to be engaged in his personal career. The profession is full of enthusiasm, and requires active exploration and continuous hard work to learn useful knowledge from super teachers and old teachers.

The top words of negative emotion average are: lectures, understanding mathematics, welfare, performance, reflection, competition and other words. This also warns teachers who are new to the teaching profession that they need to remind themselves the original intention of being a teacher, explore hard in teaching, and not to be affected by some unrelated factors outside.

We choose ten groups of words in Table 17.2 to make a bar chart, which is more intuitive for research. Table 17.2 and Fig. 17.2 are obtained.

From the above table, we can see the relationship between the principal, the student, the excellent teacher, the old teacher and so on. The key words have the greatest influence on the growth of teachers, which shows that a teacher, who wants to grow into an excellent teacher, not only depends on his own efforts, but also others' experience or help, so as to make his growth faster and better.

We can also find the same keyword, which can express different emotional emotions in different contexts, can be positive or negative. This means that the same keyword can play a positive role in the growth of teachers or a negative role.

Table 17.2 Partial sentiment analysis results

Keyword	Word frequency	Average value of positive emotion	Average value of negative emotion
优秀教（Excellentteacher）	58	0.86503	0.13496
校长（Principal）	36	0.74673	0.25219
意识（Awareness）	15	0.63535	0.36465
教授（Professor）	8	0.60773	0.39227
绩效（Performance）	7	0.29365	0.70635
热情（Enthusiasm）	4	0.99731	0.00269
师德（Teacher ethics）	4	0.36264	0.54942
环境（Surroundings）	2	0.69930	0.30070
终身学习（Life-long learning）	2	0.08594	0.91406
竞争（Competition）	2	0.46872	0.53128

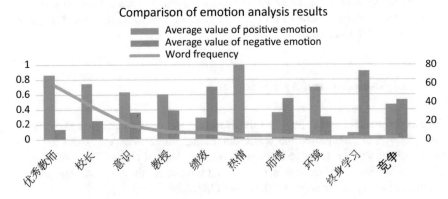

Fig. 17.2 Comparison of emotional analysis results

Table 17.3 Description table of wordcloud parameters

Parameters	Description
Width	Output canvas width, default 400 pixels
Height	Output the height of the canvas, default 200 pixels
Mask	The background of the picture (the shape of the cloud)
Scale: float	Scale up the canvas
Min_font_size	The minimum font size to display
Font_step	Font step
Max_words	The maximum number of words, defaults to 2000
Background_color	Background color, default white
Max_font_size	The maximum font size displayed, defaults to 100

17.4   Visualization of Results

17.4.1   Wordcloud

Wordcloud is not only used to display labels, but also to present keywords of the text, so as to help people understand the general content of the text concisely [9]. According to the importance of words to draw wordcloud, wordcloud can show data from different dimensions: the word itself, frequency (word size), and the color of words, making the segmentation results simple and clear. Each word is regarded as an object in wordcloud. To generate a beautiful wordcloud requires three steps: configuring object parameters, loading wordcloud text, and outputting wordcloud file.

17.4.2   Wordcloud Production

In this paper, after extracting keywords of each article, we calculate the frequency of each keyword in the corresponding article and analyze the positive and negative emotions of keywords. According to the following parameters and the final output of the three values, we get the following wordcloud effect map. The parameters used in wordcloud and their descriptions are shown in Table 17.3.

In this paper, when making the wordcloud, we define the black and white silhouette of the portrait as the shape of the image cloud, and the colour of our font is randomly assigned. From the figure, we can see different sizes of keywords to determine the importance of keywords. The result is shown in Fig. 17.3.

Fig. 17.3 Wordcloud
display results

17.5 Conclusions

In this paper, we mainly use the improved TF-IDF algorithm to extract the keywords of the interview text and analyze the emotion of the extraction results, and get the positive and negative factors that affect the growth of teachers into excellent teachers. Finally, we visualize the extraction results to see the factors that have greater influence on teachers more intuitively. This kind of research is of great significance for an ordinary teacher who has just entered the teaching industry. They can learn some experience through this summary, the personal experience of excellent old teachers, combined with their own unique views on the teaching industry, so that they can quickly grow into an excellent teacher.

However, in this paper, TF-IDF algorithm is a traditional algorithm to extract keywords, so the subsequent algorithm can be improved and innovated to make the extraction results more accurate.

Acknowledgements The work was supported by the Natural Science Foundation of China (62001328) and TJNU "Artificial Intelligence + Education" United Foundation.

References

1. H.P. Luhn, The automatic creation of literature abstracts [J]. IBM J. Res. Dev. **1**(4), 309–317 (1957)
2. N. Nazari, M.A. Mahdavi, A survey on automatic text summarization [J]. J. Artif. Intell. Data Min. **7**(1), 121–135 (2019)
3. I.H. Witten, G.W. Paynter, KEA: Practical automatic keyphrase extraction [J]. ACM (1999)
4. D.T. Peter, Learning to extract keyphrases from text [J]. DPLP (2002)
5. H. Anette, Improved automatic keyword extraction given more linguistic knowledge [J]. ACM (2007)
6. A. Muhammad, D. Jahiruddin (2011) Text mining for automatic keyphrase extraction from text documents [J]. J. Intell. Syst. **20**(4), 327–351 (2011)

7. K. Niraj, S. Kannan, Automatic keyphrase extraction from scientific documents using N-gram filtration technique [P], Document engineering. pp. 199–208, (2008)
8. Y. Jiang, X. Zhao, Research and Implementation of text-based keyword extraction [J]. China Comput. Commun. **32**(05), 51–54 (2020)
9. Y. Zhu, J. Jing, Chinese word segmentation technology based on python language [J]. Commun. Technol. **52**(07), 1612–1619 (2019)
10. Y. Wu, S. Zhao, Text classification method based on TF-IDF and cosine similarity [J]. J. Chinese Inf. Process. **31**(05), 138–145 (2017)

Chapter 18
Teacher Award Prediction Based on Machine Learning Methods

Jian Dang, Yueyuan Kang, Xiu Zhang, and Xin Zhang

Abstract With the rise of artificial intelligence, machine learning methods have been widely used in more and more fields. The main content of this chapter is the application of machine learning methods in teacher award prediction problem. The content of this chapter is mainly divided into five parts: The first part mainly introduces the development status of artificial intelligence in the field of education; The second part mainly introduces some common evaluation indexes of the learner, such as error rate and precision, precision and recall, F_β measurement, receiver operating characteristic (ROC) and area under ROC curve (AUC); The third part mainly introduces some common machine learning methods. These methods include decision trees, k-nearest neighbors, support vector machines, neural networks, and Bayesian classifiers. The fourth part is the experimental simulation as well as the discussion about the results. The fifth part is a summary. The collected data set is used to train each kind of learner, and then the evaluation criteria are used to compare each kind of learner horizontally, and to analyze the advantages and disadvantages of each learner in the teacher award prediction problem.

Keywords Artificial intelligence in education · Educational data mining · Machine learning · Teacher evaluation

18.1 The Application of Artificial Intelligence in Education

Artificial intelligence (AI) technology is widely used in the field of education, but also has the very big application prospect. At present the application of artificial intelligence in education aspects mainly includes: adaptive learning, expert system, the

J. Dang · X. Zhang (✉) · X. Zhang
Tianjin Key Laboratory of Wireless Mobile Communications and Power Transmission, Tianjin Normal University, Tianjin, China
e-mail: zhang210@126.com

Y. Kang
Faculty of Education, Tianjin Normal University, Tianjin, China

virtual assistant, student performance prediction [1], teacher performance prediction [2], etc.

The education concept according to their aptitude was proposed in a long time ago, but for the traditional education mode, it is very difficult to achieve that very accurately. The first thing to face is the cost of education, because the training cost of an excellent teacher is very high, and the training cycle is very long, the price of hiring an excellent teacher is often very high, not only that, the number of excellent teachers is very small, which makes it almost impossible to implement large-scale individualized teaching under the traditional education model. Second, in order to accurately teach students in accordance with their aptitude, a large number of students' learning data need to be collected and analyzed, and in the formulation of the program, a large number of data need to be reasonably analyzed and screened. If all these work is completed by manpower, it will require a great investment of time and energy. Adaptive learning method can solve the problem of teaching students in accordance with their aptitude. This approach by collecting data of the students, and feedback after analysis to the existing knowledge map, can accord to each student's specific conditions to develop personalized learning solutions, including providing exercises of appropriate difficulty and controlling the appropriate learning pace, it will greatly increase the students' learning efficiency. Expert system mainly uses artificial intelligence and big data technology to solve problems that can only be solved by professionals under the traditional education model. The system has collected a large amount of experience information in the corresponding field. Through the artificial intelligence algorithm, the system has a certain ability of analysis and synthesis. Moreover, the system can self-update knowledge. A typical example is the correcting website, which can correct the essays submitted by students without the help of manual workers.

The function of virtual assistant is mainly to provide students with questions, consultation, teaching assistant and other related assistance work. A typical example of a virtual assistant is music notes, which are a set of devices that combine hardware and software. Hardware devices are mainly wearable devices, whose built-in sensors can collect real-time data of piano practitioners, analyze and process the collected practice data through its artificial intelligence algorithm, and then feedback the practice effect and evaluation to users.

This paper focuses on teacher award prediction problem. Teacher award system is a way of recognition and praise by the state and society for teachers' hard work and achievements. The emotion of teachers due to the praise evaluation of the state and society is the sense of honor; on the other hand, the promotion of teachers' sense of honor is a good incentive for the majority of teachers. Teacher award system is taken by many countries. For example, the National Teacher of the Year is a kind of teacher award system in America; the Teaching Awards is a kind of teacher award system in United Kingdom; the President's Award for Teachers is a kind of teacher award system in Singapore [3]. Rare research about teacher award prediction problem could be found in the literature. In this paper, the problem is built as a multi-class classification problem. The independent variables are the quality and ability of teachers; while the label is the award levels.

18.2   Evaluation Criteria for Machine Learning Model Performance

(1)   Error rate and accuracy. Error rate and accuracy are two relative concepts, but also two commonly used metrics. Error rate refers to the ratio of the number of misclassified samples of the learner to the total number of samples. If the total number of samples is m, and the number of misclassified samples is a, the formula for the error rate is a/m. Precision, on the other hand, is the opposite of error rate. Accuracy refers to the proportion of the samples correctly classified by the learner to the total number of samples. Its calculation formula is $1 - a/m$. For continuous cases the concepts of error rate and accuracy still apply. If we assume that the distribution of the sample data is D, the probability density function is $p(\cdot)$, the calculation formulas of error rate (E) and accuracy (acc) are respectively:

$$E(f; D) = \int_{x \sim D} \prod (f(x) \neq y) p(x) dx \qquad (18.1)$$

$$acc(f; D) = \int_{x \sim D} \prod (f(x) = y) p(x) dx \qquad (18.2)$$

(2)   Precision and recall. The previous section introduced the concepts of error rate and accuracy. Although these two performance metrics are widely applicable in a variety of application scenarios, there are some cases where only the error rate and accuracy are not sufficient. For example, when testing the quality of goods, it is not possible to just know the error rate of the detected goods, because the classifier classifies the correct goods in two parts, namely, the really good goods and the really bad goods. We do not know just by error rate and accuracy of the detected goods are really good, do not know what proportion of the truly good products are correctly detected. At this time, we need other indicators, such as precision and recall. Accurate ratio, in general terms, refers to the percentage of good products picked out by a trained classifier that are truly good. Recall ratio refers to what percentage of all good products are correctly selected. In the dichotomous confusion matrix, TP, FP, FN and TN are respectively used to represent true examples, false positive examples, false negative examples and true negative examples. The calculation formulas of precision ratio (P) and recall ratio (R) are respectively:

$$P = \frac{TP}{TP + FP} \qquad (18.3)$$

$$R = \frac{TP}{TP + FN} \qquad (18.4)$$

(3) F_β measurement. Although precision and recall can measure the performance
       of the classifier well, they are often not integrated. In general, when the recall
       rate of the classifier is relatively high, the recall rate will decrease correspond-
       ingly; conversely, when the recall rate of the classifier is relatively high, the
       recall rate will also decrease. In order to comprehensively consider the accu-
       racy and recall, the concept of F_β measurement is derived. β is a real number
       greater than 0, which can be adjusted. When the value of β is equal to 1, it is
       represented as the standard F1 measurement, and the accuracy and recall are
       equally important. When the value of β is greater than 1, the recall ratio has
       a greater impact; when the value of β is less than 1, the precision ratio has a
       greater impact. In this way, the value of β can be reasonably selected according
       to the needs of practical problems.

(4)   ROC and AUC. The full name for ROC is the "receiver operating characteristic"
       curve. It originated from the radar signal analysis technology during World War
       II, and has been widely used in many fields. After normalization processing,
       in many cases the classifier output values are not binary 0 and 1 integer values.
       The output of the classifier is usually a small number between 0 and 1. At
       this point, you usually pick a threshold. If the threshold is 0.5, then output
       values greater than 0.5 are treated as 1, and output values less than 0.5 are
       treated as 0. If the samples are sorted according to the predicted results of the
       classifier, the ones most likely to be positive examples are ranked first, and then
       the classification threshold is set to the value from the first sample to the last
       sample successively, a series of different values will be obtained. If the false
       positive example rate is taken as the horizontal axis and the true example rate
       as the vertical axis, the ROC curve can be obtained. The calculation formulas
       of the false positive example rate (FPR) and the true example rate (TPR) are
       respectively:

$$FPR = \frac{FP}{TN + FP} \tag{18.5}$$

$$TPR = \frac{TP}{TP + FN} \tag{18.6}$$

AUC is the area under the ROC curve. The performance of different classifiers
can be measured by the numerical value of AUC. The higher the AUC value is, the
better the classifier performance is.

The accuracy, precision, recall, F1 score, ROC, and AUC metrics are popular in
evaluating the performance of machine learning methods [1, 2, 4, 5].

18.3   Common Machine Learning Methods

18.3.1   Decision Tree

Decision tree algorithm (tree) [6] is a commonly used classification and regression method. It was first produced in the 1960s. Common decision number algorithms include ID3 algorithm, C4.5 algorithm, CART algorithm. Because the model it builds looks like a tree, the algorithm is called decision tree algorithm. Early decision tree algorithms such as ID3 algorithm are only applicable to classification problems, and later improved C4.5 algorithm is applicable to both classification problems and regression problems.

Decision tree algorithm has strong readability and fast classification speed. When constructing the decision tree model, the model is established according to the principle of minimizing the loss function. The construction of a decision tree is usually divided into three steps: feature selection, decision tree generation, decision tree pruning. A decision tree contains a root node, several internal nodes, and several leaf nodes. The root and inner nodes represent a test property, while the leaf nodes represent the test results. The process from the root node to the internal node to the leaf node is also a process of gradually classifying the sample set. The leaves are the final categorization.

How to select the optimal attribute in the process of decision tree construction is a very key problem. According to different partitioning principles, decision tree algorithms are divided into different types. The commonly used optimal attribute classification criteria include information gain, gain rate and Gini index. The following will briefly introduce each of the three commonly used standards.

Information Gain: with the process of dividing the decision tree, we hope that each internal node of the decision tree will contain as few sample types as possible, so we need to put forward a concept of information entropy. Let's say the current sample set is D, and the proportion of the kth sample in the sample set is p_k. Then the definition of information entropy is as follows:

$$Ent(D) = -\sum_{k=1}^{|y|} p_k \log_2^{p_k} \tag{18.7}$$

Information entropy reflects the information contained in sample set D. The smaller the value is, the higher the purity of the sample set is. Let's say that property a has S different values and the sample set D is divided into S subsamples. And then you can calculate the sum of the information contained in this S subsamples. Then the information gain of this attribute division can be obtained by subtracting the sum of the information contained in the S subsamples from the information contained in the sample set D. The information gain can then be used to measure how well the samples are divided by different attributes. The larger the information gain is, the better the effect will be generated by using this attribute to partition. Information gain is defined as follows:

$$Gain(D, a) = Ent(D) - \sum_{v=1}^{V} \frac{|D^v|}{|D|} Ent(D^v) \tag{18.8}$$

Gain rate: It can be seen from the definition of information gain that the more values the attribute has, the greater the information gain is likely to be. If it is obviously not very appropriate to simply take information gain as the criterion for selecting attributes, the concept of gain rate is proposed in C4.5 algorithm of decision tree. The gain rate is defined as:

$$Gain\_ratio(D, a) = \frac{Gain(D, a)}{IV(a)} \tag{18.9}$$

$$IV(a) = - \sum_{v=1}^{V} \frac{|D^v|}{|D|} \log_2 \frac{|D^v|}{|D|} \tag{18.10}$$

It can be seen from the definition of gain rate that the less the number of values the attribute has, the greater the gain rate is likely to be. Therefore, the strategy adopted by the famous C4.5 decision tree algorithm is to comprehensively consider information gain and gain rate. The attribute whose information gain is higher than the average level is selected first, and then the attribute with the highest gain rate is selected as the dividing attribute.

Gini index: The Gini index reflects the probability that two randomly selected samples from the data set are of different categories. The smaller the Gini index, the higher the purity of the data set. Therefore, the Gini index can be used as a criterion to select the optimal attribute. For data set D, the Gini index is defined as:

$$Gini\_index(D, a) = \sum_{v=1}^{V} \frac{|D^v|}{|D|} Gini(D^v) \tag{18.11}$$

$$Gini(D) = \sum_{k=1}^{|y|} \sum_{k' \neq k} p_k p_{k'} \tag{18.12}$$

After determining the appropriate attribute selection criteria, the decision tree can be constructed. After the construction is completed, the decision tree is to be pruned. Common pruning methods include pre-pruning and post-pruning. Pre-pruning is pruning according to certain evaluation criteria before node division. Post-pruning is the pruning of the decision tree from bottom to top after the decision tree is generated.

18.3.2   Neural Network

The study of artificial neural network (net) [7] originated in the 1940s, which was inspired by the theory of brain neurology. Artificial neural network is composed of a large number of large neurons linked together according to certain weights and thresholds. Up to now, neural network has developed many types, such as Back Propagation (BP) neural network, Self-Organizing Map (SOM) network, Adaptive Resonance Theory (ART) network, Learning Vector Quantization (LVQ) network, Counter Propagation Network (CPN) network, feedback neural network, cerebellar model neural network, Principle Components Analysis (PCA) neural network and so on. In the early stage, neural networks with only a single hidden layer could only solve linear separable problems. Later, neural networks with multiple hidden layers were developed. It can be proved that the neural network can approach any function in theory when the number of hidden layers of the neuron is sufficient. Among many neural networks, BP neural network is the most classical one. BP neural network adopts the error back propagation algorithm, which includes the forward propagation of the signal and the back propagation of the error. In the training process of BP neural network, the sample signal passes through the input layer, the hidden layer, and finally reaches the output layer. Then, the sample signal is compared with the teacher signal at the output layer. The error signal is then transmitted from the output layer, the hidden layer, and the input layer in turn. During the back propagation of the error, each neuron adjusts its weight and threshold. The forward propagation process of the signal and the back propagation process of the error are repeated alternately. In this process, the weights and thresholds of the neural network are constantly corrected until the error reaches the preset range or the learning times of the learner reach the preset number.

18.3.3   Support Vector Machine

Support vector machine (svm) [8] is mainly used to solve dichotomies. The basic idea of support vector machine learning is to maximize the geometric interval. The linear separable support vector machine is mainly used to solve the linear separable problem and the nonlinear support vector machine can be used to solve the nonlinear classification problem by using the kernel technique. In general, for linearly separable problems, there are infinitely many separation hyperplanes that can properly separate the two types of samples. The solution of the support vector machine is the separation hyperplane with the largest geometric interval. The sample point closest to the separation hyperplane is called the support vector. This is where the support vector machine algorithm gets its name. For a given training data set, if one of the sample points is (x_i, y_i), the hyperplane is (ω, b). Then the geometric interval of the hyperplane with respect to the sample points is defined as:

$$Y_i = y_i \left(\frac{\omega}{\|\omega\|} \cdot x_i + \frac{b}{\|\omega\|} \right) \tag{18.13}$$

The geometric interval of the hyperplane with respect to the data set is defined as the minimum value of the geometric interval of the hyperplane with respect to all the sample points in the data set.

However, the problems encountered in the actual classification are not all linearly separable problems. For linear indivisible problems, you obviously need to do something else. The method adopted at this time is to map the low-dimensional sample space to a high-dimensional feature space, so that the sample becomes linearly separable in the high-dimensional feature space. This is the solution of support vector machine to solve linear indivisibility problems.

18.3.4 K-Nearest Neighbor

K-nearest neighbor algorithm (knn) [9] is a commonly used machine learning algorithm and a kind of supervised learning algorithm. However, knn has obvious differences with other supervised learning algorithms in some aspects. The uniqueness of knn lies in that its classifier model does not require complex training after the input of training sample data. It takes the training data as the model directly and does not deal with it accordingly.

The k-nearest neighbor algorithm has three core elements. These three elements are the determination of distance measurement standard, the selection of K value and the classification decision rule respectively. The distance measurement standards of K-nearest neighbor algorithm include Euclidean distance, Manhattan distance, Minkowski distance, etc., among which Euclidean distance is the most commonly used. Assuming that x_i and x_j are two samples in the sample set, the Euclidean distance is defined as:

$$L(x_i, x_j) = \left(\sum_{l=1}^{n} \left| x_i^{(l)} - x_j^{(l)} \right|^2 \right)^{\frac{1}{2}} \tag{18.14}$$

The selection of K value also has a great influence on the classification effect of the algorithm. Selecting the appropriate K value can significantly improve the classification effect of the algorithm. At present, the most commonly used selection method for k value is cross validation.

The most commonly used classification decision rule in the k-nearest neighbor algorithm is majority vote. That is, among the K sample points closest to the test sample, the class with the largest number of samples is selected as the category of the test sample.

18.3.5   Bayesian Classification

Bayesian classifier (cnb) [10] is a classifier designed mainly based on Bayesian formula. It is a method of estimating posterior probability by prior probability. It is assumed that the set of given category markers is y $= \{c_1, c_2, c_3...c_m\}$. For sample x, the goal of the Bayesian classifier is to calculate the probability that sample x belongs to each of the categories based on the prior probability $P(Y = c_k)$ and the conditional probability $P(X = x|Y = c_K)$, then select the category marker with the highest probability as the category marker of sample x. As you can see, the Bayesian formula is the core of the algorithm. The Bayesian formula is as follows:

$$P(Y = c_K|X = x) = \frac{P(X = x|Y = c_K)P(Y = c_k)}{\sum_{j=1}^{m} P(X = x|Y = c_j)P(Y = c_j)} \tag{18.15}$$

It is worth noting that the Naive Bayes algorithm assumes the conditional independence of the conditional probability distribution, which can significantly reduce the complexity of probability calculation.

Next, a flow chart is given in Fig. 18.1 to show the procedures of applying machine learning methods to solve teach award prediction problem.

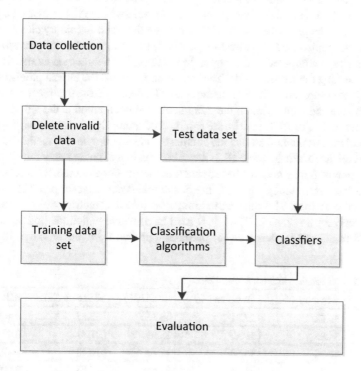

Fig. 18.1 Framework for solving teacher award prediction problem

As shown in Fig. 18.1, the first step is data collection. Then the second step is to delete the invalid data. Next, we divide the data set into training set and test set. The training set is used to train the learner, and the test set is used to test the trained model. Finally, the model is evaluated by using various evaluation criteria mentioned in Sect. 18.2. Note that the five machine learning methods are applied in classification algorithms step, thus, the framework shown in Fig. 18.1 is able to solve the problem.

18.4 Experimental Simulation

The second section of this chapter introduces several commonly used metrics of machine learning methods, such as error rate and accuracy, precision and recall, ROC curve and AUC. In the third section of this chapter, some commonly used methods in the field of machine learning are introduced. In the simulation, the tree, net, svm, knn, and cnb methods are used. Next, the method mentioned above is used to process the collected data related to teacher award prediction, and the method mentioned in Sect. 18.2 is used to evaluate the training results of several learners. Matlab software is used to simulate the experiment.

The performance of the five methods is given in Table 18.1. For precision metric, the value in Table 18.1 is the average of precision values of the four classes. So is the recall metric. The precision and recall metrics are designed for binary classification problem. For multi-class classification problem, the average value of precision and recall metrics is computed in this paper. In the table, the net method attains the best accuracy among the five methods. The tree method attains the largest precision and recall values compared with other methods. For F1 score metric, the tree method also attains the best performance; on the other hand, the net method is the worst among the five methods. For AUC metric, the cnb method attains larger value than the other methods. The tree method attains the smallest value among the five methods.

Based on the results in Table 18.1, it can be seen that a method may rank 1st for a metric; whereas it may rank the last for another metric. For example, the tree method ranks the last for accuracy and AUC metrics; while it ranks 1st for precision, recall, and F1 score metrics. The cnb method ranks 1st for AUC metric; while it does not rank the end for any metric. Thus, it is hard to conclude which method shows the best performance in the teach award prediction problem. Moreover, a hybrid or an

Table 18.1 Performance of the five classifiers

Method	Accuracy (%)	Precision (%)	Recall (%)	F1 score (%)	AUC
tree	30.62	27.31	43.56	33.57	0.4689
svm	34.85	19.40	23.63	21.31	0.4953
net	46.74	15.54	17.42	16.43	0.4903
knn	39.74	26.16	25.51	25.83	0.5001
cnb	33.39	25.43	23.18	24.25	0.5290

ensemble of several methods may be able to achieve better performance than the five methods.

The ROC curves for the four classes are shown in Figs. 18.2, 18.3, 18.4 and 18.5, respectively. For class 1, the ROC curves of the five methods are shown in Fig. 18.2. It can be seen that the curves of the five methods are intertwined. The cnb method shows better performance compared with others. For class 2, the ROC curves of the five curves are shown in Fig. 18.3. The curve of the tree method is above the curves of the other four methods. This means that the tree method attains better performance for classifying classes 2. For class 3, the ROC curves of the five curves are shown in Fig. 18.4. The curve of the svm method is above the curves of the other method. This means that the svm method attains better performance for classifying class 3. For class 4, the ROC curves of the five curves are shown in Fig. 18.5. The curves of the tree and svm method are above of the net, knn, and cnb methods. Thus, based on the four figures, it is hard to conclude which method shows overall better performance compared with others. It can be seen that the tree and svm method shows relatively good performance.

As seen from the figures, the classification ability of the classifier doesn't seem to be good enough. This is mainly due to the data set itself has no obvious category characteristics. In order to illustrate this situation, we analyze the category characteristics of the dataset. The analysis is shown in Tables 18.2, 18.3, and 18.4. In the following tables, the Euclidean distance is used to show category characteristics between classes.

As can be seen from Table 18.2, the minimum Euclidean distance of each and combination of the four categories is 1. It indicates that the minimum Euclidean

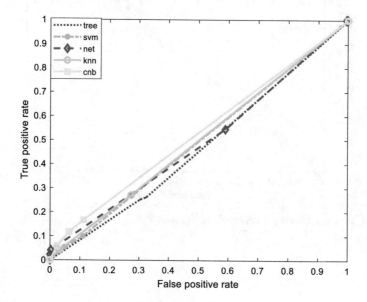

Fig. 18.2 ROC curves of the five methods for the class 1

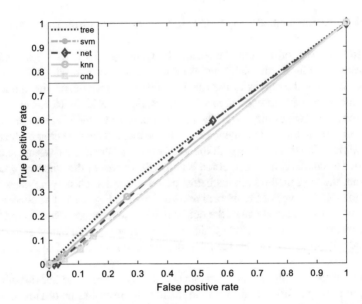

Fig. 18.3 ROC curves of the five methods for the class 2

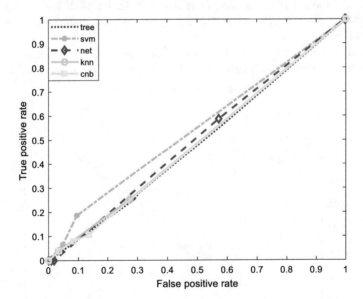

Fig. 18.4 ROC curves of the five methods for the class 3

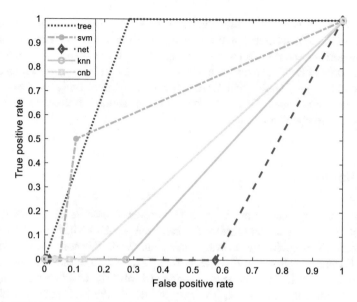

Fig. 18.5 ROC curves of the five methods for the class 4

Table 18.2 Minimum Euclidean distances between the four classes

Category	Class 1	Class 2	Class 3	Class 4
Class 1	1	1	1	1
Class 2	1	1	1	1
Class 3	1	1	1	1
Class 4	1	1	1	1

Table 18.3 Maximum Euclidean distances between the four classes

Category	Class 1	Class 2	Class 3	Class 4
Class 1	33.3317	33.3317	33.3317	33.3317
Class 2	33.3317	31.5436	31.5436	31.5911
Class 3	33.3317	31.5436	25.5343	25.5734
Class 4	33.3317	31.5911	25.5734	25.1992

Table 18.4 Average Euclidean distances between the four classes

Category	Class 1	Class 2	Class 3	Class 4
Class 1	13.5639	13.5269	13.5932	13.6092
Class 2	13.5269	13.4708	13.5142	13.5245
Class 3	13.5932	13.5142	13.6895	13.8988
Class 4	13.6092	13.5245	13.8988	13.6895

distance between samples in the data set is 1. As can be seen from each column of Table 18.3, the maximum Euclidean distance of each category after mixing with other categories is close to their own maximum Euclidean distance. And in the Table 18.4, the average Euclidean distance of each and combination of the four categories are very close. This shows that there is no very obvious category characteristic between the four classes. Therefore, for this classification problem, the upper limit of classification could not be high.

18.5 Summary

Rare research about teacher award prediction problem could be found. In this paper, five machine learning methods are used to solve the problem. The performance of the five methods is evaluated by accuracy, precision, recall, F1 score, RUC, and ROC. The ROC metric is shown in Figs. 18.1, 18.2, 18.3 and 18.4; the other metrics are shown in Table 18.1. There is no best method to solve the problem with respect to all metrics. For only one metric, it is easy to identify the best method; while it is impossible to identify the best method on all metrics. Because different methods have different ranks with respect to the metrics, thus a hybrid or an ensemble of several methods may be able to achieve better performance. An overhead is that the performance of the five methods is not good enough. For example, the accuracy is too low to be used in practice.

The methods and application examples described above are only a simple application of AI technology in the field of education. AI technology has many more complex applications in the field of education. In addition to the adaptive learning, expert system and virtual assistant mentioned above, there are also remote education, online learning, etc. It can be seen that AI technology has broad application scenarios in the field of education. Decision trees, neural networks, Bayesian algorithms, k-nearest neighbors, support vector machine, these are methods that are commonly used in the field of machine learning. There are other ways, of course, which are not covered in the text because of space. Combined with specific application scenarios, the "AI + education" market has great potential.

References

1. M. Hussain, W. Zhu, W. Zhang, S.M.R. Abidi, S. Ali, Using machine learning to predict student difficulties from learning session data. Artif. Intell. Rev. **52**, 381–407 (2019)
2. K. Kavitha, Assessing teacher's performance evaluation and prediction model using cloud computing over multi-dimensional dataset. Wirel. Pers. Commun. (2021). https://doi.org/10.1007/s11277-021-08394-3 (to appear)
3. M. Luo, A commonality research of the national teachers award system in United States, United Kingdom and Singapore. Teach. Educ. Res. **26**(5), 107–112 (2014)

4. N. Tomasevic, N. Gvozdenovic, S. Vranes, An overview and comparison of supervised data mining techniques for student exam performance prediction. Comput. Educ. **143**, Article number 103676 (2020)
5. S. García, B. Olsen, A. Simbaqueba, Teaching quality in Colombia: analysing twenty years of awarding a national best-teacher prize. Eur. J. Teach. Educ. **44**(3), 328–347 (2021)
6. L. Zhou, J. Li, Security situation awareness model of joint network based on decision tree algorithm. Comput. Simul. **38**(05), 264–268 (2021)
7. P. Yan, S. Shang, C. Zhang, X. Zhang, Classification of coal mine water sources by improved BP neural network algorithm. Spectrosc. Spectr. Anal. **41**(07), 2288–2293 (2021)
8. J. Chen, Algorithm of wireless network intrusion feature extraction based on support vector machine. Heilongjiang Sci. **12**(12), 34–35 (2021)
9. K. Luo, J. Xv, M. Yang, Improved stitching method based on KNN for UAV images. J. Wuhan Inst. Technol. **43**(03), 344–348 (2021)
10. X. Li, Z. Zhang, Fault diagnosis algorithm of transformer windings based on Bayesian classification. J. Jinan Univ. **35**(04), 412–416 (2021)

Chapter 19
A Study of the Current Status of Teachers' Core Qualities and Abilities and the Importance of Their Background Factors in Primary and Secondary Schools in Tianjin

Yueyuan Kang, Yiming Zhen, Xin Zhang, and Guangming Wang

Abstract This study intended to understand the current level of teachers' core qualities and abilities in Tianjin, China. Through questionnaire survey, stratified sampling was carried out for 4,903 teachers from 36 primary and secondary schools in 8 districts of Tianjin, China, with 4,661 valid samples. Reliability and validity analysis, descriptive statistical analysis, and confirmatory factor analysis were conducted. In combination with machine learning algorithms, clustering analysis, abnormal case screening, importance analysis of background factors. were performed. As indicated by the results, primary and secondary school teachers in Tianjin overall had good core qualities and abilities. In descending order of scores, teachers' core qualities and abilities were: ideological accomplishment, moral cultivation, educational ideal spirit, communication and cooperation ability, educating and teaching ability, humanistic, scientific and technological literacy, learning and development ability, and research and innovation ability. Phase of studying had a large effect on teachers' qualities and abilities, while urban/rural had only a small effect. As the most prominent differences, teacher education background had a significant impact on the top 30% samples, but had little impact on the bottom 30%; Gender exerted the largest impact on the bottom 30% samples, but exerted little impact on the top 30%.

Keywords Teachers' core qualities · Teachers' core abilities · Background factors · Importance analysis · Artificial intelligence

Y. Kang · Y. Zhen · G. Wang (✉)
Faculty of Education, Tianjin Normal University, Tianjin 300387, China
e-mail: bd690310@163.com

X. Zhang
Tianjin Key Laboratory of Wireless Mobile Communications and Power Transmission, Tianjin Normal University, Tianjin 300387, China

© The Author(s), under exclusive license to Springer Nature Singapore Pte Ltd. 2021
W. Wang et al. (eds.), *Artificial Intelligence in Education and Teaching Assessment*,
https://doi.org/10.1007/978-981-16-6502-8_19

19.1 Introduction

In the 1980s, assessments of teachers' professional competencies became prevailing in developed countries in Europe and the United States. In the 1990s, there was an upsurge in research into the professional development of teachers. At the turn of the century, countries in Europe and the United States worked to rebuild the professional philosophy and systems of teachers with the aim of demystifying educational success through the lens of teacher professional development. Since the twenty-first century, the world has witnessed an era of "great change, development and integration", with unprecedented international concern about teachers' qualities, especially the Teaching and Learning International Survey (TALIS) launched by the Organization for Economic Co-operation and Development (OECD), which brought research on teacher professional development to a climax. According to the *Education 2030 Framework for Action* released by the United Nations Educational, Scientific and Cultural Organization, this is called for "sound planning of teacher policies and norms to ensure that highly qualified, experienced and motivated teachers are engaged in education", highlighting the role of teachers' core qualities and abilities in current education. In February 2016, when the OECD published TALIS's results, Shanghai teachers received attention from researchers for their outstanding performance. Scholars proposed that to cultivate talent that meets the requirements of the future and the world, teachers are first expected to have an international perspective, to adapt to the general trend of internationalization in education, and to take the initiative to explore the effective integration of international experience with local practices.

From the above, enhancing teachers' professionalism and vigorously promoting their professional development has always been a national priority in education. Efforts should be made to accurately assess teachers' core qualities and abilities, and to identify the strengths and weaknesses of primary and secondary school teachers for targeted improvement.

Based on the above policy background, practical significance and research trends, this study has two main focuses, namely "factual" and "relational" questions. On the one hand, the factual questions are about the current situation. What is the current status of teachers' core qualities and abilities in Tianjin's primary and secondary schools? What is the current situation of the first-level dimensions of teachers' core qualities and abilities in Tianjin's primary and secondary schools? On the other hand, as for the relational questions, how do teachers' background factors contribute to their core qualities and abilities?

19.2   Literature Review

19.2.1   Studies on the Assessment of Teachers' Core Qualities and Abilities

Research on the assessment of teachers' core qualities and abilities has been conducted from different perspectives. From an international perspective, according to the *Common European Principles for Teacher Competences and Qualifications* issued by the European Union, teachers should possess three abilities, namely the ability to work with others, the ability to make full use of knowledge, technology and information, as well as the ability to closely relate to society [6], which are subdivided into different branches to promote the integration of teacher quality and ability standards across member states. Nevertheless, this lays small emphasis on teachers' personal internals, while their value consciousness drives their constant growth in professional development. The *Competency Framework For Teacher* [5] published by the Australian Department of Education and Training, divides teacher development into three stages and suggests that teacher qualities consist of professional attributes, professional knowledge and professional practice. On the whole, there has been an evaluation framework that takes into account both explicit abilities and internal qualities of teachers, with abilities such as education and teaching, communication and cooperation, self-development, etc., and qualities such as moral cultivation, information technology, beliefs, etc.

19.2.2   Factors Influencing Teachers' Core Qualities and Abilities

Regarding the factors influencing teachers' core qualities and abilities, a large number of researchers have been committed to exploring the factors that influence teachers' professional development (e.g., [1, 10, 11, 13]). For example, based on the 2013 Teaching and Learning International Survey (TALIS), there was an empirical examination of teachers' professional development in 36 countries and regions. It was found that background factors such as gender, length of teaching and education, as well as professional development needs of teachers had a significant impact on their professional development [4]. According to TALIS data, studied have found that the efficacy of teacher professional development was primarily influenced by the time and manner in which teachers engage in professional development, teachers' needs, teaching philosophies and approaches, school climate, evaluation and feedback on teachers' work, and principals' instructional leadership [15]. Besides, a study from Vermunt et al. [12] found that lesson study had a positive impact on teachers' professional learning, especially in terms of meaning and practice. As can be seen, existing studies have discussed the factors that influence teacher development from internal and external perspectives, yet they tend not to take into account the ranking of the importance of these factors.

19.2.3 Theoretical Framework

Based on the fourth-generation assessment theory [7] and stakeholder theory [2], which are both people-oriented and multi-care, this paper assesses teachers' core qualities and abilities by considering national teacher education policy-making and teacher development decisions, and integrating the needs of key stakeholders such as government, schools, and teachers, and provides targeted improvement initiatives based on this.

This study takes the double helix model of teachers' core qualities and abilities constructed by the research group of "A Study on the Teachers' Core Qualities and Abilities in China", a key tendering project of National Social Science Foundation of China for education in 2017, as the theoretical framework. Chinese teachers' core qualities and abilities comprise of ideological accomplishment, moral cultivation, humanistic, scientific and technological literacy, educational ideal spirit, educating and teaching ability, research and innovation ability, communication and cooperation ability, learning and development ability (see Fig. 19.1). The four core qualities and four core abilities are similar to the phosphoric acid and nucleobases in DNA, while teacher education, daily teaching and teaching and research activities are similar to phosphodiester linkages in DNA. Teachers' core qualities and abilities are alternately connected through these phosphodiester linkages and interconnected to realize its double helix and multi-way coupling, and rotating around the common axis of "strengthening moral education and cultivating people", thus forming a double helix structure model of teachers' core qualities and abilities [14].

19.3 Methodology

19.3.1 Participants

Focusing on primary and secondary school teachers in Tianjin, China, this study adopted stratified sampling and obtained data by filling answer sheets offline. According to statistics, the survey involved 4,903 teachers from 36 schools of different disciplines and levels in primary and secondary schools in Tianjin. 4,903 questionnaires were returned, with a return rate of 96.82%, of which 4,661 were valid, with a validity rate of over 95%. Among all participants, 1,969 (42.2%) were elementary school teachers, 1,520 (32.6%) were middle school teachers, and 1,116 (23.9%) were high school teachers, with 56 missing (see Table 19.1).

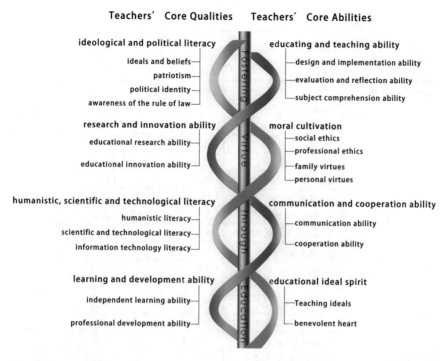

Fig. 19.1 The "double helix" model of teachers' core qualities and abilities

19.3.2   Instrument

According to Wang et al. [14], this paper identifies the first-level dimensions of teachers' core qualities and abilities assessment, namely ideological accomplishment, moral cultivation, humanistic, scientific and technological literacy, educational ideal spirit, educating and teaching ability, research and innovation ability, communication and cooperation ability, and learning and development ability (see Fig. 19.1). The adjusted index system consists of 8 first-level dimensions, 22 s-level indexes and 58 third-level observations, each of which contains a number of key attributes or behaviors.

19.3.2.1   Reliability Analysis

SPSS 24.0 was introduced to perform the internal consistency reliability test on the whole scale and the eight first-level dimensions, with a Cronbach's α of 0.979. As the Cronbach's α of each dimension was found to be greater than 0.7 (see Fig. 19.3), the questionnaire as a whole and the first-level dimensions had high internal consistency (see Table 19.2).

Table 19.1 Samples overview

Basic characteristics of teachers			
Category		Sampling number of teachers	Validity percent (%)
Town (township)	City	2,424	52.01
	Towns and villages	2,237	47.99
Gender	Male	809	17.4
	Female	3,794	81.4
	Missing value	58	1.2
Age	Under 30 years old	909	19.5
	31–40 years old	1,385	29.7
	41–50 years old	1,653	35.5
	51 years old and above	691	14.8
	Missing value	23	0.5
Length of teaching	10 years or less	1,359	29.2
	11–20 years	1,225	26.3
	21–30 years	1,397	30.0
	31 years and above	643	13.8
	Missing value	37	0.8
Education	College and below	201	4.3
	Bachelor's degree	3,612	77.5
	Master's degree	788	16.9
	Doctoral degree	28	0.6
	Missing value	32	0.7
Teacher education background	No teacher education experience	440	9.4
	Part-time teacher education background	905	19.4
	Full teacher education background	3,216	69.0
	Missing value	100	2.1
Professional title	Unrated or primary	896	19.2
	Intermediate	2,433	52.2
	Senior	1,275	27.4
	Full senior	34	0.7
	Missing value	23	0.5
Phase of studying	Primary school	1,969	42.2
	Middle School	1,520	32.6
	High school	1116	23.9

(continued)

Table 19.1   (continued)

Basic characteristics of teachers			
Category		Sampling number of teachers	Validity percent (%)
	Missing value	56	1.2
Honor	School-level honors or below, or no honors at present	2,237	48.0
	District-level honors	1,925	41.3
	Tianjin city-level honors	401	8.6
	National honors	65	1.4
	Missing value	33	0.7

Table 19.2   Reliability coefficient alpha of dimensions

Dimensions		Cronbach's alpha for internal consistency
The questionnaire as a whole		0.979
First-level dimensions	Ideological accomplishment	0.928
	Moral cultivation	0.849
	Humanistic, scientific and technological literacy	0.895
	Educational ideal spirit	0.868
	Educating and teaching ability	0.955
	Research and innovation ability	0.797
	Communication and cooperation ability	0.881
	Learning and development ability	0.880

19.3.2.2   Validity Analysis

(1)   Correlation matrix analysis

To further examine the construct validity of the test scale, Pearson correlation analysis was conducted for the eight first-level dimensions and the questionnaire as a whole, and the correlation matrix is shown in Table 19.3. Among the eight first-level dimensions, the highest correlation coefficient was 0.773, and the lowest was 0.277, both within the range of 0.27–0.78, suggesting a moderate correlation among the first-level dimensions. The correlation coefficients between each first-level dimension and the questionnaire as a whole were in the range of 0.69–0.90, implying a medium to high correlation between the first-level dimensions and the questionnaire

Table 19.3 Correlation coefficient matrix

	Whole	Ideological accomplishment	Moral cultivation	Humanistic, scientific and technological literacy	Educational ideal spirit	Educating and teaching ability	Research and innovation ability	Communication and cooperation ability	Learning and development ability
Ideological accomplishment	0.697	1.000							
Moral cultivation	0.797	0.621**	1.000						
Humanistic, scientific and technological literacy	0.870	0.545**	0.706**	1.000					
Educational ideal spirit	0.866	0.605**	0.678**	0.749**	1.000				
Educating and teaching ability	0.896	0.426**	0.631**	0.723**	0.745**	1.000			
Research and innovation ability	0.719	0.277**	0.389**	0.540**	0.519**	0.773**	1.000		
Communication and cooperation ability	0.842	0.444**	0.623**	0.686**	0.720**	0.758**	0.647**	1.000	
Learning and development ability	0.823	0.391**	0.534**	0.692**	0.648**	0.771**	0.725**	0.752**	1.000

** Significantly correlated at level 0.01 (double-tailed)

as a whole. Since each dimension was relatively independent and highly correlated with the questionnaire as a whole, the questionnaire had good construct validity.

(2)   **Confirmatory factor analysis (CFA)**

Confirmatory factor analysis was made to further validate the structural soundness of the scale, and software AMOS was employed to test the construct validity of the 8 first-level dimensions of teachers' core qualities and abilities in turn. As shown in Table 19.4, with the exception of some indexes (RMSEA), the other fitting indexes were all greater than or close to 0.9. The model is acceptable because it is basically consistent with the theoretical framework. The model was acceptable as it was generally consistent with the theoretical framework.

As indicated by the results of the confirmatory factor analysis above, the first-level dimensions of teachers' core qualities and abilities all had good model fits, implying an overall ideal construct validity of the test instrument.

19.3.3   Data Analysis

Basic descriptive statistical analysis was first conducted by SPSS 24.0, and quantitative studies such as confirmatory factor analysis were performed by AMOS. In combination with machine learning algorithms, MATLAB was adopted to carry out the analysis of data.

19.3.3.1   Empirical Cumulative Distribution Function

Cumulative distribution function can completely describe the probability distribution of a random variable [8]. The empirical cumulative distribution (ECDF) is an estimate of the cumulative distribution function of a sample of data, whose main purpose is to use the sample to infer the state of the aggregate, and thus the empirical cumulative distribution function is an approximate estimate of the probability distribution of the problem under study. According to the Glivenko-Cantelli theorem, the empirical cumulative distribution converges to the true distribution function when the probability is 1. In the data analysis, this study used the empirical cumulative distribution function to estimate the true distribution function for each dimension to observe the status of the teachers in general.

19.3.3.2   Clustering Analysis

The Gaussian Mixed Model (GMM) method [9] was used for clustering analysis, which is a linear combination of multiple Gaussian distributions, and ideally it can approximate any type of probability distribution that can aggregate the data into k

Table 19.4 Fitting indexes of confirmatory factor analysis

	χ^2	Df	IFI	TLI	NFI	GFI	CFI	RMSEA
Standard model			>0.9	>0.9	>0.9	>0.9	>0.9	<0.05
Ideological accomplishment	3437.211	29	0.806	0.698	0.804	0.761	0.805	0.212
Moral cultivation	448.486	14	0.936	0.872	0.934	0.959	0.936	0.109
Humanistic, scientific and technological literacy	731.147	24	0.925	0.888	0.923	0.938	0.925	0.106
Educational ideal spirit	209.150	8	0.967	0.937	0.965	0.975	0.967	0.098
Educating and teaching ability	359.267	11	0.976	0.953	0.975	0.961	0.976	0.110
Research and innovation ability	39.015	4	0.993	0.982	0.992	0.994	0.993	0.058
Communication and cooperation ability	223.129	8	0.968	0.939	0.966	0.972	0.968	0.102
Learning and development ability	91.353	13	0.989	0.981	0.987	0.990	0.989	0.048

categories. In this study, the Davies-Bouldin Index (DBI) was used to measure the clustering results, i.e., to optimize the size of k-value by calculating the ratio of the sum of intra-class distances to inter-class distances, thus avoiding the situation of local optima in other algorithms due to the calculation of the objective function only. In the data analysis, this study used GMM and DBI to categorize the sample of tested teachers to derive the optimal number of categories for the sample and the proportion of samples in each category, thus screening for convergent and abnormal groups in the sample.

19.3.3.3   Classification Analysis

Random Forest (RF) method was used for classification analysis, which contained classifiers with multiple decision trees, and the final classified category is determined by the plurality of the categories output from the multiple decision trees. Among them, Decision Tree (DT) is a typical classification method that used inductive algorithms to generate readable rules and decision trees, and then used the rules and decisions to classify new data. In the data analysis, this study used the Random Forest method proposed by Breiman [3], where the resampling was performed by the self-help method, and several decision trees were generated based on the training of the resampled sample set and formed a random forest, where each tree had the same distribution and the classification error was influenced by the classification ability of each tree and the correlation between trees. Specifically, in this study, the importance of background variables was first analyzed using the Random Forest method, and then, the importance of background factors for all samples and samples in the top 30% and bottom 30% of the score of teachers' core qualities and abilities were randomly simulated using Matlab, and then the random results were averaged to obtain the ranking results of the importance of background factors. Finally, a random simulation analysis of the paths of influence of background variables was conducted separately for different groups of teachers whose scores were in the top 30% (denoted as 1) and the bottom 30% (denoted as 0) using the Random Forest method.

19.4   Results

19.4.1   Analysis of the Overall Status of Teachers' Core Qualities and Abilities in Tianjin

To get a general picture of the questionnaires, the total score of each questionnaire was counted for descriptive statistical analysis, and the data were plotted as the following frequency histogram (see Fig. 19.2). The scores mostly fell between 600 and 700, with a mean score of 644.7 and a full score of 756, a scoring rate of 85.3%

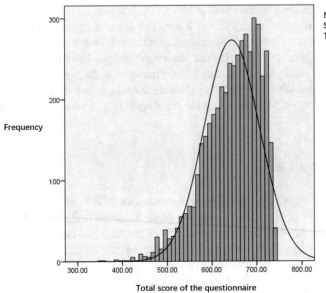

Fig. 19.2 Frequency histogram of the total score of the questionnaire

(scoring rate = mean score/full score), indicating a satisfactory overall situation. As the highest score of 743, near full mark, suggests, there are outstanding performers in the faculty. There was a minimum score of just 347 but with low frequencies, in contrast to high frequencies of high scores (see Table 19.5).

Descriptive analysis was carried out for the 8 first-level dimensions mentioned above (see Table 19.6). As the comparison of their means shows, ideological accomplishment scored the highest (3.6147) among the 8 dimensions, and research and innovation ability scored the lowest (2.8989). Since the mean value of qualities (3.50) was slightly higher than that of abilities (3.24), teachers' core qualities and core abilities were analyzed separately. This was found that among teachers' core qualities, ideological accomplishment scored the highest (3.6147), and humanistic, scientific and technological literacy scored the lowest (3.3504); Among teachers' core abilities, communication and cooperation ability scored the highest (3.4096), and research and innovation ability scored the lowest (2.8989).

Table 19.5 Descriptive statistics of the total score of the questionnaire

	N	Minimum	Maximum	Mean	Standard deviation	Total score of the questionnaire	Scoring rate
Total score of the questionnaire	4,661	347.00	743.00	644.7474	61.88079	756	85.3%

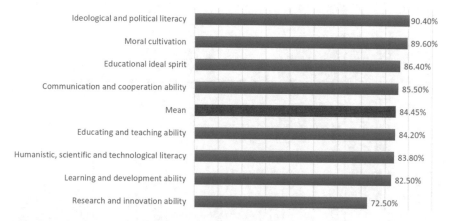

Fig. 19.3 Bar chart of the scoring rate of first-level dimensions

Further, descriptive analysis was conducted on the average score for each person of the 4,661 teachers involved in the survey. According to the calculation of scoring rate, ideological accomplishment had the highest scoring rate (90.4%), and research and innovation ability had the lowest (72.5%). Since the scoring rate of qualities (87.6%) was slightly higher than that of abilities (81.2%), teachers' core qualities and core abilities were analyzed separately. It was found that among teachers' core qualities, ideological accomplishment had the highest scoring rate (90.4%) and humanistic, scientific and technological literacy had the lowest (83.8%). Among teachers' core abilities, communication and cooperation ability had the highest scoring rate (85.5%), and research and innovation ability had the lowest (72.5%).

The scoring rates of the 8 first-level dimensions were plotted as a bar chart and arranged in descending order of their scores. As shown in Fig. 19.3, the top four first-level dimensions were all higher than the mean, with the top three being core qualities, i.e., three of the last four first-level dimensions were core abilities, ranking 6th, 7th, and 8th. This suggests that teachers' core abilities are more in need of improvement than core qualities, which explains why core qualities were analyzed separately from core abilities next.

19.4.2   Empirical Cumulative Distribution Function

The empirical cumulative distribution function expresses the distribution of samples. As shown in Fig. 19.4, samples of the 6th dimension (research and innovation ability) scored significantly different from other dimensions.

According to the clustering results of each first-level dimension, except for the 6th dimension, more than 99% of the samples of the remaining dimensions fell in the same category, indicating that the majority of teachers were of the same type. The

Table 19.6 Analysis of the average score of first-level dimension questions

First-level dimensions	Minimum	Maximum	Standard deviation	Mean of questions	Mean of core qualities	Mean of core abilities	Scoring rate (%)	Scoring rate of core qualities	Scoring rate of core abilities
1. Ideological accomplishment	1.51	4.00	0.33632	3.6147	3.50	–	90.4	87.7%	–
2. Moral cultivation	1.85	4.00	0.32347	3.5857			89.6		
3. Humanistic, scientific and technological literacy	1.32	3.90	0.35451	3.3504			83.8		
4. Educational ideal spirit	1.78	4.00	0.37572	3.4583			86.4		
5. Educating and teaching ability	1.46	4.00	0.46844	3.3467	–	3.24	84.2	–	81.2%
6. Research and innovation ability	1.21	4.00	0.45787	2.8989			72.5		
7. Communication and cooperation ability	1.50	4.00	0.45114	3.4096			85.5		
8. Learning and development ability	1.31	4.00	0.50176	3.2923			82.5		

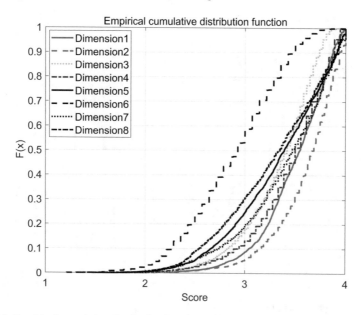

Fig. 19.4 Empirical cumulative distribution function of first level dimensions

Table 19.7 Clustering of first-level dimensions

Dimensions	1	2	3	4	5	6	7	8
Number of clusters	2	3	2	2	5	5	3	5
Largest proportion (%)	99.98	99.94	99.98	99.90	99.51	97.89	99.90	99.72

largest proportion of clusters of the 6th dimension (research and innovation ability) was 97.89%, implying that more than 2% of the samples distinguished themselves from the majority (see Table 19.7).

19.4.3   Screening of Abnormal Samples

Exploratory analysis was conducted to obtain z-scores for sample data, and then to screen out extreme values and outliers.

As shown in Fig. 19.5, the long lower tails and plus signs indicate the asymmetry of sample data, and it can be determined that samples of the 6th dimension (research and innovation ability) were quite different from the other dimensions.

From the outliers reflected in the box plot and identified in z-score calculation, there were respectively 22, 51, 82, 37, 60, 17, 7, 23 and 9 outliers in the whole and 8 dimensions in the 8 first-level dimensions. Quantitatively, the 1st, 2nd, and 4th

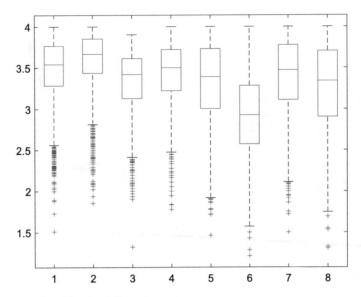

Fig. 19.5 Box plot of first-level dimensions

dimensions (i.e., ideological accomplishment, moral cultivation, and educational ideal spirit) had more outlier samples.

19.4.4 Analysis of the Importance of Background Factors

Random simulation was performed with MATLAB to determine the importance of background factors for all samples and samples in the top 30% and bottom 30% of the score of teachers' core qualities and abilities. The random results were then averaged to get the ranking of importance of background factors. Regression analysis was conducted using the Random Forest method, with background factors (teacher education background, length of teaching, phase of studying, age, professional title, honor, urban/rural, gender, and education) as the independent variable, and the total score of core qualities and abilities as the dependent variable. As can be seen from Table 19.8, the top 5 influencing factors in general were phase of studying, teacher education background, age, education, and length of teaching, which exerted a greater influence on teachers' core qualities and abilities than other factors. Correspondingly, honor, professional title, and gender had smaller and insignificant effects on teachers' core qualities and abilities.

Random forest was reintroduced to analyze the importance of background factors for samples in the top 30% and bottom 30% of the total score of teachers' core qualities and abilities. As shown in Table 19.9, for samples in the top 30% of the total score, teachers' core qualities and abilities were more influenced by length of

Table 19.8 Ranking of importance of background factors of teachers' core qualities and abilities of all samples

Ranking	Result 1	Result 2	Result 3	Result 4	Composite
1	Phase of studying	Phase of studying	Phase of studying	Phase of studying	Phase of studying
2	Education	Length of teaching	Age	Teacher education background	Teacher education background
3	Age	Teacher education background	Teacher education background	Age	Age
4	Teacher education background	Age	Urban/rural	Gender	Education
5	Length of teaching	Education	Length of teaching	Education	Length of teaching
6	Honor	Urban/rural	Education	Length of teaching	Urban/rural
7	Urban/rural	Honor	Professional title	Urban/rural	Honor
8	Professional title	Professional title	Honor	Professional title	Professional title
9	Gender	Gender	Gender	Honor	Gender
Regression error	1.19e7	1.28e7	1.35e7	1.35e7	

teaching, teacher education background, phase of studying, age and professional title, and less influenced by urban/rural, gender and education. For samples in the bottom 30% of the total score, teachers' core qualities and abilities were more influenced by gender, phase of studying, education, age, and honor, and less influenced by teacher education background, professional title, and urban/rural (see Table 19.10).

Based on the analysis of samples in the top 30% and bottom 30% of the total score, phase of studying had a large effect on teachers' qualities and abilities, while urban/rural had only a small effect. As the most prominent differences, teacher education background had a significant impact on the top 30% samples, but had little impact on the bottom 30%; Gender exerted the largest impact on the bottom 30% samples, but exerted little impact on the top 30% (see Fig. 19.6).

In the last row, "0" denotes the bottom 30% samples and "1" denotes the top 30%. The top of the tree is the length of teaching variable. If the length of teaching is 2 (11–20 years), then turn to the left to determine the teacher education background. If the teacher education background is 1 (no teacher education background), then turn to age. If the age is 2 (31–40 years old), the result shall be "0", implying that it falls in the bottom 30% categories. Taking the education variable as another example, it all corresponds to "1", meaning that teachers in primary schools without

Table 19.9 Importance of background factors corresponding to the top 30% of total score

Ranking	Result 1	Result 2	Result 3	Result 4	Composite
1	Teacher education background	Length of teaching	Phase of studying	Length of teaching	Length of teaching
2	Length of teaching	Teacher education background	Teacher education background	Phase of studying	Teacher education background
3	Phase of studying	Phase of studying	Length of teaching	Teacher education background	Phase of studying
4	Age	Age	Age	Professional title	Age
5	Professional title	Honor	Honor	Urban/rural	Professional title
6	Honor	Professional title	Professional title	Honor	Honor
7	Urban/rural	Urban/rural	Urban/rural	Age	Urban/rural
8	Gender	Education	Education	Gender	Gender
9	Education	Gender	Gender	Education	Education
Regression error	1.77e5	2.00e5	2.10e5	2.17e5	

11–20 years of teaching experience, regardless of their education, fall in the top 30% after classification, and so on (see Fig. 19.7).

19.5 Conclusion

As indicated by the research findings, teachers in primary and secondary schools in Tianjin had overall good core qualities and abilities. Among core qualities, teachers performed best in ideological accomplishment (ranked 1st) and moral cultivation (ranked 2nd), better in educational ideal spirit (ranked 3rd), and worst in humanistic, scientific and technological literacy (ranked 6th); Among core abilities, teachers performed better in communication and cooperation ability (ranked 4th) and educating and teaching ability (ranked 5th), and worse in learning and development ability (ranked 7th), and worst in research and innovation ability (ranked 8th). By examining the effect of background factors on teachers' core qualities and abilities, this was found that phase of studying had a large effect on teachers' qualities and abilities, while urban/rural had only a small effect. As the most prominent differences, teacher education background had a significant impact on the top 30% samples, but had little impact on the bottom 30%; Gender exerted the largest impact on the bottom 30% samples, but exerted little impact on the top 30%.

Table 19.10 Importance of background factors corresponding to the bottom 30% of total score

Ranking	Result 1	Result 2	Result 3	Result 4	Composite
1	Age	Gender	Phase of studying	Phase of studying	Gender
2	Gender	Education	Gender	Gender	Phase of studying
3	Length of teaching	Age	Length of teaching	Education	Education
4	Education	Teacher education background	Professional title	Honor	Age
5	Phase of studying	Honor	Honor	Teacher education background	Honor
6	Honor	Professional title	Teacher education background	Professional title	Length of teaching
7	Professional title	Length of teaching	Education	Age	Teacher education background
8	Teacher education background	Phase of studying	Age	Length of teaching	Professional title
9	Urban/rural	Urban/rural	Urban/rural	Urban/rural	Urban/rural
Regression error	1.26e6	1.47e6	1.64e6	1.76e6	

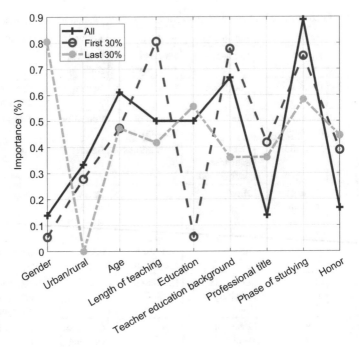

Fig. 19.6 Importance Comparison of background factors

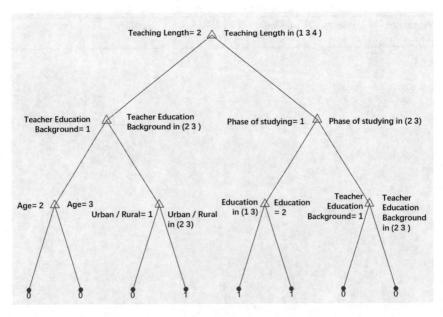

Fig. 19.7 An example of tree structure in the Random Forest method

Acknowledgements This paper was supported in part by the key project of the National Social Science Foundation of China "A Study on the Teachers' Core Qualities and Abilities in China" (Project No. AFA170008).

References

1. F. Barrera-Pedemonte, High-quality teacher professional development and classroom teaching practices. *OECD Education Working Papers*, No. 141. (OECD Publishing, Paris, 2016)
2. J.R. Boatright, Contractors as stakeholders: reconciling stakeholder theory with the nexus-of-contracts firm. J. Bank. Finance **26**(9), 1837–1852 (2002)
3. L. Breiman, Random forests. Mach. Learn. **45**(1), 5–32 (2001)
4. C. Chen, Teacher professional development and its influential factors on the international perspective: evidences from TALIS data. Int. Comparat. Educ. **39**(6), 84–92 (2017) (in Chinese)
5. Department of Education and Training, *Competency Framework for Teachers*. Strategic Human Resources (2014), https://www.education.wa.edu.au/dl/ojlqqk2
6. European Commission, *Common European Principles for Teacher Competences and Qualifications* (2005), http://www.pef.uni-lj.si/bologna/dokumenti/eu-common-principles.pdf
7. E.G. Guba, Y.S. Lincoln, *Fourth Generation Evaluation* (Sage, New York, 1989)
8. J.F. Lawless, *Statistical Models and Methods for Lifetime Data* (Wiley, Hoboken, NJ, 2011)
9. G.J. McLachlan, S.X. Lee, S.I. Rathnayake, Finite mixture models. Annu. Rev. Stat. Appl. **6**(1), 355–378 (2019)
10. K.M. Soine, A. Lumpe, Measuring characteristics of teacher professional development. Teach. Dev. **18**(3), 303–333 (2014)
11. B. Torff, D. Sessions, K. Byrnes, Assessment of teachers' attitudes about professional development. **65**(5), 820–830 (2005)
12. J.D. Vermunt, M. Vrikki, N. van Halem, P. Warwick, N. Mercer, The impact of lesson study professional development on the quality of teacher learning. Teach. Teach. Educ. **81**, 61–73 (2019)
13. C.S. Wallace, M. Priestley, Teacher beliefs and the mediation of curriculum innovation in Scotland: a socio-cultural perspective on professional development and change. J. Curric. Stud. **43**(3), 357–381 (2011)
14. G. Wang, W. Huang, L. Wu, Q. Wei, The double helix model of teachers' key competencies and abilities. Curric. Teach. Mater. Method **39**(9), 132–138 (2019) (in Chinese)
15. M. Zhao, The status and implications of teachers' professional development in an international perspective: based on the results of TALIS 2013. Teach. Educ. Res. **27**(3), 100–106 (2015) (in Chinese)

Chapter 20
The Analysis Path of Classroom Teacher Behavior Supported by Artificial Intelligence

Libao Wu, Yanan Cao, Qing Du, and Tingting Han

Abstract The analysis of classroom teacher behavior mainly focuses on teacher's performance in classroom teaching with the aim of exploring the occurrence rule of teaching behavior. Supported by Artificial Intelligence (AI), it is possible to raise analytical efficiency, enrich analytical content, innovate developing form, and realize intelligent analysis of classroom teacher behavior. Based on development and implementation of current text categorization, human posture estimation, facial expression recognition and other technologies, this paper studies and builds an integrated practice process of classroom behavior analysis under AI. This process mainly includes three modules: acquisition and analysis, feedback and improvement, and external conditions guarantee, so as to realize automatic collection, calculation, analysis and evaluation of classroom teacher behavior, which can guide teacher's behavior improvement, promote teacher's professional development, and enhance classroom teaching quality and student's learning effect.

Keywords Classroom behavior · Classroom language · Classroom posture · Facial expression analysis · Analysis path

20.1 Introduction

As the organizer of classroom teaching activities, teacher can demonstrate and guide student's behavior and emotion even with a subtle body movement. Teacher's behavior in the classroom can initiate teaching activities and affect educational phenomena, quality of classroom teaching, as well as emotion and quality of student's learning. Focusing on teacher's performance in classroom teaching, the analysis of classroom teacher behavior explores the occurrence rule of teaching behavior,

L. Wu · Y. Cao · Q. Du (✉)
Faculty of Education, Tianjin Normal University, Tianjin 300387, China

T. Han
Tianjin Key Laboratory of Wireless Mobile Communications and Power Transmission, Tianjin Normal University, Tianjin 300387, China

which can guide teacher's behavior improvement, promote teacher's professional development, and enhance classroom teaching quality and student's learning effect.

Since the concept of AI was first put forward in 1956, it has been developing quickly owing to the rapid development of modern science and technology. With the help of its fast computing and massive storage capacity, now it is moving towards the goal of enabling machines to acquire, process and apply knowledge autonomously like human brain and accelerating its integration and application with other fields. Education is an important part of AI application fields, which can be illustrated by the research carried out in this paper. The application of AI technology in the analysis of classroom teacher behavior not only enlarges the radiation scope of AI application, but also enables the intelligent analysis of teaching behavior. Based on collection, calculation, analysis and evaluation of classroom behavior, it can provide teachers with the improvement scheme concerning personalized teaching behaviors, observable tools and platforms used to improve teachers' teaching ability, as well as personalized and accurate quantitative data supporting the evaluation of teaching ability.

To sum up, the research conducted in this paper will sort out the researching progress of intelligent recognition algorithm for the analysis of classroom teacher behavior and explore the analytical path supported by AI, constructing the integrated practice process of classroom behavior analysis, so as to facilitate teacher's professional development.

20.2 Related Research

20.2.1 Application of AI in Education

AI technology provides strong technical support for the reform of pedagogical teaching approach and the improvement of educational teaching quality. Up to now, applications of AI in the field of education have covered four scenarios: teaching, learning, evaluation and management. In terms of intelligent teaching, AI technology can be used to create virtual famous teachers and carry out interactive teaching. Virtual teaching assistants can replace teachers to arrange personalized learning content for students and realize "double teacher classroom". In the aspect of intelligent learning, Intelligent Tutoring System (ITS) can collect and analyze data of student's learning process by using data mining technology such as character recognition and natural language processing, thus realizing the analysis of student's learning situation and providing personalized learning scheme. As for intelligent evaluation, some achievements have been made in automatic evaluation system for classroom teaching, for example, oral assessment system for speaking test, and intelligent examination paper marking system for written examination. In particular, oral assessment and intelligent marking have already been applied in daily learning, oral English test and large-scale examination paper marking. As far as intelligent management is concerned, AI is used to build a smart campus to complete the integrated management of identity authentication, classroom attendance, campus security, logistics service and other multi-scene data exchange. Based on what has been discussed above, it can be concluded that AI technology has been explored and applied in many aspects of education, and the more in-depth integration of AI and education is the trend of future research. However, the current practice is mostly based on guiding and evaluating student's learning, so there are still some deficiencies on how to apply AI technology to analyze teacher's behavior, which definitely needs further research and exploration.

20.2.2   Technical Support for the Analysis of Classroom Teacher Behavior

Classroom teacher behavior is an observable and explicit activity mode that teachers adopt to complete teaching task, and it is the behavior that teachers show in the process of classroom teaching [1]. Previous analysis and research of classroom behavior have divided different observable classroom teaching behaviors through the decomposition of those behaviors, and have recorded the frequency of various behaviors manually in the classroom teaching scene or through the teaching video, so as to obtain the evaluation result of classroom teacher behavior. On the one hand, it takes researchers a lot of time to count the frequency of those behaviors; on the other hand, some subtle behaviors may be neglected due to the limitation of human observation ability. Thanks to the rapid development of information technology, it is possible to carry out the intelligent analysis of classroom teacher behavior. Through the installation of ultra-clear cameras in the classroom to collect data concerning voice and image in the classroom, it is possible to improve the analytical efficiency, enrich the content of behavior analysis, innovate the form of research, and realize the intelligent development of teacher's classroom behavior with the help of intelligent recognition algorithm. At present, recognition algorithms that can be applied to the analysis of classroom teacher behavior mainly include text categorization, human posture recognition and facial expression recognition.

(1)   **Text categorization**

Language is the medium of delivering content, expressing intention and emotion. In terms of processing voice signal, the first step is to use automatic speech recognition technology to obtain the signal, transform it into corresponding text and carry out further task of linguistic text categorization, thus realizing the intelligent analysis of teacher's classroom language structure. With the development of machine learning, deep learning has made a new breakthrough in natural language processing and image recognition, acting as the guarantee for automatic categorization of class-room linguistic text. Zhang et al. [2] proposed adopting a method of text analysis: Character-level Convolutional Networks (ConvNets). Lu et al. [3] put forward

Sentence-based Automatic Coding (SAC) for teacher-student interaction. By using the input text of teacher-student dialogue, the teacher-student discourse can be automatically coded on the basis of the established classification framework of interactive behavior, which greatly saved the time needed for manual coding. Li and Dong [4] integrated Convolutional Neural Network (CNN) with Bi LSTM network to establish a feature fusion model, which not only extracted local features of text, but also took global features of context into consideration, greatly improving the accuracy of text categorization.

(2) Human posture estimation

Human posture estimation is to understand and reflect human state or intention by recognizing gesture, action and movement, whose key step is the recognition algorithm of posture. Nowadays the recognition algorithm of human posture in single picture mainly includes regression-based method, instance-based method and model-based method. Regression-based method is to establish the mapping relationship between human image feature and posture model with the help of regression model, so as to complete the process of recognition. Instance-based method is to build a huge instance database of human posture, then use the input human image to compare and match with it, and take the closest instance as the result of human posture recognition. Model-based method is to model, fix and segment human body structure, and get the overall posture recognition result by determining the position relationship of each part [5]. Yang et al. [6] developed a gesture recognition algorithm based on the spatial distribution feature of gesture, which could recognize human gesture in real time under complex background.

(3) Facial expression recognition

Facial expression is the emotional information that human shows during the process of expressing and communicating. Through the recognition of facial expression, machines can identify and analyze human emotion, and understand signal and intention revealed by facial expression. The continuous development in the field of computer vision, as well as the gradual maturity of face detection and recognition technology, provides the basis for the development of facial expression recognition technology. The research of facial expression recognition mainly focuses on the selection of expression features, which can be divided into two categories. One kind is the recognition of local facial features. By locating and analyzing features of eyebrows, eyes, nose, lips and other key points, 32 facial muscle movements are divided to classify facial expressions [7]. The other kind is the recognition of overall facial features. CNN can be used for feature matching of facial expressions, later the traditional neural network has been improved and the attention mechanism has been introduced to reduce the interference of other factors on expression recognition, thus achieving better recognition effect.

20.3   The Analysis Path of Classroom Teacher Behavior Supported by AI

Combined with the existing research foundation, an analytical model of classroom teacher behavior has been built in this paper from the perspective of AI, as is shown in Fig. 20.1.

Centering on the classroom teaching practice, this model collects, analyzes and stores the data information in the process of classroom teaching by means of AI technology, providing feedback and improvement scheme which in turn acts on classroom teaching practice. Its analysis data comes from the classroom, and which also contributes to the requirement of actual classroom teaching improvement. At the same time, the whole process needs to be developed under the guidance of educational theory and technical specifications, and under the premise of personal privacy data protection, so as to build an integrated practice process of teacher's classroom behavior analysis, thus realizing the enhancement of classroom teaching quality and teacher's professional development. Three modules will be illustrated in the following part: acquisition and analysis, feedback and improvement, and external conditions guarantee.

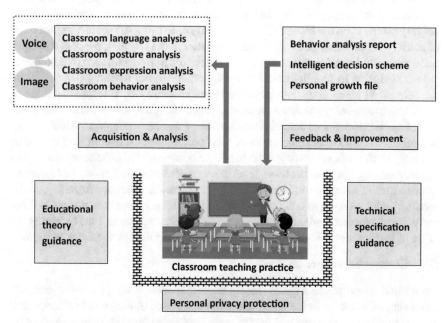

Fig. 20.1   The integrated practice process of analyzing classroom teacher behavior supported by AI

20.3.1 Acquisition and Analysis

(1) Data collection

Accurate and real data collection is the basis of conducting intelligent analysis, so this paper studies how to record the classroom teaching process by installing high-definition cameras in the classroom and collects teacher's voice and image data in classroom teaching, which can function as the basis of subsequent intelligent behavior analysis. Among those data, voice data serve as the guarantee for classroom language analysis. As for image data, on the one hand, the whole body's movement image can be used to conduct classroom posture analysis; on the other hand, the facial image is expected to be extracted to conduct classroom expression analysis. Classroom teaching behavior analysis will comprehensively apply those data of voice, body image and facial image to carry out multimodal teaching behavior analysis.

(2) Classroom language analysis

Language is the main form of communication in classroom teaching activities and teachers use it to transfer knowledge to students and organize teaching activities. Teacher's capacity to use classroom language reasonably and properly is an important element of teaching ability. On the one hand, the analysis of teacher's classroom language starts from the type of teacher's language. To be more specific, the adoption of guiding, stimulating and questioning language in the teaching process can stimulate student's learning enthusiasm. Too much imperative and narrative language is not conducive to highlight student's subjectivity in the teaching process. With the help of AI technology, it is possible to automatically code teacher's language according to several types that have already been set, get to know the overall situation of application and structural characteristic of teacher's language, which can be helpful for teachers to become aware of their problems in classroom language, thus assisting teachers in correcting their language behaviors and enhancing classroom teaching quality. On the other hand, from the perspective of interaction, the amount of teacher-student discourse and interaction in the process of classroom teaching can be counted under AI so as to reflect whether teacher's language causes student to think and observe whether student's speech gets the teacher's response, thus obtaining the value of teacher's questioning behavior and the actual effect of feedback behavior.

(3) Classroom posture analysis

Earlier and recent psychological studies show that 55% of the process of human's conveying information to the outside world is composed of nonverbal behavior, and body movement is an important part of nonverbal behavior. The proper application of body movement in teaching can convey more semantic information to students, mobilize their attention and improve their learning effect [8]. Inappropriate teacher posture is not conducive to the construction of teacher-student relationship in classroom. For instance, crossed arms in front of the chest may give students a feeling of dominance, both hands placed behind the back may highlight the teacher's authority, a single finger pointed at students may mean disrespect, etc. Human posture recognition technology can be used to judge teacher's body shape and gesture in the process of classroom teaching, help teachers recognize their body postures which are not easy to detect, and give feedback to teachers, so as to timely correct their inappropriate body movements. Consequently, it can directly reflect classroom posture of teachers, help teachers correct improper teaching posture, enhance the quality of classroom teaching and promote teacher's professional development.

(4)   **Classroom expression analysis**

The process of classroom teaching is not only the procedure of teacher's imparting knowledge to students, but also the step of emotional interaction between teacher and student. Teacher's facial expressions in the classroom convey his or her emotional state, which will affect the whole classroom teaching process to a certain extent. The facial recognition function of AI is used to capture facial images of teachers and initiate facial expression matching, obtain the category and time distribution of teacher's emotional expressions, and see a whole picture of teacher's emotional expressions in the whole class. At the same time, every emotional change is combined with the actual teaching event at the same time so as to analyze the cause of that emotional change and endow the result of teacher's emotional analysis with pedagogical significance, thus revealing educational phenomena reflected by analyzing the application of teacher's classroom facial expression.

(5)   **Classroom behavior analysis**

As has been discussed above, classroom language analysis, classroom posture analysis and classroom expression analysis are carried out from perspectives of language, posture and expression, which are all based on single modal analysis. In the classroom teaching environment, teachers interact with students through multiple senses and levels. Specifically speaking, initially, teacher's classroom language is the direct way to carry out teaching activities. Additionally, body movement is the action orientation of classroom teaching. Moreover, facial expression is the recessive infiltration of classroom teaching atmosphere. As a consequence, data collection of multimodal classroom behavior, comprehensive application of a variety of identification and analysis technologies, realization of automatic collection, calculation, analysis and evaluation, as well as exploration of internal relationship between various kinds of data, can comprehensively and stereoscopically restore the appearance of teacher's behaviors in classroom teaching and excavate educational significance and value behind classroom behavior, which can be regarded as the fundamental goal of application and development of classroom teacher behavior analysis under AI, eventually guiding teachers to mind and improve their teaching behaviors.

Different teacher's classroom teaching behaviors can lead to different educational phenomena [9], thus affecting the form of teaching activities, classroom teaching quality and student's learning effect. S-T analysis is a commonly used method to analyze classroom teaching behavior. It is a quantitative analysis method adopted to objectively and effectively reflect the teaching process in the form of graphics by means of recording the behavior of teachers and students, together with analyzing and studying the teaching process. Through identification and analysis of classroom behaviors, the developing process of classroom teaching activities can be figured out. In practice, the face recognition technology can be used to test facial features such as the number of faces and outlines of teachers and students. In this way, teacher's behaviors such as explanation, demonstration, blackboard-writing, media presentation, questioning, roll call and inspection, together with student's behaviors such as speech, thinking, notes and homework, can be identified so as to draw S-T curve and distinguish different kinds of classroom teaching modes [10]. Only in this way can we help teachers optimize classroom teaching behavior, mobilize student's learning enthusiasm, and make students fully participate in classroom teaching activities, eventually enhance the quality of classroom teaching. Luo and Zhang [11] established an automatic evaluation system of classroom teaching based on teacher-student dialogue text and computer vision technology including expression recognition and gaze estimation, which could be regarded as the attempt to carry out classroom teaching behavior analysis on the basis of multimodal data.

20.3.2   Feedback and Improvement

The analysis of teacher's behavior comes from classroom teaching, and its research results should in turn be applied to the actual classroom teaching and implemented in the improvement and promotion of teacher's classroom behavior, so as to enrich practical significance of the research and make AI technology truly act on teacher's classroom teaching. As a result, feedback and improvement scheme can be provided on the basis of data collection and behavior analysis. Feedback mode and improvement approach will be presented through the following three aspects: behavior analysis report, intelligent decision scheme and personal growth file.

(1) **Behavior analysis report**

Based on the analysis of language, posture, expression and teaching behavior, the system can automatically generate the analytical result of teacher's personal behavior, presenting teacher's performance in many aspects during the teaching process of a whole class. Meanwhile, comparative analysis among different teachers can also be conducted to explore common characteristics of excellent teachers in the application of behavior category, scenario, time distribution and so on. For instance, behavior comparison between novice teachers and skilled teachers can be carried out to help inexperienced novice teachers find the differences between themselves and teachers with rich teaching experience, so as to adjust their classroom language usage, classroom posture performance, classroom expression mobilization and teaching behavior performance, ultimately boosting the rapid growth of novice teachers.

(2)   **Intelligent decision scheme**

Thanks to the development and application of information technology, high-capacity storage, high-speed computing and expert decision-making system, based on a large number of collected data concerning classroom teacher behavior, a database of teacher's classroom behavior performance has been established. The expert decision-making system is used to give a teacher the matching content of excellent teachers' classroom behaviors which are consistent with the current classroom teaching content and similar to the teacher's teaching style, and provide intelligent optimization scheme of classroom behavior for teachers, eventually helping teachers optimize classroom teaching behavior and enhance the quality of classroom teaching.

(3)   **Personal growth file**

With further integration of AI and education, an analytical system of classroom teacher behavior supported by AI will be set up in daily classroom in the future to realize real-time collection and identification of behavior data during the teaching process. After class, teachers can view the analytical report of their teaching behavior on electronic device, as well as the intelligent behavior improvement scheme provided by AI expert decision-making system, which can greatly improve the feedback speed and therefore help teachers adjust and improve their teaching behaviors in time. The large capacity storage space of the network cloud platform makes it possible to store teacher's behavior analysis during the daily teaching process, establish teacher's personal growth file, and record the track of teacher's professional development.

20.3.3   *External Conditions Guarantee*

Education is a complicated social activity, so the integration of AI and education needs to be carried out in an orderly manner under the guidance of educational theory and technical specifications, so as to meet personalized and diversified needs of teaching activities. In the process of dividing and interpreting those collected data, we need to consider different classroom teaching fields and different student's learning state, take root in the actual classroom teaching, and set up personalized research norms to adapt to the quantitative analysis of teacher's behaviors. Research experience is expected to be summarized in practice, which can in turn promote the innovation of educational theory and algorithm, eventually realizing the two-way development of AI and education. At the same time, we are supposed to fully inform students and teachers of important rules before collecting data, standardize reasonable usage and safe storage of data in the whole analytical process, pay attention to the protection of personal privacy security, and explore new changes brought by AI technology for education and teaching on the premise of ensuring information security.

20.4 Discussion and Conclusion

In order to analyze classroom teacher behavior with the system mentioned above, we just need to collect voice and image data through ultra-clear cameras installed in the classroom, and then carry out analytical research on teacher's language, posture, expression and teaching behavior. Compared with the traditional way of analyzing teacher's behavior, the present researching process has been greatly improved and more subtle behaviors that are not easy to detect by human eyes can be captured with the help of AI technology, powerful data mining and computing analytical ability. In the meanwhile, more objective and accurate data of teacher's classroom performance are expected to be collected, in order to obtain personalized analytical results, provide decision-making materials for teaching behavior improvement and promote the development of teacher's professional ability.

"AI + education" is a hot topic in current research and relevant researchers are actively exploring ways to apply AI technology to the field of education, as a result of which intelligent technology are expected to better assist the development of educational activities. At present, related researches on the integration of AI and education are mostly carried out in laboratory and several pilot researches have already been conducted in some schools, but those researches still have not been widely promoted in daily classroom teaching. With more breakthroughs and achievements made in relevant fields, AI technology can truly be applied to classroom teaching practice and will be of great help to the development and improvement of teaching activities in the future.

Acknowledgements This work was supported by the National Social Science Foundation of Education Key Project under Grant No. AFA170008, by the Tianjin Science and Technology Planning Project under Grant No. 20JCYBJC00300, by the National Natural Science Foundation of China under Grant No. 11404240, and by Tianjin Philosophy and Social Science Planning Project under Grant No. TJJX17-016.

References

1. L. Yan, Classroom teaching behavior: connotation and research framework. Glob. Educ. **36**(S1), 39–44 (2007)
2. X. Zhang, J. Zhao, Y. LeCun, Character-level convolutional networks for text classification, in *Proceedings of the 28th International Conference on Neural Information Processing Systems* (2015)
3. J. Lu, D. Wang, Z. Luo, Automatic evaluation of teacher-student interaction based on dialogue text, in *2nd International Conference on Education, Sports, Arts and Management Engineering* (2017)
4. Y. Li, H. Dong, Text sentiment analysis based on feature fusion of convolution neural network and bidirectional long short-term memory network. J. Comput. Appl. **38**(11), 3075–3080 (2018)
5. S. Li, Y. Zhao, Q. Zhao, W. Yan, Algorithm of human posture action recognition and imitation for robots. Comput. Eng. **39**(8), 181–186 (2013)

6. B. Yang, X. Song, Z. Feng, X. Hao, Gesture recognition in complex background based on distribution features of hand. J. Comput. Aided Des. Comput. Gr. **22**(10), 1841–1848 (2010)
7. M. Pantic, L.J.M. Rothkrantz, Facial action recognition for facial expression analysis from static face images. IEEE Trans. Syst. Man Cybern.-Part B **34**(3), 1449–1461 (2004)
8. Z. Pi, J. Hong, J. Yang, Effects of the instructor's pointing gestures on learning performance in video lectures. Br. J. Edu. Technol. **48**(4), 1–10 (2017)
9. L. Wang, Y. Li, Research on teaching phenomena based on big data of classroom teaching behavior. e-Educ. Res. **38**(4), 77–85 (2017)
10. Q. Liu, H. He, L. Wu et al., Classroom teaching behavior analysis method based on AI and its application. China Educ. Technol. **9**, 13–21 (2019)
11. Z. Luo, D. Zhang, Auto-evaluation of classroom teaching & learning and its preliminary research findings. Mod. Educ. Technol. **28**(8), 38–44 (2018)

Chapter 21
A Survey of Automated Essay Scoring System Based on Naive Bayes Classifier

Chen Liang, Bo Zhang, Xiaoyang Gong, Menglin Li, Hui Guo, and Rui Li

Abstract Most language exams have requirements for testing candidates' writing ability, such as CET-4 and CET-6. However, large-scale manual scoring requires a lot of manpower, material resources, and time costs, and it also has some unfairness due to the subjective preference of the scoring teacher. To solve the problem, natural language processing (NLP) has attracted more and more attention, and its application-automated essay scoring (AES) has been developed, using NLP technology instead of manual labor. The AES system is reviewed in the paper and the principle of the commonly used classifier 'Naive Bayes Classifier' is described.

Keywords Automated essay scoring · bayesian classifier · natural language processing · text categorization

21.1 Introduction

Natural language processing is a discipline including computer science, artificial intelligence, linguistics, etc. and can be traced back to 1940s, when scholars created conjectures and preliminary theories and generated two different directions based on rules and basic probability, respectively [1, 2]. In 1960s, NLP made a great progress, and came to a relatively mature stage in 1980s. Until 1990s, the era of early manual definition of rules to classify text was ended, the appearance of machine translation provides new solutions and it gradually changes early rules of classifying

C. Liang · B. Zhang (✉) · M. Li · H. Guo · R. Li
Tianjin Key Laboratory of Wireless Mobile Communications and Power Transmission, College of Electronic and Communication Engineering, Tianjin Normal University, Tianjin 300387, China
e-mail: b.zhangintj@tjnu.edu.cn

X. Gong (✉)
Faculty of Education, Tianjin Normal University, Tianjin 300387, China
e-mail: xgong@tjnu.edu.cn

247

texts manually. With the development of NLP, its application AES has attracted more and more attention. In [3], a large-scale PEG (Project Essay Grade) was described for more efficient essay scoring, followed by an intelligent essay assessor (IEA) system based on latent semantic analysis technology. In [4], Electronic Essay Rater (E-Rater) created in the late 1990s was reviewed, and it has been used for TOEFL essay scoring since 2005. In [5], an AES system "IntelliMetricTM" based on artificial intelligence (AI) was reviewed. Based on probability theory, the Bayesian Essay Test Scoring sYstem (BETSY) was described in [6, 7], and essays were divided into four levels: unqualified, qualified, good, and excellent.

The remaining part of this paper is structured as follows. A review of AES system is given in Sect. 21.2. Its core classification technology Naive Bayes Classifier is described in Sect. 21.3, with conclusions drawn in Sect. 21.4.

21.2   Review of automatic essay scoring system

As shown in Fig. 21.1, the flowchart of an AES system can be divided into the following five steps.

1. Text acquisition: Get the text by crawler or local import. In AES system, the obtained text is the student's essay.

2. Corpus pre-processing: Segment the text, remove modal particles and stop words, and mark each word with part-of-speech tagging. In AES system, deleting stop words and extracting roots are mainly used in this step. Stop word deletion is to delete a large number of prepositional pronouns from the feature set. Extracting root is to organize the similar words of the same root into one form.

3. Feature processing: Convert the words after word segmentation into a form that the computer can understand and calculate, generally represented in a mathematical vector form. Here, we need to establish the correspondence between words and mathematical vectors. Bag of Word (BOW) and word vector models are two commonly used representation models, where the bag-of-words model puts each word in a set, and counts the number of occurrences without considering the order of words, while the word vector model converts words into a vector matrix. At present, the most commonly used is one-hot encoding technology, but it cannot reflect the relevance between words. Word embedding technology can well express the similarity and relevance between words and solve this problem. The American company Google created a Word2vec word embedding tool, which includes two training models: Skip-Gram Model (SGM) and Continuous Bag-of-Words (CBOW).

4. Model training: Different algorithms can be selected for different purposes and application scenarios. Here, we have machine learning model algorithms, including naive Bayes, proximity algorithms, logistic regression, and deep learning algorithms, including convolutional neural networks, recurrent neural networks, etc.

5. Model evaluation: After the model is established, certain tests and evaluations need to be carried out to judge the pros and cons of the algorithm.

21.3   Principle of Naive Bayes Classifier

Classifier can specifically assign the data in the database to a certain category according to the characteristics of the data, which can be used for data prediction. In this section, we introduce Bayesian classifier, a general term for a class of classification algorithms based on Bayes' theorem. Equation 21.1 is known for Bayesian formula calculating $P(B|A)$ based on the known conditional probability $P(A|B)$. Suppose event B is divided into $B_1, B_2, \ldots, B_n$, then for any event A, we have

$$P\left(B_i \mid A\right) = \frac{P\left(B_i\right) P\left(A \mid B_i\right)}{\sum_{j=1}^{n} P\left(B_j\right) P\left(A \mid B_j\right)} \tag{21.1}$$

Naive Bayes Classifier (NBC) is the most common classification method in Bayesian classifiers, and is a supervised learning algorithm. The feature conditions are independent of each other, and the essence is to compare the probability of a certain text in different types of text libraries; in other words, by calculating the joint probability distribution of several feature words from this text in different types of text databases, we identify the text library with the greatest possibility of text occurrence and determine the most likely text category.

The following Eq. 21.2 used in NBC algorithm shows the probability of the text with the characteristic words $w_1, \ldots, w_d$ belonging to the category c_i $(i \in [1, n])$. Here we suppose d characteristic words are in the text represented by $W = [w_1, \ldots, w_j, \ldots, w_d]$ with n categories represented by $c = [c_1, \ldots, c_i, \ldots, c_n]$, then the joint probability distribution of multiple feature words is given by

$$
\begin{aligned}
P\left(c_i \mid W\right) &= \frac{P\left(\mathbf{c}_i\right) P\left(W \mid c_i\right)}{P(W)} = \frac{P\left(\mathbf{c}_i\right) P\left(w_1, \ldots, w_d \mid c_i\right)}{P(W)} \\
&= \frac{P\left(c_i\right) P\left(w_1 \mid c_i\right) \cdots P\left(w_j \mid c_i\right) \cdots P\left(w_d \mid c_i\right)}{P(W)} \\
&= \frac{P\left(c_i\right)}{P(W)} \prod_{j=1}^{d} P\left(w_j \mid c_i\right)
\end{aligned}
\tag{21.2}
$$

21.4   Conclusions

In this paper, automated essay scoring system was reviewed and its core classification technology Naive Bayes Classifier was briefly described. With the development of natural language processing, its application-AES system is becoming more and more popular, since the new technology can reduce the workload of teachers, eliminate the difference caused by subjective differences of teachers and can make the essay scoring process more fair.

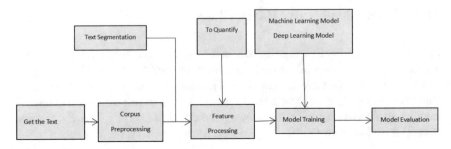

Fig. 21.1 The flowchart of an AES system

References

1. L. Yang, Y. Wu, J. Wang, Y. Liu, Xun huan shen jing wang luo yan jiu zong shu [summary of recurrent neural network research]. J. Comput. Appl. **38**(S2), 1–6+26 (2018)
2. H. Liu, T. Zhang, P. Wu, G. Yu, Zhi shi zhui zong zong shu [overview of knowledge tracking]. J. East China Normal Univ. (Nat. Sci.) **05**, 1–15 (2019)
3. X. Chen, S. Zhu, Zi dong zuo wen ping fen yan jiu zong shu [summary of research on automatic essay scoring]. J. PLA Univ. Foreign Lang. **05**, 78–83 (2008)
4. M. Liang, Q. Wen, Wai guo zuo wen zi dong ping fen xi tong ping shu ji qi shi [overview and enlightenment of comments on automatic scoring system of foreign essays]. Technol. Enhanced For. Lang. Educ. **5**, 18–24 (2007)
5. N. Han, Ji ge ying yu zuo wen zi dong ping fen xi tong de yuan li yu ping shu [principles and comments on several automatic scoring systems for english essays]. J. China Exam. **3**, 38–44 (2009)
6. J. Tang, Betsy zai zi dong zuo wen ping fen zhong de yuan li yu ying yong [principle and application of betsy in automatic essay scoring]. Contemp. For. Lang. Stud. **01**, 48–51+66 (2011)
7. K. He, Ji yu zi ran yu yan chu li de wen ben fen lei yan jiu yu ying yong [research and application of text classification based on natural language processing]. Ph.D. dissertation, Nanjing University of Posts and Telecommunications (2020)

Chapter 22
Curriculum Reform and Exploration Under the Background of Artificial Intelligence and New Engineering

Baoju Zhang, Jin Zhang, Cuiping Zhang, and Youchen Sun

Abstract College courses play a fundamental role in cultivating high-quality talents. With the rapid development of artificial intelligence technology, the existing engineering curriculum knowledge system and teaching methods can no longer meet the needs of talent training, so this paper selects the School of Electronics and Communication Engineering of Tianjin Normal University as the research object, and actively explores and tries from four aspects: teaching content, teaching form, teaching methods and evaluation methods. Teaching adds artificial intelligence content; adds extended experimental content; uses heuristic, inquiry, and group discussion teaching methods; combines online and offline, uses online software to assist teaching, and uses WeChat groups for teacher-student interaction, Use artificial intelligence technology for data analysis, and arrange assignments according to the learning situation; conduct teacher-student mutual evaluation through software. Teaching practice shows that the exploration of curriculum teaching under the background of "artificial intelligence + new engineering" improves the quality of teaching, and provides theoretical and practical basis for cultivating new engineering talents.

Keywords Artificial intelligence · New Engineering Course · Teaching Reform

B. Zhang (✉) · J. Zhang · C. Zhang (✉) · Y. Sun
College of Electronic and Communication Engineering, Tianjin Normal University, Tianjin 300387, China
e-mail: wdxyzbj@163.com

C. Zhang
e-mail: zcptjnu@163.com

Tianjin Key Laboratory of Wireless Mobile Communications and Power Transactions, Tianjin Normal University, Tianjin 300387, China

22.1   Introduction

The new engineering course is based on the new requirements of national strategic development, international competition situation, and new requirements of Lide to cultivate people, that is, to respond to changes and shape the future as the construction concept, to cultivate diversified, innovative and applied talents [1]. Traditional curriculum teaching content and teaching methods can no longer meet the needs of current talent training. On the one hand, with the rapid development and widespread application of artificial intelligence in recent years, this has brought certain difficulties to the teaching of courses. It is necessary to formulate the important and difficult points of learning based on the actual development of the current situation and the latest technological research. On the other hand, artificial intelligence is empowering all walks of life, and education is no exception. In terms of teaching, learning, assessment, management and other aspects, artificial intelligence can make education diversified in form and content, so adopt appropriate The teaching method has become an important part of teaching in various colleges and universities [2] Teachers need to continuously summarize the experience, adjust and optimize teaching plans, accelerate the construction of a comprehensive curriculum system such as academic research, innovation and practicality, and deliver excellent engineering and technical talents to the society [3].

22.2   Current Situation of Curriculum

New engineering courses generally include two parts: theoretical teaching and experimental teaching. Taking the course "Video Signal Fundamentals and Applications" as an example, theoretical learning mainly includes visual characteristics and the principle of three primary colors, the basic principles of TV image transmission, the principle of analog color TV, the principle of digital TV video compression and coding, the principle of digital TV transmission and digital TV The receiving principle. Experimental teaching is mainly related to theoretical teaching. Through the practical operation, students will deepen their understanding of the knowledge taught in the classroom and exercise their practical skills.

In terms of theoretical teaching, engineering courses mostly adopt task-driven teaching methods. While teaching in class, some learning tasks will be assigned to supervise students to complete. In the process of completing tasks, groups are usually used as a unit, which not only enables students to learn knowledge, but also cultivates students' ability to collaborate in groups. Students focus on tasks and analyze, discuss, and solve problems in the process of completing tasks [4]. In terms of practical teaching, experimental cases related to theoretical teaching are often used to help students understand abstract concepts more deeply and master knowledge better.

Compared with traditional teaching methods, the current teaching methods have made great progress, but there are still some problems in the teaching process, which can be divided into the following four categories.

(1) The content is outdated and cannot keep up with the times. Textbook knowledge is limited and it is difficult to adapt to the current rapid development of science and technology. Especially in the field of computer and artificial intelligence, the updated speed of course teaching content generally lags behind the speed of the development of frontier knowledge of the subject, which seriously restricts the improvement of the quality of talent training.

(2) The teaching model is old and single. The traditional teaching model is mainly based on the teacher's teaching, the process is relatively monotonous, lacks practical application, the teaching effect is average, and it is difficult to adapt to the current social development.

(3) Experiments are mostly confirmatory experiments, which are not attractive and challenging to students. Engineering courses are courses that focus on practical applications. In addition to theoretical teaching, practical teaching is also very important. However, confirmatory experiments will make students have a poor sense of experience and are not conducive to exerting students' autonomy.

(4) The form of assessment and evaluation is single. Students usually do not take the initiative to review, they only make surprise reviews before the exam, and the knowledge is quickly forgotten after the exam. The source of teacher evaluation is limited and limited to local peer teacher evaluation, which is not conducive to teaching reform.

22.3 Teaching Reform

Engineering courses cover rich types of knowledge, complex content, and abstract concepts. Students generally feel that it is difficult to learn. Therefore, the use of appropriate and effective teaching methods is particularly important for stimulating students' interest in learning, helping students to effectively master the knowledge they have learned, and cultivating learning ability and innovative thinking. With the advancement of science and technology, teaching methods have been updated and improved. Especially the rapid development of artificial intelligence nowadays provides more possibilities for the improvement of teaching methods. We can integrate artificial intelligence technology into classroom teaching, solve some problems in traditional teaching methods, and improve teaching quality.

22.3.1 Teaching Content Optimization

With the rapid development of information technology, textbooks and teaching materials can no longer fully meet the needs, so it is necessary to innovate the teaching content. In the actual teaching process, the proportion of teaching of new technologies will be appropriately increased, and the development of related technologies will be tracked and reflected in the teaching content. At present, artificial intelligence is a research hotspot of machine learning, so in practice teaching, it is necessary to combine artificial intelligence-based algorithms with traditional algorithms for learning and comparison, inspiring students to further research.

Experimental teaching can fully stimulate students' interest in learning and exercise their hands-on ability. In view of the problems of simple implementation and lack of challenges in the current experiments, additional experiments related to the course content are added. Students can independently choose related topics for research, such as using convolutional neural for video image registration and deep learning for pedestrian gait detection, Vehicle type recognition, etc. It is realized as a group to improve students' ability to find and solve problems in the process of realization, which can stimulate students' sense of innovation and increase their enthusiasm for learning.

22.3.2 Teaching Form Reform

The traditional teaching method is limited to offline, with teachers as the main body, completing the teaching through the teacher's teaching method, which is not conducive to stimulating students' interest in learning. Therefore, the new teaching method will take students as the main body, adopt artificial intelligence-based online and offline teaching methods, and teach through heuristic, inquiry, and group discussions.

(1) Take students as the main body. Colleges and universities should regard students as the main body in the cultivation of new engineering talents, be guided by their needs and interests, give students a certain degree of freedom, mobilize students' enthusiasm, increase their interest in majors, and enhance students' learning and innovation capabilities.

(2) Heuristic and inquiry teaching mode. In order to deepen students' mastery of various knowledge points, the designed cases and questions can be sent to students in advance, and through classic case analysis, explanation and discussion, students' interest in learning can be stimulated and students can be inspired to further research. According to the degree of difficulty of teaching, multi-level teaching is carried out, from easy to difficult, to guide students to actively think and explore.

(3) Adopt a group discussion mode. In the classroom, students are arranged scientifically and reasonably to discuss and interact with teachers and students, fully mobilize the enthusiasm of students, let students participate, and activate the classroom atmosphere. Group students with different interests to complete different experiment contents, and improve students' ability to learn independently and collaborate with others.

(4) Pay attention to practical teaching. The practical activities of engineering courses are indispensable. In order to ensure the quality of education, practical teaching must be emphasized. On the one hand, the teacher designs experimental courses related to theoretical teaching in the course; on the other hand, the school should enhance the openness of the laboratory, so that students can obtain experimental venues and experimental facilities when they need experiments, so as to promote students' Cultivation of independent practice and independent exploration spirit [5].

22.3.3 Teaching Method Reform

The new teaching method uses artificial intelligence-based online and offline teaching methods, as shown in Fig. 22.1, using artificial intelligence technology and online software to assist teaching to help students better learn and master knowledge.

Before the class, the teacher can conduct targeted learning, not only can learn the knowledge and teaching methods that need to be taught, and continuously improve the teaching content and teaching methods, but also understand the latest research progress in the field, and insert cutting-edge technologies into the course teaching process. Teachers send the knowledge that needs to be previewed to students through WeChat groups in advance, which can be online classrooms, encyclopedia links, video pictures, PPT files, PDF files, etc., in various forms, which fully stimulate students' interest in learning. Students learn independently through software and use big data technology to learn relevant knowledge efficiently. Preview the test before the software release class, and understand the student's preview situation through the background data analysis.

In class, the entire teaching environment is carried out with the Internet. The software can provide teachers with richer teaching methods, and can arbitrarily call a large number of high-quality learning resources in the background, and show them to students in various forms. The abstract and difficult concepts in teaching can be displayed through animation and other means to help students understand. For new

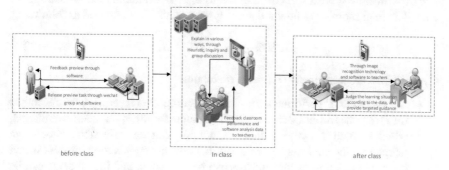

Fig. 22.1 Teaching methods in the context of artificial intelligence

ideas or questions generated by teachers and students during class, you can directly search and answer them.

After class, use software to collect students' daily learning situation and data generated in the process of completing homework, use artificial intelligence technology to analyze data, accurately understand the mastery of each student's knowledge points, predict student performance, and assign homework in a targeted manner, To achieve the effect of teaching students in accordance with their aptitude. At the same time, students use the software to check for leaks. Through the knowledge point test, the software will judge the knowledge points that the students have not mastered based on the data generated, and enable students to conduct targeted reviews through push explanations or test questions.

At the same time, image recognition technology can also be used to further improve teaching efficiency. Students can take pictures of textbook content or homework questions on their mobile phones, analyze photos and texts, and display the corresponding points and difficulties. Use software to submit homework, use image recognition technology to judge the homework submitted by students and generate data feedback to the teacher. The teacher can analyze the extracted information and data to have a clear understanding of the student's learning mastery.

22.3.4 Evaluation Method Reform

Effective teaching management is an important component of course teaching. Teaching management mainly includes assessment of student learning and mutual evaluation of teachers and students. Traditional student assessment methods focus on the final grades and results, and have a certain degree of contingency. Therefore, in the final assessment, we must not only pay attention to the final result, but also the process.

This course adopts the evaluation method of combining theoretical learning with experimental innovation, and determines the final score S in the form of weighted average, mainly including the performance score in class S1, accounting for 30%; The experimental score S2, accounting for 40%; Final evaluation S3, accounting for 30%. The final score s is a hundred point system, which is composed as follows:

$$S = S_1 \times 30\% + S_2 \times 40\% + S_3 \times 30\% \tag{22.1}$$

(1)   Classroom performance score S1 evaluation

Assess students' performance in class, including attendance a1, which accounts for 20%; classroom Q&A a2, which accounts for 40%; innovation ability a3, which accounts for 40%. In this way, not only can the professional knowledge learned by the students be evaluated, but also the cooperation awareness and class participation of the students can be evaluated, and the students can be inspected in many aspects.

$$S_1 = a_1 \times 20\% + a_2 \times 40\% + a_3 \times 40\% \qquad (22.2)$$

(2) Experimental score S2 evaluation

According to the students' learning attitude, completion degree, and innovation ability in the experiment process, the student's performance is evaluated, specifically including experimental verification b1, accounting for 30%; extended experiment b2, accounting for 40%; experimental report b3, accounting for 30%. The experiment includes basic experiments and extended experiments. The extended experiment takes the group as a unit. The students can choose the subjects they are interested in and study the practice. In the process of practice, they can exercise the ability to find and solve problems. The final experimental results should not only consider whether to achieve, but also consider the difficulty of the subject and the process performance of students.

$$S_2 = b_1 \times 30\% + b_2 \times 40\% + b_3 \times 30\% \qquad (22.3)$$

(3) Final test S3 evaluation

The final assessment mainly consists of two parts: the group semester summary c1 and the final exam c2, which account for 30% and 70% respectively.

$$S_3 = c_1 \times 30\% + c_2 \times 70\% \qquad (22.4)$$

Teachers and students can evaluate each other through software. On the one hand, the teacher puts forward different evaluations for different students, which helps students fully understand themselves and further improve, so as to teach students in accordance with their aptitude. On the other hand, students' evaluation of teachers can enable teachers to fully understand students' needs and learning conditions and further improve teaching methods.

22.4 Teaching Practice Process

The central idea of the organization and implementation is "student-centered, independent experiment, intelligent and efficient". The teaching method uses heuristic, inquiry, and group discussion methods; the teaching organization form is online + offline based on artificial intelligence. In the classroom, teachers provide students with corresponding teaching resources for further study and absorption, highlight the central position of students, mobilize students' learning enthusiasm, and enhance the effectiveness of course teaching. Through the teaching reform, the teaching concept has been transformed from knowledge instillation to the combination of self-inquiry and learning ability; the teaching method has been transformed from a single form of teaching to diversified methods; the teaching evaluation has been transformed from a single evaluation to an intelligent evaluation. By combining the curriculum with artificial intelligence, the challenge of the curriculum is improved, and the learning ability of the students, the construction of the curriculum connotation and the quality of the curriculum are improved.

Through teaching, students apply the content learned in class to extracurricular scientific and technological activities to obtain rewards. For example, in an electronic design competition, students use the theoretical knowledge and practical experience learned in class to design a combination of software and hardware, and obtain A good result. And because of the study of this course, students have developed a strong interest in image and video research. Through the expansion of artificial intelligence content in the classroom and the application of artificial intelligence technology, students have a preliminary understanding of artificial intelligence and current development in my country, and express that they want to continue to study this topic. This fully demonstrates the effectiveness of the teaching reform of this course, and encourages teachers to further study the teaching content and teaching methods, and strive to cultivate high-quality talents.

22.5 Summary and Outlook

The current rapid development of artificial intelligence will continue to affect education reform and become an important auxiliary force for education. The personalization achieved by artificial intelligence will make full use of teaching resources, so as to teach students in accordance with their aptitude and keep pace with the times. In response to the rapid development of artificial intelligence technology and the needs of countries and industries, this article improves the "Video Signal Fundamentals and Applications" course from four aspects: teaching content, teaching form, teaching methods, and evaluation methods. After trying, improved teaching The method works well. The online and offline teaching based on artificial intelligence technology is student-centered, which fully stimulates students' interest in learning, broadens students' horizons, and enhances students' practical and innovative abilities.

In the future, the use of artificial intelligence technology can also achieve matching between peer teachers. Artificial intelligence will intelligently screen and match teachers across the country based on grades, subjects, teaching content, etc. After the matching is successful, online communication and teaching demonstrations can be carried out. Through the demonstration, peer teachers will give their opinions and evaluations based on the teaching effect. This not only avoids the embarrassment of putting forward opinions face-to-face, but also makes the acquisition of suggestions no longer limited to regional restrictions, and promotes the exchange and development of subject teaching. With the continuous development of artificial intelligence, education has gradually become intelligent.

Acknowledgements This work was supported in part by the Second Batch of New Engineering Research and Practice Projects of Ministry of Education under Grant E-DZYQ20201408, and in part by the School-level Key Teaching Reform of Tianjin Normal University under Grant JGZD01219013

References

1. X. Shuangyun, H. Rumei, C. Chunling, Research and practice on the cultivation of innovative applied talents of mathematical modeling under the background of new engineering subjects [c]. shenyang municipal committee of the communist party of China, Shenyang Municipal People's Government, in *Proceedings of the 17th Shenyang Academic Annual Conference. Shenyang Municipal Committee of the Communist Party of China, Shenyang Municipal People's Government: Shenyang Science and Technology Association*, 2020(3), pp. 1609–1611
2. W. Ping, Yu. Shao, W. Yang, Li. Qiang, Teaching framework and experimental platform construction of antenna design course for electronic information engineering majors. J. Changchun Norm. Univ. **39**(10), 21–28 (2020)
3. H. Yujing, H. Li, Research on cultivating innovative talents of new engineering disciplines in practical teaching in comprehensive universities [C]. Fujian Business Association. South China Education Informatization Research Experience Exchange Conference 2021 Paper Collection (5). Fujian Provincial Business Association: Fujian Provincial Business Association, 2021(3), pp. 25–27
4. J. Zhao, Exploration of artificial intelligence curriculum teaching reform under the background of new engineering. Comp. Knowl. Technol. **16**(33), 111–112+127 (2020)
5. H. Chen, F. Feng, S. Liu, Create online and offline hybrid electrical courses experimental teaching courses under the background of new engineering disciplines [C]. Fujian Business Association, in *South China Education Informatization Research Experience Exchange Conference 2021 Paper Collection (3). Fujian Provincial Business Association: Fujian Provincial Business Association*, 2021(4), pp.77–80

Chapter 23
Dynamics, Hot Spots and Future Directions of Educational Research in the Intelligent Era

Libao Wu, Mingxue Jiang, Qing Du, Zheng Jiang, and Yongjian Zhang

Abstract With the rapid development of Artificial Intelligence (AI) technologies, the third round of development boom in AI has come, and its integration and application in education have also acquired new opportunities to develop. Using the software CiteSpace, this study adopted literature analysis and a scientific knowledge map to analyze 749 articles concerning educational research in the intelligent era. The results revealed the dynamics and hot spots of the existing studies in three aspects: (1) the application of deep learning in education, (2) the application of AI technologies in education, (3) the development of educational informatization, and (4) new forms of future education. Future directions relevant to teaching, learning, and evaluation are also raised accordingly: intelligent personalized learning to develop innovative talents, intelligent machine teaching to promote changes in teachers' roles, and intelligent evaluation to explore professional indices.

Keywords Artificial Intelligence · Deep learning · Intelligent education · Scientific knowledge map

23.1 Introduction

With the third round of development of Artificial Intelligence (AI), 2017 marks the first year of it. Following computational intelligence, perceptual intelligence, and cognitive intelligence, AI research and relevant industrial innovation have acquired various support from different fields, such as the research and innovation on brain science and deep learning, the product development and iteration relevant to automatic driving and intelligent medical treatment, and the formulation and promulgation of government documents [1]. As a representation of AI and education, the deep integration of cutting-edge technologies, such as intelligent speech recognition, computer vision, machine learning, and other AI technologies, has gradually

L. Wu · M. Jiang · Q. Du (✉) · Y. Zhang
Faculty of Education, Tianjin Normal University, Tianjin 300387, China

Z. Jiang
Mathematics & Science College, Shanghai Normal University, Shanghai 200234, China

© The Author(s), under exclusive license to Springer Nature Singapore Pte Ltd. 2021
W. Wang et al. (eds.), *Artificial Intelligence in Education and Teaching Assessment*,
https://doi.org/10.1007/978-981-16-6502-8_23

changed the new ecology of future education. "AI + Education" has increasingly attracted researchers' attention. This paper conducted bibliometrics and visual analysis of relevant literature on educational research in the intelligent era and revealed the dynamics, hot spots, and trends of the existing studies. Some future directions pertinent to this field were also proposed.

23.2 Methods

23.2.1 Strategy for the Literature Search

The CNKI academic journal database and "AI * Education" as search terms were used to retrieve relevant literature. In addition, targeted journals were required to be included in "A Guide to the Core Journal of China" and "Chinese Social Sciences Citation Index (CSSCI)", and the publication date of articles were needed to range from January 2000 to July 2021. A total of 1040 articles were retrieved firstly. After literature reading and screening, conference information, notice, and many other articles irrelated to AI and education were removed. Finally, 749 valid articles were included for analysis. After eliminating repeated authors and keywords, 1271 authors and 1770 keywords were identified (see Table 23.1).

Table 23.1 Publication dates, authors, and keywords of 749 articles

Year	Author	Keywords	Number of articles	Year	Author	Keywords	Number of articles
2001	1	3	1	2012	3	13	1
2002	9	16	6	2013	0	0	0
2003	4	15	3	2014	16	24	6
2004	5	8	2	2015	5	14	3
2005	9	16	5	2016	15	30	7
2006	4	14	3	2017	89	100	30
2007	11	23	5	2018	224	420	128
2008	14	23	8	2019	393	563	204
2009	6	16	4	2020	411	603	213
2010	5	16	4	2021	236	373	114
2011	6	10	2	Total	1271	1770	749

23.2.2 Data Analysis Methods

To better understand the application and development of education in the intelligent era, scientific knowledge map and bibliometrics analysis of relevant literature were conducted with the visualization software Citespace 5.7.R5 which was developed by Professor Chen Meichao [2]. These methods could intuitively present changing trends in the number of publications, distribution of authors and research institutions, and hot spots in educational research on AI.

23.3 Dynamics in Educational Research in the Intelligent Era

23.3.1 Changes in the Annual Number of Articles

Analyzing the annual number of published articles helps understand development stages and changing trends of research on AI and education. As shown in Fig. 23.1, the number of AI-related publications in education experienced a trend from gentle fluctuation to rapid growth between 2001 and 2021. In and before 2016, the annual number of published articles fluctuated between 0 and 10, which indicates an exploratory stage of AI technology. After 2016, with research perspectives and AI and big data strategies being various, an increasing number of AI-related educational research has been conducted. As described in Fig. 23.1, the annual number of published articles peaked in 2020 (i.e., 213), while it also achieved 114 in July 2021. A total of 531 papers have been published between 2019 and July 2021, accounting for 70.89% of the total. This phenomenon indicates that AI educational research is experiencing rapid development like a raging fire in mainland China.

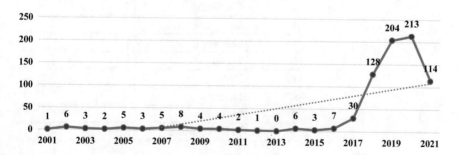

Fig. 23.1 The annual distribution of literature quantity

23.3.2   Analysis of Study Authors

The core authors of literature research mainly referred to those researchers who played an essential role in the relevant field. For example, their research directions were the focus of the area. According to Price's Law [3], the minimum number of papers m_p equals 0.749 $\sqrt{n_{pmax}}$ where $n_{p\,max}$ is the maximum number of papers published by a certain author in the analyzed literature. If the number of an author's articles is identical or larger than m_p, the author is called core author. After analysis, it was found that Ren Youqun published the largest number of articles (i.e., 9) during the period from 2001 to 2021. Therefore, authors who published three or more papers can be considered as the core authors. In total, 83 authors published more than three papers, accounting for 6.53% of the total number of authors. These results suggested that there has been no stable core group of authors in the field of AI education, and the top 10 authors are listed in Table 23.2.

It can be found through the research that those authors' collaboration relationship is weak. In other words, the top ten core authors seldom interacted or collaborated with each other. Moreover, their research directions in the same field are divergent. Similarly, most of the other researchers also published articles independently, with some exceptions. There were some existing collaboration groups. Ren Youqun's and Wan Kun's collaboration group paid more attention to the informatization development of basic education, while the collaboration group represented by Zhu Zhiting and Peng Hongchao focused more on the deep learning of the smart classroom. The collaboration group consisting of Liu Jin, Lv Wenjing, and other researchers took the evolution and trend of AI as their main research direction.

Table 23.2 Publications of core authors

Sort	Author	Number of articles
1	Ren Youqun	9
2	Gu Xiaoqing	8
3	Zhu Zhiting	7
4	Huang Ronghuai	7
5	Liu Bangqi	6
6	Liu Jin	6
7	Xu Ye	6
8	Liu Kai	6
9	Li Haifeng	6
10	Zhong Shaochun	6

23.3.3   Analysis of Research Institutions

The analysis of the collaboration between research institutions uncovered that a large number of publications were from universities, including the School of Education of Tianjin University, the School of Intelligent Education of Jiangsu Normal University, and the Faculty of Education of Beijing Normal University. The research institutions are widely distributed in mainland China. In addition, institutions with solid collaboration were generally in the same department or the same city. By contrast, there were few inter-provincial collaborations.

23.4   Research Hot Spots and Frontier Trends

23.4.1   Hot Spots of Educational Research in the Intelligent Era

Keywords of articles usually summarized full texts, indicating core research content. In this sense, the analysis and interpretation of keywords could provide insights into hot spot information in relevant research.

In Fig. 23.2, keywords are represented by the cross node in the graph. The larger the node is, the higher the occurrence frequency is, and the stronger the centrality is. As shown in Fig. 23.2, educational research from the perspective of AI mainly focuses on a variety of aspects, such as AI education, big data, intelligent education, future education, educational informatization, educational application, deep learning, educational technology, personalized learning, and so on. Combining co-occurrence of keywords with literature reviewing, this study found that hot spots of educational research in the intelligent era could be divided into the following four fields:

Fig. 23.2 Keywords co-occurrence map

(1) *Application of deep learning in education*

Deep learning, as an AI technology, has promoted the application of AI in various fields. In particular, it has enabled education to shift from the traditional way to an intelligent direction and facilitated the realization of educational reform [4]. Deep learning refers that drawing on existing knowledge, learners critically and actively learn new knowledge and process information deeply to build a new knowledge system and solve complex problems [5]. So far, the classic models of deep learning consist of Deep Belief Network (DBN), Convolutional Neural Network (CNN), and Recursive Neural Network (RNN), among which CNN and RNN have been widely applied to sentiment classification and language modeling.

During teaching and learning, deep learning can classify different kinds of data (e.g., images, speech, texts) and then apply them to educational data mining. The application of deep learning in the field of education mainly includes: (1) tracking and predicting students' learning and providing automatic feedback to improve teaching and its quality; (2) teaching aids based on deep learning; for example, MOOC learning platform can predict students' dropout rate and offer personalized learning resources according to students' conditions [6]; (3) making examination more convenient, such as automatic marking of compositions or mathematics and intelligent design of test items [7]. In the future, deep learning will further promote the rapid development of intelligent learning, intelligent examination, intelligent educational robot, and so on. On-going attention to deep learning will also benefit the integration and innovation of AI and education.

(2) *Application of intelligent technologies in education*

Technology empowers education, and education drives science and technology. The new generation of information technology, such as AI, big data, 5G, blockchain, educational robots, and virtual platforms, are important tools to support educational development and reform. For example, virtual platforms can promote public collaboration and communication as well as a realization of wisdom sharing [8]. Big data can provide reliable data support and diagnostic intervention for students' learning processes, learning outcomes, and evaluation. Moreover, AI technology can capture students' behaviors during the class, analyze their emotional states, and then alert them. In this intelligent era, supported by cutting-edge technologies represented by AI, intelligent campuses and intelligent society have acquired an overall development. These changes, in turn, create an environment for technological development. In summary, technological innovation and change definitely bring about educational innovation and change.

(3) *Development of educational informatization*

Generally, educational informatization has experienced three stages: (1) audition education in the embryonic period, (2) information technology education in the initial period, and (3) intelligent education in the present period. So far, information technology and education have been deeply integrated.

In particular, AI technology has facilitated the achievement of an intelligent teaching environment, diversified educational evaluation, and intelligent educational management [9]. The continuous development of information technology has promoted educational modernization effectively. AI technologies (e.g., big data) have played an important role in the new stage of educational informatization, and accurate, intelligent decision-making has gradually been identified as one of the characteristics in this stage [10]. With AI developing from computational intelligence, perceptual intelligence to cognitive intelligence, educational informatization has also become the core element of educational reform [11]. In the era of educational informatization, four types of efforts are necessary: (1) exploring a new model of education governance, (2) promoting the reform of education governance in the context of Internet + and big data, (3) ensuring the data security of the information environment, establish a standard, intelligent, and open education data system, and (4) opening a new era of intelligent education.

(4)   *New forms of future education*

In the context of the intelligent age, future education needs to realize the reform and innovation of education. The deep integration of technology and education can accelerate the reshaping of the future education form. At present, future education will be characterized as three new forms. The first one is flexible teaching and active learning. During the pandemic of COVID-19, online learning has been conducted widely, enabling learning at any time and place. Flexible teaching space and time have become a basic feature of future education [12]. In this case, to ensure effective curriculum implementation, learners need to have the ability to learn actively and participate in teaching activities positively. The second one is mobile online education. It refers that learning resources are obtained through mobile phones and other smart devices when the Internet network is available. This new form provides a new pathway for personalized learning and accelerates the development and integration of online education and offline education. The third one is 5G-based intelligent education. With the popularization of 5G technology, a variety of 5G application scenarios have emerged, such as 5G+VR virtual training, 5G+ smart classroom, 5G+ dual-teacher classroom, and so on [13]. In the future, supportive policies, innovative ideas, and new technologies will further promote smart education, shaping forms of future education together.

23.4.2 Evolution Trends of Educational Research in the Intelligent Era

The keyword time zone map (see Fig. 23.3) and the keyword information graph (see Fig. 23.4) present the evolution process of the existing studies and the changes in keywords.Based on the knowledge map and previous research, three stages of frontier topics were recognized in educational research on AI.

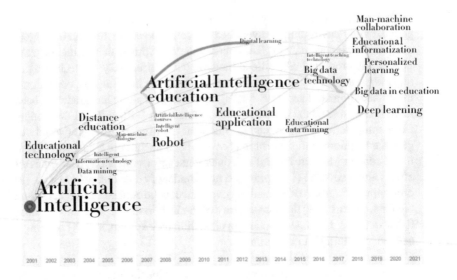

Fig. 23.3 Keyword time zone map

Top 10 Keywords with the Strongest Citation Bursts

Keywords	Year	Strength	Begin	End	2000 - 2021
Learning	2000	5.02	2001	2014	
Educational technology	2000	2.14	2002	2006	
Distance education	2000	5	2003	2008	
Robot	2000	3.46	2005	2014	
Knowledge engineering	2000	1.95	2005	2008	
Learning analysis	2000	3.33	2014	2018	
Big data in education	2000	2.78	2016	2018	
AI	2000	2.35	2017	2018	
Deep learning	2000	2.16	2017	2018	
Educational informationization	2000	2.98	2018	2019	

Fig. 23.4 Keyword information graph

(1) *Stage one: 2000–2005*

In this stage, "educational technology", "distance education", "data mining", and "intelligent" were the frontier keywords of the studies. In the 1980s and 1990s, machine learning had made some progress. For example, the supercomputer "Dark Blue" defeated the first-class chess player in the world. However, most people still believed that AI was rather far from their daily lives. At the beginning of the 21st century, technological exploration continued, and the big data set played an important role in machine learning. Many experts and scholars realized that enough data support could solve various problems, for instance, poor algorithm performance [14]. With the help of electronic communication technology and computer technology, distance education significantly affects education. However, due to the imperfect service system and teachers' and students' lack of network knowledge, educational informatization was faced with certain difficulties and challenges [15]. The application of AI in education was also explored continuously.

(2) *Stage two: 2006–2015*

In this stage, "Artificial Intelligence education", "robot", "educational application", and "big data technology" were the research frontier keywords. In 2006, Hinton proposed Deep Belief Network (DBN), the optimization problem of Deep Neural Network (DNN) was hence solved. With the continuous development of computer technology, the constant accumulation of data, and the optimization of DNN, researchers made great strides in deep learning. AI education was also developed. For example, relevant research shifted to robot teaching, AI-aided education, and other aspects. Intelligent robots were also entering the classroom, assisting education and teaching [16].

(3) *Stage three: 2016 to present*

"Deep learning", "personalized learning", "educational informatization", and "human-machine collaboration" are the research frontier keywords in this stage. In 2016, Google's AI program AlphaGo defeated the Go player Mr. Lee Sedol, the winner of 18 world titles, marking that AI had entered a new era. Following this, governments and departments worldwide issued a number of strategic plans and relevant documents [17]. With the rapid development of AI, the application scenario of AI in education is undergoing qualitative changes. Multiple technologies like deep learning and big data are being applied to teaching, learning, management, and assessment. Various AI products are produced successively and applied to different aspects of education. Taking advantage of teacher and machine teaching, human-machine collaborative education facilitates personalized teaching, constructs a smart campus and intelligent teaching environment, and integrates scale education with personalized education [18].

23.5 Future Directions

With the integration of AI and education, educational informatization has entered the era of intelligent education. Based on the analysis of current dynamics, hot spots, and evolution trends of educational research in the intelligent era, this study proposed future directions in three aspects: application of AI in learning, teaching, and evaluation.

23.5.1 Intelligent Personalized Learning to Develop Innovative Talents

The U.S. Department of Education defines personalized learning as "instruction in which the pace of learning and the instructional approach are optimized for the needs of each learner" in the National Educational Technology Plan [19]. Historically, due to the limitation of the class teaching system, it is challenging to implement individualized learning to meet every learner's needs. However, the development and innovation of education and technologies (e.g., AI, big data) enables personalized pathways for individuals' learning. For instance, online education platforms can recommend appropriate learning content for learners through AI and big data technology, improving personalized experiences and learning quality [20]. In future classrooms, smart technologies and educational data will create a smart learning environment and eventually make personalized learning come true. Smart devices (e.g., camera and eye tracker) can offer real-time analysis and feedback relevant to learning. By contrast, as behavioral traces of learners, educational data can provide personalized feedback and guidance after intelligent analysis. Future education should follow this trend, promoting the development of learners and educational theories. With the support of the educational information ecosystem in the new era, it is essential to implement instruction that conforms to the natural learning process, provides personalized content, and cultivates innovation [21].

23.5.2 Intelligent Machine Teaching to Promote Changes in Teachers' Roles

With the continuous maturity of AI technology, machine learning and teaching have become one of the major trends of educational research in the intelligent era. The degree of intelligence and humanization of educational and teaching robots is getting higher and higher. In the future AI era, collaborative teaching between humans and machines will be the main trend, and their roles and tasks vary with stages [22]. In the stage of weak AI, the teacher plays a key role, while the machine works on simple imitations. In the stage of strong AI, both the teacher and machine are in charge of teaching, based on their expertise. In the stage of super AI, machines exceed that of human beings in terms of execution. Hence, machines are responsible for teaching knowledge, while teachers are responsible for educating people. In the age of AI, although machine teaching will not completely replace teachers, the teacher's traditional role cannot meet the needs of the intelligent era. Therefore, teachers are required to improve their professional literacy and re-position themselves. In the context of AI, massive educational resources owned by machines far exceed that of teachers. In this stage, instead of transmitting knowledge, teachers need to propose targeted suggestions to create a beneficial learning environment and select appropriate learning resources for students [23]. Although AI can provide some personalized services that teachers cannot do, it cannot give students emotional care. Therefore, teachers should make full use of their specialties and promote students' development together with AI.

23.5.3   Intelligent Evaluation to Explore Professional Indices

Classroom teaching evaluation with AI technology can promote changes in evaluation subject, evaluation content, evaluation mode, and evaluation result, providing precise suggestions for decision-making [24]. Speech recognition, facial recognition, and other technologies can be used to analyze and evaluate the language and behaviors of teachers and students in the teaching process, strengthening the feedback function of evaluation. In addition to the mastery of knowledge, intelligent education needs to focus on students' attitudes and emotions. AI and other technologies can analyze teachers' and students' emotions and interactions and establish harmonious teacher-student relationships. These AI technologies (e.g., data mining) can also afford the real-time situations and data of the classroom, replacing the traditional evaluation form (i.e., in-class observation) with intelligent evaluation. Apart from academic scores, the intelligent evaluation will fully capture classroom events, generate comprehensive evaluations, and provide prompt reports and personalized suggestions, with the support of big data technology. Emerging intelligent technologies will enrich evaluation methods, scientize evaluation process, and generate accurate evaluation results. Based on these, exploring a professional evaluation system and indices is essential to interpret the collected data quantitatively and facilitate the practical innovation of teaching evaluation in the intelligent era.

Acknowledgements This work was supported by the National Social Science Foundation of Education Key Project under Grant No. AFA170008, by Tianjin Philosophy and Social Science Planning Project under Grant No. TJJX17-016, by the Tianjin Science and Technology Planning Project under Grant No. 20JCYBJC00300, and by the National Natural Science Foundation of China under Grant No. 11404240.

References

1. W. Lv, L. Xu, J. Liu et al., A 10-year review of AI research in China—based on literature metrology and knowledge graph analysis from 2008 to 2017. Tech. econ. **37**(10), 73–38 (2018)
2. Y. Chen, C. Chen, Z. Liu, Z. Hu, X. Wang, Methodological functions of CiteSpace knowledge graph. Sci. Sci. Res. **33**(02), 242–253 (2015)
3. S. Zong, Evaluation of core authors based on Pryce law and composite Index method: a case study of chinese journal of science and technology. Chinese J. Sci. Technol. **27**(12), 1310–1314 (2016)
4. Y. Liu, Q. Li, C. Yu, Deep learning technology applications in education: current status and prospects [J]. Res. Open Educ. **23**(5), 113–120 (2017)

5. X. Wu, H. Zhang, C. Ni, Reflective deep learning: connotation and process [J]. Res. Audio-visual educ. **35**(12), 23–28, 33 (2014)
6. W. Xing, D. Du, Dropout prediction in MOOCs: using deep learning for personalized intervention. J. Educ. Comp. Res. **57**(3), 547–570 (2019)
7. D. Chen, Y. Zhan, B. Yang, Application analysis of deep learning technology in the field of educational big data mining. Res. Audio-visual Educ. **40**(2), 68–76 (2019)
8. C. Guan, C. Chen, X. An, The trend of educational innovation in the intelligent age and its enlightenment for future education. China Audio-visual Educ. **4**(7), 13–21 (2021)
9. X. Xing, New ideas of basic education information development towards intelligent education. Res. Audio-visual Educ. **41**(7), 108–113 (2020)
10. Y. Wang, Y. Li, D. Li et al., The situation analysis and prospect of the strategic planning of educational informationization in the fourteenth Five-year Plan. Modern Educ. Technol. **31**(6), 5–13 (2021)
11. Y. Meng, S. Wu, J. Wei, Current status, hot spots and trends of AI education research—based on data analysis of 1,043 AI education literatures from 1979 to 2019 [J]. Modern Edu. Technol. **30**(3), 120-123 (2020)
12. R. Huang, Y. Wang, H. Wang et al., New forms of teaching for future education: flexible teaching and active learning. Mod. Dist. Educ. Res. **32**(3), 3–14 (2020)
13. R. Huang, Y. Wang, Y. Jiao, Educational reform in the era of Intelligence—a proposition on the two-way empowerment of science and technology and education. China Audio-visual Educ. **4**(7), 22–29 (2021)
14. X. Feng, Y. Wang, Y. Wu, New developments in the application of AI in education. Mod. Educ. Technol. **28**(12), 5–12 (2018)
15. R. Huang, J. Sha, Reflections on the development of educational technology in China. China Audio-visual Educ. **4**(1), 5–11 (2005)
16. P. Zhang, Intelligent robot assisted education and its application. China Audio-visual Educ. **4**(2), 84–86 (2009)
17. H. Li, W. Wang, Research progress and hot spots in the international field of AI + education—also on the development strategy of AI + education in China. J Dist. Educ. **37**(2), 63–73 (2019)
18. R. Xiao, H. Xiao, J. Shang, AI and educational change: prospects, difficulties, and strategies. China Audio-visual Educ. **4**(4), 75–86 (2020)
19. U.S. Department of Education, Reimagining the role of technology in education: 2017 national education technology plan update. Washington, DC: U.S. Department of Education. Retrieved on July 30, 2021, from https://tech.ed.gov/files/2017/01/ NETP17.pdf (2021)
20. Y. Liu, B. Hu, X. Gu, What future of learning will AI bring: qualitative Meta-analysis based on core international education journals and development reports. Dist. Educ. China **4**(6), 25–34, 59 (2021)
21. X. Liu, R. Huang, From Knowledge to Wisdom: wisdom education from the perspective of real learning. China Audio-visual Educ. **4**(3), 14–20 (2016)
22. X. Zhang, X. Dong, Man-machine Symbiosis: the development trend of AI and its education. Res Audio-visual Educ. **41**(4), 35–41 (2020)
23. T. Zou, R. Kang, P. Tan, The role crisis and reconstruction of teachers in the era of AI. Contemp. Educ. Sci. **4**(6), 88–95 (2021)
24. L. Wu, Y. Cao, Y. Cao, The framework construction of AI—enabled classroom teaching evaluation reform and technology realization. China Audio-visual Educ. **4**(5), 94–101 (2021)

Chapter 24
"AI and Practice Teaching" Electronic Information Innovative Training Model in the Context of Exploring

Baoju Zhang, Man Wang, and Cuiping Zhang

Abstract As a frontier discipline of society, electronic information has a great demand for such innovative talents in national strategy and industry development. Higher education schools should continuously improve the capabilities of technological innovation, talent training and international cooperation and communication in the field of artificial intelligence, to promote higher-quality entrepreneurial employment for college graduates. This project is aimed at the background of "AI plus", with practical teaching as the central idea, through the establishment of an open and innovative laboratory platform, with diversified discipline competitions as the starting point, the use of information resources and artificial intelligence technology to organize discipline professional technical associations. Improve the innovative consciousness, practical ability and comprehensive quality of engineering students, explore the training mode of innovative talents in electronic information, and finally point out the results obtained under this mode, and provide new ideas for adapting to the development of the industry and the demand for innovative talents.

Keywords Artificial intelligence · Electronic information · Talent training

24.1 Introduction

In 2019, the "Notice on Implementing the "Double Ten Thousand Plan" for the Construction of First-Class Undergraduate Majors" [1] issued by the General Office of the Ministry of Education of the People's Republic of China pointed out the basic

B. Zhang (✉) · M. Wang · C. Zhang
Tianjin Key Laboratory of Wireless Mobile Communications and Power Transactions, Tianjin Normal University, Tianjin 300387, China
e-mail: wdxyzbj@163.com

C. Zhang
e-mail: zcptjnu@163.com

College of Electronic and Communication Engineering, Tianjin Normal University, Tianjin 300387, China

concept of continuous improvement of the practical teaching mechanism, strengthening of practical teaching, and improving the achievement of the goal of talent training. The eighth item in the "China Education Modernization 2035" [2] issued by the General Office of the State Council of the People's Republic of China in February 2019 also stated that "using modern technology to accelerate the reform of the talent training model and achieve the organic combination of large-scale education and individualized training" is an education governance plan. One of the effective paths of change. It further explains that the innovative talent training model should be combined with the "Artificial Intelligence" technology proposed in the "the 13th Five-Year Plan for Education Informatization", and implement the concept of taking students as the main body [3], focusing on practice, and aiming at success.

As one of the important supporting majors of engineering majors, the discipline of electronic information has a wide range of professional technology and knowledge, rapid product update, and new technologies and new applications emerge in an endless stream. It not only requires high qualifications and teaching levels of professional teachers [4], but also many large enterprises and companies have a large demand for this professional and innovative talent. Therefore, in the training of such applied innovative talents, colleges and universities should transform the training model, fully integrate with practice, and use subject competition as a carrier to cultivate students' innovative practical ability and promote professional development [5], using open and innovative experimental platforms. Organize and participate in diversified subject competitions, organize professional extracurricular clubs, conform to the development prospects of artificial intelligence technology, and comprehensively cultivate innovative talents in electronic information to adapt to industry development and changes in corporate needs. As shown below (Fig. 24.1).

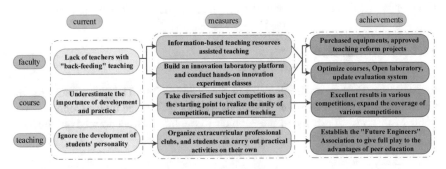

Fig. 24.1 Exploring the formation of the talent training model

24.2 Current Status of Traditional Talent Training

In the traditional engineering teaching process, it mainly revolves around classrooms, teaching materials, and teachers to complete the teaching goals [6, 7]. The main problems include the following three aspects:

24.2.1 In Terms of Teachers, There is a Lack of Teachers with "Back-Feeding" Teaching

Traditional engineering colleges and universities need not only solid theoretical knowledge, but also the practical teaching ability of scientifically using artificial intelligence technology and information technology to realize "back-feeding" teaching and the ability to solve practical problems. However, in engineering colleges, especially local colleges and universities, the lack of such dual-ability talents makes colleges and universities unable to satisfy the cultivation of innovative talents.

24.2.2 In Terms of Curriculum, the Importance of Development and Practice is Underestimated

In the context of the increasingly diversified curriculum of colleges and universities, colleges and universities have gradually realized the importance of practical courses in the cultivation of talents. However, in the traditional course teaching process, it is still a common situation to attach importance to theoretical teaching and despise practical teaching. A large proportion of basic knowledge teaching and lack of transitional courses that are progressive and adapt to the development of the information age. As a result, students who have a poor grasp of knowledge, are out of touch with the needs of social talents and have difficulties in finding employment after graduation.

24.2.3 Teaching Methods Ignore the Personality Development of Students

In 2018, the Ministry of Education released the "Action Plan for Artificial Intelligence Innovation in Higher Education Institutions" [8], In recent years, teaching methods have become increasingly diversified. Although there are applications of teaching methods such as group discussions and case teaching, the most common teaching method is theoretical indoctrination. It has failed to cater to the rapid development of the artificial intelligence era, and the demand for technical talents. In the classroom, teachers are still in a dominant position, leading to the neglect of the development of students' personality and the inability to give full play to individual initiative.

24.3 Methodology

"AI plus" is a kind of vitality that came into being after the introduction of artificial intelligence in the era of artificial intelligence, which is fully integrated with all walks of life and promotes the continuous change of economic patterns. It is the use of artificial intelligence technology and Internet platforms, information and communication technology, to integrate artificial intelligence with all walks of life, including traditional industries. Since the outbreak of the COVID-19 during the Spring Festival in 2020, artificial intelligence and Internet technologies have provided many conveniences for our epidemic life and solved many daily needs. t is the disruption and recombination of these mature technologies and the practice and development of new technologies that have made my country's economy the only country in the world with a positive growth trend under the epidemic. Giving full play to the role of "Artificial Intelligence" technology in society and strengthening practical teaching are not only an important part of improving the quality of innovative talents in colleges and universities, but also the cultivation of College Students' Innovative entrepreneurship and social responsibility.

24.3.1 Faculty Training Model

1. Build an innovative laboratory platform and conduct teaching models such as hands-on innovative experimental courses. In the current training program for engineering students, there are still problems that the curriculum is focused on theoretical professional courses and the practical links are weak. By adjusting the course evaluation system, with the help of innovative experimental platforms, adding open practice questions, adjusting the weights of experimental course assessment and experimental results evaluation, arousing students' enthusiasm for learning, and comprehensively improving students' practical ability.

2. Use information-based teaching resources to assist teaching. Make full use of professional advantages and the application status quo of modern "Artificial Intelligence" technology, introduce animation into the more difficult-to-understand course content system, and improve the intuitiveness of content understanding. Guide and give full play to the subjective initiative of students, encourage students to combine their own creativity to produce animations that are in line with the curriculum, help students understand the principles that are not easy to understand, and increase students' interest in learning and interest in active learning.

24.3.2 Course Optimization Model

Taking diversified subject competitions as the starting point, using competitions to promote training, competitions to promote teaching, and competitions to promote learning, to achieve the organic unity of competition, practice, and teaching. According to the basic professional level of the participating students, combined with the requirements of the subject competition and the current status of the development of "Artificial Intelligence" technology and the actual needs of society, professional basic training, professional improvement training and real-question training will be carried out. Encourage more students to actively participate in subject-related professional competitions and innovation and entrepreneurship competitions. At the same time, professional teachers are required to provide professional guidance and training to participating students to maximize their self-learning abilities.

24.3.3 Teaching Innovation Model

Organize extracurricular professional clubs, and students can carry out practical activities on their own. With the help of open laboratories, students can form a good style of study from " Make me to learn" to "I want to learn", strengthen the construction of the teaching staff, and increase the professional construction. Utilizing the advantages of peer education and the academic disciplines, outstanding students will give back to the lower grade students what they have learned in the laboratory for four years at the university, promote the talent training and selection plan, and stimulate the enthusiasm of the lower grade students for the electronics major.

24.4 Results and Discussions

24.4.1 Equipment, Course, System

1. The teaching team has successfully purchased "4G mobile communication system", "5G mobile communication test system" and other system equipments, which are exactly the same as the core network equipment used by operators such as China Mobile and China Unicom. By introducing the learning of this equipment into courses such as "Course Design of Communication Principles", students are required to complete the network architecture and configuration on the basis of actual equipment, providing students with opportunities to contact real communication networks. With a real experimental teaching system, the effect of experimental teaching is greatly improved. At the same time, relying on Tianjin International Union Center and Tianjin Key Laboratory, it can provide equipment such as laser plate making machine, 63 GHz high-end oscilloscope,

59 GHz spectrum analyzer, 128×128 array antenna, etc., which is convenient for students to engage in various practical learning. By reducing the proportion of closed-book exams at the end of the term, comprehensive evaluation will be carried out through various methods such as experimental courses and scientific research competitions to further enhance students' practical ability.

2. Relying on the "Exploration and Practice of OBE Model Artificial Intelligence Professional English Course Teaching Mode" teaching reform project, and "Exploration and Practice of International Innovative Talent Cultivation Model of Electronic Information Based on Outcome-Oriented Education Concept" new engineering exploration and research project, Curriculum reform and teaching integration were carried out, and the course "Professional English" was selected as the 2021 Tianjin University Curriculum Ideological and Political Demonstration Course.

24.4.2 Various Competitions Results

At present, the main subject competitions arranged to participate in are the "Internet plus" competition, the innovation and entrepreneurship competition, the national college student electronic design competition, the challenge cup, and the Tianjin college student electronic design competition. Later, we will depend on the condition of entry, and actively expand the entries, so that more students to enhance their professional practice from competition in order to become an innovative talent pool conditions necessary for society.

Under the background of the 2020 epidemic, college students will actively participate in the sixth "Internet plus" competition international track, giving full play to their professional advantages and the advantages of college personnel. Participating projects "Intelligent War Epidemic" System based on Pedestrian Retrieval", "Belters Health——Intelligent remote TCM diagnosis and treatment for "One Belt And One Road" countries" are based on the facts during the new coronavirus epidemic, combined with professional advantages and the national development strategy designed the "intelligent pedestrian detection" and "intelligent Chinese medicine diagnosis and treatment" systems, which won the national bronze award and the second prize of Tianjin City respectively; In addition, the 2020 Tianjin University Student Electronic Design Competition (TI Cup) won the second prize at the provincial and ministerial level.

24.4.3 "Future Engineers" Association

Now the electronics major of the college has organized the "Engineers of the Future" association, with the help of the college's open laboratory, making it a learning garden for students, enabling students to carry out practical activities independently.

At present, the Student Open Laboratory and the "Future Engineers" Association have jointly launched the "Nursery Project", using the advantages of peer education, outstanding students will give back to the junior students what they have learned in the laboratory for four years in the university, and give full play to their professional advantages, Combining Internet hotspot technologies, issues and social needs, to stimulate the enthusiasm of the junior students for the electronics major.

24.5 Conclusion

Higher engineering education, which occupies an important position in higher education in my country, is a solid foundation for building a strong engineering education country and deepening engineering education reform, exploring and optimizing the training of electronic information professionals, improving the level of engineering literacy of graduates, and serving and supporting my country's economy. The transformation and upgrading are of great significance.

However, with the increasing opening of society and the rapid development of new technologies, the training goals and training plans of traditional engineering education have exposed many problems, such as: students are weak in practical skills, unable to meet the needs of social development, shallow understanding of frontier knowledge, and slow updating of the knowledge structure. Propose the exploration of the training mode of innovative talents in electronic information under the background of " AI and practice teaching ", relying on the Internet background and artificial intelligence technology to fully understand the cutting-edge technology of society. With the help of the college's characteristic laboratory, balance the proportion of theoretical teaching and practical teaching, so that the teaching effect can be maximized, while stimulating students' enthusiasm for electronics majors, and better promoting students' overall development; Through the way of promoting training, teaching and learning through competitions, the students' practical ability can be stimulated to the greatest extent, and the innovative consciousness, comprehensive quality and practical ability of engineering students can be improved; Organize professional associations, use information resources and artificial intelligence technology, give full play to the subjective initiative of students, and combine the needs of industry development and enterprise development to better achieve the goal of training innovative talents in electronic information.

Acknowledgements This work was supported in part by the Second Batch of New Engineering Research and Practice Projects of the Ministry of Education under Grant E-DZYQ20201408, and in part by the School-level Key Teaching Reform Project of Tianjin Normal University under Grant JGZD01219013.

References

1. The General Office of the Ministry of Education of the People's Republic of China issued the "Notice on Implementing the "Double Ten Thousand Plan" for the Construction of First-class Undergraduate Majors". http://www.moe.gov.cn/srcsite/A08/s7056/201904/t20190409_377216.html
2. The Central People's Government of the People's Republic of China, the General Office of the State Council of the People's Republic of China issued the "China Education Modernization 2035". http://www.gov.cn/xinwen/2019-02/23/content_5367987.htm
3. M. Wang, X. Wang, H. Xin, J. Zhu, "Internet + Maker Education" Chain integrated teaching research and practice——taking electronic information specialty as an example[J]. China Inf. Technol. Educ. **2020**(Z4), 179–181 (2020)
4. N. Zhu, B. Song, J. He, H. Chen, C. Wang, Y. Li, The construction of a "golden course" of electronic information based on industry-university cooperation under the background of the "Double Ten Thousand Project"[J]. J. Higher Educ. **35**, 38–41 (2020)
5. L. Tong, Promoting teaching with competition, promoting learning with competition—exploration of the cultivation mode of college students' practical and innovative ability[J]. Technol. Wind **33**, 32–33 (2020)
6. L. Geng, W. Yang, Exploring the teaching mode of cultivating new engineering talents[J]. Heilongjiang Sci. **11**(09), 58–59 (2020)
7. S. Li, J. Yao, Analysis on the talent training path of engineering colleges under OBE theory[J]. Educ. Forum **22**, 78–79 (2020)
8. The Ministry of Education of the People's Republic of China, The Ministry of Education issued the "Action Plan for Artificial Intelligence Innovation in Higher Education Institutions". http://www.moe.gov.cn/srcsite/A16/s7062/201804/t20180410_332722.html

Chapter 25
Overview of Intelligent Tutoring System

Sen Li, Ying Tong, Simbarashe Tembo, and Baozhu Han

Abstract An intelligent tutoring system is an adaptive support system that uses artificial intelligence to allow computers to act as virtual tutors to impart knowledge to learners. How to better realize the application of artificial intelligence in education is a hot topic of current research. This article mainly discusses the basic framework of ITS (Intelligent Tutoring System), the trend of ITS and summarizes some suggestions for the future development of ITS.

Keywords Artificial intelligence · Education · ITS

25.1 Introduction

Intelligence Tutoring System (ITS) uses artificial intelligence to guide learners to acquire knowledge and skills without a human tutor. It was born in the early nineteenth century. With the development of cognitive science, computer science and technology, and educational science, it has been constantly updated and developed many representative systems. In the new century, with the development of complex computing, distributed cognition, pattern recognition, knowledge representation, natural language understanding, network computing and computer visualization, it is facing a new period of rapid development. In recent years, researchers in the field of artificial intelligence education have made many explorations in the perspective of principle, application mode and technology. At the application level, there are also many excellent intelligent tutoring systems and educational robots. However, AI education still faces many problems and challenges. Overall, the combination of AI and education is still in its infancy.

Research on ITS abroad has a history of more than 30 years and is relatively mature. Many countries and regions, such as the United States, the United Kingdom, Canada, Europe, and Japan, attach great importance to the research, development and application of ITS. They have invested a lot of manpower and financial resources, and

S. Li · Y. Tong (✉) · S. Tembo · B. Han
Tianjin Key Laboratory of Wireless Mobile Communications and Power Transmission, Tianjin Normal University, Tianjin 300387, China
e-mail: tongying2334@163.com

© The Author(s), under exclusive license to Springer Nature Singapore Pte Ltd. 2021
W. Wang et al. (eds.), *Artificial Intelligence in Education and Teaching Assessment*,
https://doi.org/10.1007/978-981-16-6502-8_25

have established a large number of ITS-related research institutions and academic publications. Compared with developed countries, China's research in the field of ITS started late. The research work is mainly carried out in a few universities and research institutions, and the results are mostly "demonstration" systems. There are not many systems that have been deployed for teaching practice.

Most international research in the field of education technology integrate artificial intelligence technologies such as machine learning, problem solving, logical reasoning, natural language processing, automatic programming, expert system, pattern recognition, machine learning, data mining in ITS for teaching, learning, and decision-making. The system supports to build learning situation, standardize learning behavior, promote learning participation, provide learning support, evaluate academic level and ability structure, formulate personalized learning path and content, etc. It aims to help teachers to support differentiated teaching, improve teaching effect, optimize teaching mode and path. According to the individual specific situation, difficulties and needs, the system provides personalized learning services. These research results provide methodological guidance and research paradigms for us to develop artificial intelligence teaching products.

However, it is not difficult to find that the performance and application scope of artificial intelligence tutoring system are still far from people's expectations, and there are narrow and fragmented problems. It is necessary to pay attention to diversified application situations, change the application status of artificial intelligence tutoring centered on teaching, practice and testing, so as to avoid artificial intelligence becoming a tool to simply strengthen exam-oriented education. The research on the application of artificial intelligence tutoring is mostly located in a specific aspect of teaching or learning, such as text evaluation, learning ability structure evaluation, adaptive and personalized learning system, etc., which ignores the improvement and development of learners' overall quality, the research of human–computer collaborative teaching mechanism, etc. [1–3].

25.2 Basic Framework of ITS

ITS mainly consists of four parts, which are student module, expert module, curriculum and diagnosis module, communication module. Figure 25.1 depicts the basic components of the ITS and their mutual contacts.

25.2.1 Students Module

Student module is an important concept of ITS, which represents the situation of learners in the system. The student module is very important in order to obtain the learner's understanding or state of the knowledge. Generally, it is a systematic description of the learner's knowledge state. There are many ways to acquire learners'

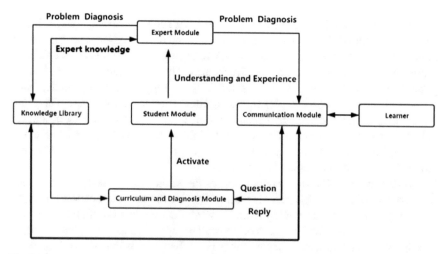

Fig. 25.1 Basic components of the ITS and their mutual contacts

knowledge, but it is difficult to save learners' behavior as a data resource. However, if the learner's behavior is explained first, it is easier to obtain relevant inferences. Therefore, the researcher should form an explanation of the learner's current behavior state based on the previous and latest explanations.

There is no agreement on what should be included in the student module or whether the student module is necessary for teaching. However, an ideal student module should include some of this information, such as the elements associated to the learner's past learning, the state of progress in course learning, the type of learning, etc. Implementing such a student module is difficult, so many systems mainly simulate learners according to the content of subject. McCalla made an in-depth discussion on clear and fuzzy student module. He thinks that the clear student module is the description of the learner in the learning system, which can be used to obtain the instructional decision. The fuzzy student module reflects the instructional decision, which is the viewpoint of the system designer about the learner. For example, the symbols and icons used in human–computer interfaces usually reflect the designer's understanding of learner. Artificial intelligence researchers are usually more interested in clear student module. In order to ensure that the system is more suitable for individual learner, a clear student module is particularly needed. Without a clear student module, the decisions to adapt to the environment can only be made by a simple impression of the learner's behavior. The clear student module allows the system to store relevant knowledge of the learners. On this basis, providing the system to adapt to the learner's decision-making. Moreover, the behavior pattern of learners stored by the clear student module is the basic element of intelligentization and individualization.

Traditional computer-aided learning systems (CAL) store quantitative scores for knowledge tests. Most ITSs store domain knowledge in the form of overlay or mal-rules. Some ITSs represent learners in the form of subset of domain cognitive module.

Some ITSs represent individual learners' attributes, such as learning style, influence state, special knowledge or characteristics of different individual learners. In the traditional CAL, the learner presents unprocessed, unstructured data, such as quantized scores on tests or binary judgments of responses. These data can be used to identify possible program branches or loops, but lacking the support of tutor module, which cannot be used to support complex reasoning about learner's current state. Therefore, the problem of imitating students cannot be solved, instead, the teaching design can only be combined with the content of the field through simple branched and loops.

Student module in ITS usually include three types: overlay module, differential module, perturbation module (deviation module).

Overlay module: Overlay module regards the knowledge owned by learner as a subset of expert knowledge, and the teaching goal is to establish the closest connection between them. In the overlay module, the student module is built by comparing the learner's behavior with expert's behavior. This approach assumes that the difference between the learner's behavior and expert's behavior is due to a lack of skills; therefore, the learner's knowledge is viewed simply as a subset of the expert knowledge (as shown in Fig. 25.2). The learner in the overlay module describes a simple inference mechanism that supports related inference between the cognitive state of learner and ideal domain expert. It can be well applied to a class of system that transfers knowledge from expert to learner. But the main problem of the overlay module is that it thinks that learner's knowledge is only a subset of expert knowledge, which is inconsistent with the real state of students' learning. Beginners are always unable to handle problems in the same way as experts. They usually use surface analogies between two problems, while experts use deep functional analogies.

Differential module: Differential module is an improvement of the overlay module, so it is also a kind of overlay module in essence. This module divides the knowledge of learners into two categories, namely the knowledge that learners can obtain and the knowledge that is not expected to be obtained (as shown in Fig. 25.3). Therefore, the differential module differs from the overlay module is that it does not assume that all differences in the student module are equally unexpected. Differential module acknowledges and attempts to express explicitly the learner's knowledge and

Fig. 25.2 Overlay module

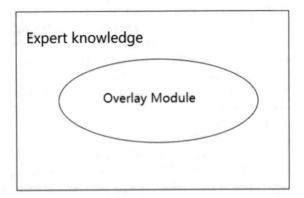

Fig. 25.3 Differential
module

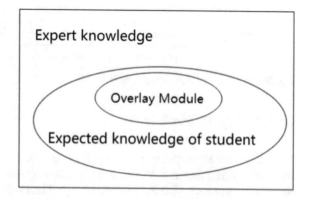

the difference between learner and expert. This module is considered to overlay the
expected knowledge, and it is also a subset of the expert module in essence.

Perturbation module (Deviation module): Overlay module represents learner in
correct knowledge, while perturbation modules usually combine standard overlay
pattern with biased knowledge. In the Perturbation module, learner is no longer
regarded as a subset of experts, but the potential of learner's knowledge processing
is different from expert's knowledge in terms of quantity and quality. The general
technique for implementing the perturbation model is to present the expert knowledge
firstly, and then supplement the statement based on additional potentially misleading
knowledge. Thus, the student module is superimposed on an extended ordinary
module (as shown in Fig. 25.4). The Perturbation module contains a closed link
between the learner and the expert module, and it also represents the knowledge
state of the learner beyond the scope of the expert module.

Fig. 25.4 Perturbation
module

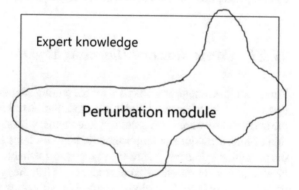

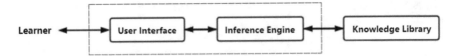

Fig. 25.5 Simple structure of expert system

25.2.2 Expert Module

Early ITS was combined with the expert system, and many ITSs were built on the basis of existing expert systems. The goal of a representative expert system is to provide the same solution as the expert for problem solving in a particular domain. Expert systems should deal with uncertain and imperfect information, and explain their decisions. Figure 25.5 is a simple structure of expert system.

The expert system consists of three components: user interface, inference engine and knowledge library. The role of the user interface is to provide smooth communication between the learner and the system. Inference engine is the interpreter of the knowledge library, producing results and explanation for the problem presentation. The inference engine and the user interface are seen as a separate part, the shell of the expert system. The core and decisive component of an expert system is the knowledge library. The knowledge library is independent of the expert system framework and can be used by other applications. The expert system contains knowledge representation transmitted to students. It not only contains the description of different concepts and skills of experts in a particular domain but also contains a dynamic form of expert module implemented in the domain. However, it is much more than just a description of data. It is a skillful presentation of knowledge in a particular area. The use of the expert module is to point out the learner's difficulties by comparing the learner's plan with the expert's plan.

25.2.3 Curriculum and Diagnosis Module

This module provides a mechanism for presenting adaptive knowledge in the tutoring system. In order to ensure the adaptive presentation of knowledge, the system adjusts the curriculum by comparing domain knowledge with student's responses. The function of the curriculum and tutor module includes three aspects: first, it must control the presented resources, its order and type must suitable for student. Second, it must be able to answer questions from students. Third, the type of help given to students must be determined. The global counseling strategies should be based on reasonable educational and psychological principles. These need to be identified by the student's diagnostic process and fed back to the student as a result of guidance and remedial teaching. Diagnosis is the process of forming and updating student module by analyzing the data, and applying this module in the system.

25.2.4 Communication Module

The function of the communication module is to ensure the interaction between the system and learner, mainly including dialog and screen design. The communication module occupies an essential position in ITS system, and becomes an important symbol to determine the practicability of ITS system. Generally speaking, communication module is designed to facilitate the use of learners. In order to improve the performance of human–computer interaction, the communication module in ITS adopts an interactive system based on semantic and context processing.

The development of human–computer interface is mainly reflected in two aspects: one is that learners become direct participants in the field; The other is to control domain knowledge by teaching the system to execute the required actions. The goal of interface design in ITS system is to realize semantic visualization in the domain. Special support is provided to learners for knowledge acquisition and to the conceptual model of communication by building complex domain models. Additionally, various graphic techniques can be used to represent the module, especially when they are associated with different conceptual stages, because they have different levels of abstraction and fidelity.

Another development direction of human–computer interface is to develop interface toolbox, which mainly includes direct operation technology, natural language interface, voice processing, video disc, touch screen technology and interface integration technology. Miller believes that the future development of human–computer interface in ITS is mainly manifested in three-dimensional graphics, continuous speech processing and massive data presentation. Matching between content and interface will help interface technology facilitate integration between different modules of ITS [4–7].

25.3 The Trend of ITS

25.3.1 Emotion Perception

In the process of learning, the intelligent tutoring system obtain the learners' facial expressions and other action characteristics to find out whether the learners are frustrated or interested in the problem, so as to help them overcome difficulties. By analyzing students' various physiological indicators, the intelligent tutoring system can roughly understand the students' emotional state.

25.3.2   Diagnostic Control Function

At present, the diagnostic function of the intelligent tutoring system is weak, and further optimization is needed. The user can get the corresponding diagnosis report in the intelligent tutoring system. The diagnosis report needs to show the learner's answering time, the frequency of checking the prompts and whether the answer is correct. Because the content expressed by the student is inaccurate, it is difficult for the tutor to know exactly what the student has learned. In this case, the tutor cannot make timely and accurate changes. This problem can be solved by using the intelligent tutoring system. When the system detects that the student has not mastered the relevant knowledge points, in order to enhance the student's confidence, the system will give some hints and help, and it can also reduce the difficulty of the question. When the system detects that the student has mastered the relevant knowledge points, it will reduce the prompts and increase the difficulty of the question.

25.3.3   Dynamic Interactive Tutoring

In the traditional tutoring system, the tutoring mode is that students learn step by step with the system, which leads to repeated learning of the knowledge already mastered by students, thus greatly reducing the learning efficiency. In the intelligent tutoring system, due to the existence of dynamic interactive tutoring, learners can click on the guidance button at a certain problem-solving step according to their personal needs and have a dialogue with the system.

25.3.4   Collaborative Learning Environment

Since the depth and breadth of individual learners' knowledge of a problem is limited by their own conditions and level of understanding, collaboration is a necessary ability in the current knowledge society. The intelligent tutoring system should not only be a learning environment to help individual learners, but also an open learning place to develop collaborative learning skills. Although there are already some intelligent tutoring systems with collaborative learning environments, the technology is still not mature enough and needs further in-depth exploration.

25.4 Suggestions for ITS Development

Although the research and application of artificial intelligence education have made some progress, the intelligent tutoring system is still in the weak artificial intelligence stage. In order to break through the bottleneck of China's artificial intelligence education and develop to a deeper level, we can start from the following aspects.

(1) Pay attention to the application of artificial intelligence in the field of education, provide policy support and increase capital investment. The information age requires education to be individualized and precise, especially emphasis on individualized teaching and lifelong education. Artificial intelligence can well avoid the teaching similarity and generalization caused by class-teaching system in the process of education. The development of artificial intelligence cannot be separated from the support of funds, so more funds should be invested to attract talent to actively participate in the construction of artificial intelligence education.

(2) We should strengthen the construction of cooperation community and explore the joint point between artificial intelligence and education. It is not enough to rely on traditional teachers to improve the quality of education but also by using artificial intelligence. At present, front-line teachers have little understanding of artificial intelligence, so it is difficult to find the combination point between artificial intelligence and education. Therefore, it is impossible to apply artificial intelligence in education and teaching. School-enterprise cooperation is one of the important ways to make artificial intelligence better promote the development of education. Enterprises can provide users and technical support for universities, while universities use artificial intelligence technology to reorganize knowledge and conduct intelligent analysis of learning behaviors to achieve mutual benefit and win–win results. Therefore, the cooperation between enterprises and universities should be strengthened to form a cooperative community to help AI promote the development of education.

(3) Standardize data processing standards and promote data sharing. Artificial intelligence is based on big data. With the development of technology, a large number of online resources appear. The online learning process will generate a large amount of data, the efficiency of data processing is low, and the risk of data leakage is high. Big data processing technology can process a large amount of data with complex structure, improve the efficiency of data processing, and optimize the storage of processed data. However, there are no unified standards and regulations for data management in schools. In order to prevent data leakage, there are almost no data sharing between enterprises and schools, causing obstacles to the development and research of artificial intelligence education. Therefore, it is urgent to standardize data processing standards and realize data sharing.

(4) Artificial intelligence training should be carried out on teachers to improve their awareness and ability of applying artificial intelligence. At present, teachers

have little understanding of artificial intelligence technology, and the application of artificial intelligence technology in education and teaching is not clear, so that it is difficult to carry out artificial intelligence education activities. Therefore, attention should be paid to the professional development of teachers and the level of artificial intelligence education of teachers should be improved through training. Pay attention to the explanation of the application cases of artificial intelligence in education, cultivate teachers' awareness of artificial intelligence, enable them to have the awareness and ability of artificial intelligence application, so as to promote the application and research development of artificial intelligence education.

(5) Establish an effect tracking and evaluation system for ITS to discover problems in time and optimize them quickly. At present, the omni-directional effect tracking and evaluation system of the intelligent tutoring system has not been fully established. It is not enough to use student' knowledge as an evaluation indicator. Students' autonomous learning, psychological development, changes in values, etc., should be taken as evaluation indicators. In a longer period, examine the impact of ITS on students.

(6) The hints of multivariate thinking path, enhance innovative thinking ability. At present, the intelligent tutoring system is mainly centered on knowledge learning, which often provides students with deterministic, standardized and procedural knowledge, but lacks guidance and development for students' innovative thinking. By providing the hints of multiple thinking path, students can explore and think independently to get their own understanding, meanwhile, the system gives positive feedback and encouragement, so as to cultivate innovative consciousness and innovation ability imperceptibly. Additionally, the exploration process of students can be recorded to form an innovative materials library for later data mining [8–18].

25.5 Conclusion

The development of ITS is full of twists and turns. From the initial people's desire to establish an "all-powerful" ITS to the realization of the importance of breaking through the bottleneck of local restrictions. To ITS structure, it mainly includes four components: student module, expert module, curriculum and diagnosis module, communication module.

The twenty-first century is the era of digitalization, the explosion of knowledge as well as the universalization of human education requirements of the times, objectively requires the replacement of traditional classroom teaching through advanced ITS in part or all. With the rapid development of computer science, intelligent teaching system will certainly continue to improve. However, we must clearly understand that intelligent teaching systems at this stage are still in their initial stage. The development characteristics of intelligent technology need to progress in iteration and require a large amount of practical data, but education cannot take students as experiments, and every student must not become a test subject of immature intelligent teaching system. There is still a long way to go for developing intelligent tutoring systems, and the abuse of technology must be eliminated while developing at high speed.

Acknowledgements This work was supported by Youth Research Project of Tianjin Normal University (52XQ2101), Teaching Reform Project of Tianjin Normal University (JGYB01220075).

References

1. T. Chen, J. Zhang, Research status of intelligent tutoring system (ITS) and ITS development in China. China Educ. Technol. (02), 95–99 (2007)
2. J. Guo, G. Rong, J. Hao, A review of foreign artificial intelligence tutoring application research. E-Educ. Res. **41**(02), 91–98+107 (2020)
3. Y. Zhang, W. Zhang, Hotspot, trend, and enlightenment of educational artificial intelligence research abroad. Open Educ. Res. **25**(04), 43–58 (2019)
4. J. Jiao, L. Xu, K. Dai, Applications of AI in ITS. Comput. Int. Manuf. Syst. (08), 49–51+54 (2003)
5. L. Wang, H. Feng, A discussion of the intelligent tutoring system based on the teaching process. Comput. Eng. (05), 64–65+105 (2000)
6. G. Xu, W. Zeng, C. Huang, Research on intelligent tutoring system. Appl. Res. Comput. **26**(11), 4019–4022+4030 (2009)
7. L. Liu, R. Zhang, Research and summary of intelligent tutoring system based on web. Comput. Knowl. Technol. **5**(09), 2474–2475 (2009)
8. M. Zhou, Y. Ma, F. Cen, A summary of application research on intelligent learning guidance system. China Comput. Commun. **33**(05), 115–117 (2021)
9. L. Chen, Y. Kang, H. Chen, Study on evaluation of learning effect in intelligent tutoring system. J. Fujian Comput. (05), 25+6 (2007)
10. J. Jia, Q. Meng, Evaluation and selection of intelligent tutoring systems. Digital Educ. **5**(03), 1–9 (2019)
11. Y. Yu, Y. Liu, X. Yu, H. Wei, Prospect on Intelligent teaching system under educational artificial intelligence. Heilongjiang Sci. J. **10**(15), 14–15 (2019)
12. Y. Liu, Intelligent teaching system based on big data analysis technology. Modern Electr. Tech. **44**(07), 178–182 (2021)
13. P. Lu, Based on intelligent teaching platform of expert system research. China CIO News (04), 148–150 (2021)
14. J. Jia, Artificial intelligence empowers education and learning. J. Dist. Educ. **36**(01), 39–47 (2018)
15. J. Li, Z. Zhou, New developments of intelligent tutoring system. Appl. Res. Comput. (12), 21–26+32 (2005)
16. D. Liu, J. Du, N. Jiang, R. Huang, Trends in reshaping education with artificial intelligence. Open Educ. Res. **24**(04), 33–42 (2018)
17. Q. Wang, W. Li, AI-empowered personalized education: practical mistakes and countermeasures. Modern Dist. Educ. Res. **33**(03), 12–17+43 (2021)
18. Y. Ma, Analysis of the relationship between school teachers and students from the perspective of artificial intelligence. J. Teach. Manage. **21**, 67–69 (2020)

Chapter 26
Study on Intelligent Evaluation of High School Mathematics Teachers' Teaching Reflection

Yueyuan Kang, Fan Yang, Wei Wang, Xinyuan Zhang, and Weiwei Liu

Abstract Developing the evaluation index system for teaching reflection and carrying out evaluation practice play a critical part and serve as an important breakthrough point in facilitating teachers' professional development. To evaluate efficiently, we developed an intelligent evaluation system for high school mathematics teachers' reflection, by integrating artificial intelligence (AI) technologies with the evaluation index system and evaluation model, and making use of the semantic similarity algorithm based on the Chinese National Knowledge Infrastructure (CNKI). Then the system was tested and applied with an accuracy reaching over 80%. This indicates the preliminary realization of the development, design and application of the intelligent evaluation system for high school mathematics teachers' teaching reflection.

Keywords High school mathematics · Teaching reflection · Intelligent evaluation

26.1 Introduction

In recent years, teachers' professional development has become a hot topic in international teacher education, and teaching reflection, as a core factor of teachers' professional development and personal growth, has been frequently mentioned in registration and professional standards for teachers in various countries. In 2012, the Ministry of Education of the People's Republic of China (MOE) issued *the Professional Standards for Middle School Teachers* (*Trial*), asking teachers to "continue to practice, reflect, practice again and reflect again, to constantly improve their professional ability [1]". The evaluation index system for teachers established by National

Y. Kang · W. Liu
Faculty of Education, Tianjin Normal University, Tianjin 300387, China

F. Yang (✉)
Tongyun Primary School, Beijing 101100, China
e-mail: yfanny66@163.com

W. Wang · X. Zhang
College of Artificial Intelligence, Tianjin 300387, China

Board for Professional Teaching Standards (NBPTS) highlights that teachers should "reflect systematically and learn from experiences". British Columbia in Canada issued in 2019 the *Professional Standards for British Columbia Educators*, requiring that "educators engage in professional learning and reflective practice to support their professional growth". In addition, deepening education evaluation and teacher evaluation is also the only way for teachers' growth in the new era. In 2020, the Central Committee of the Communist Party of China (CCCPC) and the State Council issued *the Overall Plan for Deepening the Reform of Education Evaluation in the New Era*, in which "reforming teacher evaluation [2]" is proposed.

With technological development, education has become one of the important sectors in which AI technologies are applied. In 2017, CCCPC and the State Council issued the notice of *Development Plan for the New Generation of Artificial Intelligence*, emphasizing "promotion of integration of AI with related basic subjects". Between 2016 and 2018, the United States released successively three reports on AI strategies including *Preparing for the Future of Artificial Intelligence, the National Artificial IntelligenceResearch and Development Strategic Plan* and *a National Machine Intelligence Strategy for the United States*, all of which highlighted the need for the integration of education and AI technologies. In 2019, United Nations Educational Scientific and Cultural Organization (UNESCO) launched the *Beijing Consensus on artificial intelligenceand education*, in which it's pointed out that "we are committed to leading appropriate policy responses aimed at the systematic integration of AI and education to innovate education, teaching and learning".

It can be seen that, in the information age, the integration of education with AI technologies has become a hot topic of current researches. However, viewing from existing researches, there are a certain amount of studies on theories and practices of reflective ability and reflective thinking, and some scholars have established the examination model for rural teachers' ability of teaching reflection against the background of "Internet+ [3]". Quite a few studied the integration of AI technologies with educational researches, which came down to evaluations of teachers' teaching, students' learning level and students' test results, and intelligent evaluation of educational management. From the perspective of the technological supply of AI, in the education evaluation field, video recognition, natural language process, text similarity comparison and computer-based visualization have been widely applied [4–7]. However, there are barely any studies on intelligent evaluation of teachers' abilities, or those that combine AI technologies with the evaluation of mathematics teachers' teaching reflection.

Therefore, it's necessary to study the establishment of the evaluation index system for teachers' teaching reflection, targeting at mathematics and taking the high school phase as an example. The support of AI technologies can not only enrich research content to a certain extent, deepen research methods, and facilitate diversification of studies on teaching reflection, but also make the evaluation of teachers' teaching reflection more scientific and convenient.

26.2 Definition and Theoretical Framework

26.2.1 Definition

Etymologically, in *Collins Learners' English-Chinese Dictionary*, "reflect" and "rethink" can be interpreted as "反思" (reflect in Chinese), and the prefix re- represents "again" and "once again", indicating that "reflect" means thinking twice and reviewing. Psychologically, teachers' reflection on teaching practices is an implicit metacognitive process, and Dewey was the first to put forward the concept of reflection in Western academia: an individual's repeating, serious and persistent consideration of any problem in the mind. Based on M. Griffiths and S. Tann, Chinese scholar Zhao Mingren defined different levels of teaching reflection, and from the time perspective, divided it into while-teaching reflection and post-teaching reflection, and the latter into three types including reviewing, study and re-theorization. Compared to implicit reflection while teaching, post-teaching reflection is more explicit, measurable and practicable. Therefore, focusing on post-teaching reflection, namely reflection after lesson, and taking reflection, the last module of teaching design, as the research subject, this paper selects the dimension of teachers' "reviewing", to conclude the concept of teaching reflection as follows: teaching reflection is the cognitive process of teachers actively evaluating, reviewing, and generating new understanding from finished teaching activities, and the re-construction of teaching experience.

26.2.2 Theoretical Framework

A good evaluation model is necessary for the scientific evaluation of high school mathematics teachers' teaching reflection, and this study chooses the CIPP model as the theoretical basis. CIPP (Context evaluation, Input evaluation, Process evaluation, Product evaluation) model (see Fig. 26.1) was put forward by American scholar Stufflebeam D.L. According to Stufflebeam, the CIPP model is a "comprehensive framework for guiding formative and summative evaluations" (p. 2) [8]. Three concentric circles describe basic elements of the CIPP model, with the inner circle representing core value. The wheel surrounding core value is divided into four evaluation focuses: goal, project, process, and product. The outer wheel indicates evaluation types of four focuses, namely context evaluation, input evaluation, process evaluation and product evaluation, while the double-sided arrows reveal the relationship between certain evaluation focuses and respective evaluation types.

CIPP model puts emphasis on process evaluation and includes the actual performance of teachers in teaching practice into the scope of the evaluation. It also features a dynamic evaluation of project, organization, implementation and recirculation, and the evaluation is targeted at development, which conforms to requirements and goals of the evaluation of teaching reflection. Thus, it provides a framework

Fig. 26.1 CIPP model

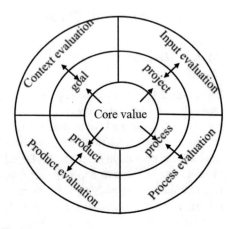

for compiling the evaluation index system for high school mathematics teachers' teaching reflection.

26.3 Compiling the Evaluation Index System for High School Mathematics Teachers' Teaching Reflection

26.3.1 Compile the Evaluation Index System

The evaluation index system for high school teachers' teaching reflection drafted based on theoretical analysis consists of 4 primary indexes and 12 secondary indicators. To ensure a scientific index system, the Delphi method is used to consult experts in related fields.

The amount of experts is usually 10–50 to ensure good validity of expert. After consultation [9] we use Excel 2019 and SPSS 24.0 for statistics and calculation of the active coefficient of the experts, authority coefficient of the experts and Kendal's coefficient of concordance of consultancy, thus ensuring scientificity and effectiveness of the Delphi method [10].

The active coefficient of experts is represented with questionnaire collection rate, expressed as the active coefficient of experts = collected amount/distributed amount. The figure is greater than 70% in two rounds of opinion polls, suggesting that the experts take active participation in this research.

The experts' familiarity with and diagnosis about this research decide their authority coefficient, expressed as $C_r = \frac{C_s + C_a}{2}$. The greater C_r is, the more accurate the prediction would be. According to the statistical requirements, data is reliable when $C_r \leq 0.70$.

There are five levels of familiarity, namely very familiar, familiar, average, a little bit familiar and not familiar, with the scores being 1, 0.8, 0.5, 0.2 and 0. Based on the

Table 26.1 Quantized values of expert familiarity and diagnosis references

Familiarity C_a		Diagnosis C_s			
Classification	Quantized value	Classification	Quantized value		
			Significant	Moderate	Small
Very familiar	1	Practice experience	0.5	0.4	0.3
Familiar	0.8	Theoretical basis	0.3	0.2	0.1
Average	0.5	Popularity among peers	0.1	0.1	0.0.5
A little bit familiar	0.2	Individual instincts	0.1	0.1	0.05
Not familiar	0.0	Sum	1	0.8	0.5

credibility of the scored items, the diagnosis references are classified into practice experience, theoretical basis, popularity among peers, and individual instincts. If the sum of diagnosis reference coefficients is 1, then the factor has significant impact on expert diagnosis; if the sum is 0.8, then the impact is moderate; and if 0.5, small. The quantized values of familiarity coefficients and diagnosis reference coefficients are listed in Table 26.1.

According to the self-evaluation data of experts, the experts' familiarity about issues in two opinion polls is greater than 0.7, diagnosis reference greater than 0.8, and authority greater than 0.8. Therefore, the experts' comments about indicators are reliable (Table 26.2).

The indicators shall meet designated requirements, ensuring that the indicator system is feasible. In line with the statistical requirements and research conditions, mean, standard deviation, coefficient of variation and full score frequency are taken as the measurements. The mean, standard deviation, coefficient of variation and full score frequency of experts' recognition about the feasibility of indicators shall be above 3, less than 1, less than 0.2 and above 50%, respectively. All requirements need to be met at the same time.

Based on data analysis and experts' opinions, amendments are made. While the primary indexes remain unchanged, "resource allocation" and "teaching efficiency" are deleted, "design of the process" is added to teaching preparation, and "classroom culture" is transferred to "teaching process". Index description is also improved.

Table 26.2 Statistics of expert authority coefficient

Round	Familiarity C_a	Diagnosis C_s	Authority C_r
First round of Delphi method	0.76	0.89	0.83
Second round of Delphi method	0.72	0.88	0.80

Table 26.3 Rationality analysis of secondary indicators in the first round of Delphi method

Name of indicator	Average	Standard deviation	Coefficient of variation	Full mark frequency (%)
Curriculum standard requirements	3.86	0.36	0.09	85.71
Understanding of teaching materials	3.43	0.65	0.19	57.14
Student situation	3.79	0.43	0.11	78.57
Teaching objectives	3.64	0.63	0.17	71.43
Points and difficulties	3.64	0.50	0.14	64.29
Design of the process	3.71	0.47	0.13	71.43
Teacher's teaching	3.93	0.27	0.07	92.86
Student learning	3.93	0.27	0.07	92.86
Classroom culture	3.79	0.43	0.11	78.57
Teacher development	3.93	0.27	0.07	92.86
Student development	3.86	0.36	0.09	85.71

Consisting of 4 primary indexes and 11 secondary indicators, the amended system is used for the second round of consultation.

Analysis of opinions on secondary indicators is shown in Table 26.3, with the average of each index being over 3, standard deviation less than 1, coefficient of variation less than 0.2. All of them are in accordance with statistical requirements.

In this round of consultation, some experts mentioned that: ① "teaching materials", which is not in line with indicator description, should be changed into "understanding of teaching materials", and as a result, the name of the indicator is changed. ② "Teaching objectives" should take into account the relationship between unit objectives and class objectives. ③ In the evaluation criterion for "classroom culture", ideological political instructions can be integrated into mathematics classes, so they are added into the criterion respectively. Consequently, an evaluation index system consisting of 4 primary indexes and 11 secondary indicators is complied with (see Fig. 26.2 for the amended evaluation framework).

26.3.2 Testing the Evaluation Index System

To guarantee analyzability of teaching reflection samples, based on three publications under the guidance of *High School Mathematics Curriculum Standards* (*2017*) and

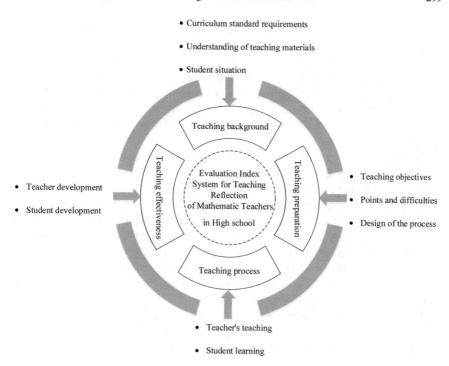

Fig. 26.2 Evaluation indexes for high school mathematics teachers' teaching reflection

articles of example lessons published on CNKI, we choose the part of teaching reflection (or "teaching postscript" or "teaching perception") in teaching design as the coding object. The basic process of coding for 73 texts of high school mathematics teaching reflection with NVivoll software is: text import → text coding → code testing → result summary. The study has two coders who code independently, and the coding consistency is over 80%, which is in accordance with coding requirements, and verifies the rationality of the index system.

26.3.3 Calculating Weightings of Evaluation Indexes

The weight can be calculated by subjective and objective weighting: the former relies on the experts' opinions to judge the importance of indicators, and the latter on data analysis and calculation. As the evaluation indicator system on the teaching reflection of high-school math teachers is a hierarchical system. The actual conditions of the math teachers should be taken into consideration when the weight is calculated. As most items to be evaluated have no clear boundaries among each other, no accurate classification can be made.

To ensure reasonable weight calculation, it is not suggested to rely on the current data distribution. The AHP method is employed in weight calculation. Proposed by the American operational research expert Saaty, AHP calls for "decomposing first and summing up late [11]". It designs a hierarchy, compares the relative importance of two indicators at the same level, and then makes calculation based on the comparison results of experts, thus determining the weight, i.e. relative importance, of each indicator. This is a subjective weighting method, which combines the qualitative and quantitative approaches [12].

Analytic Hierarchy Process, as a subjective weighting method, needs consultation with experts in relevant fields. For this purpose, with the compiled evaluation index system for high school mathematics teachers' teaching reflection as the framework, we designed a questionnaire with pairwise comparison among indexes of each level, and thus compiled *the Questionnaire on Weighting of Evaluation Indexes for High School MathematicsTeachers' Teaching Reflection*. In terms of fields involved and positions, recipients of the questionnaire are mainly professors and associate professors whose research interests are in mathematics education (teacher education) in universities, and high school mathematics teachers with senior titles or above. Questionnaires are sent to 14 experts via e-mail.

Data analysis is made after receiving feedback from experts. 13 valid questionnaires are collected and the recovery rate is 92.9%. The process of calculating weightings by AHP method is divided into three steps:

(1)   Design the diagnosis matrix of indicators

Saaty et. al came up with the diagnosis matrix (consistency matrix), where experts compare and score two indicators to determine the relative importance of indicators, arriving at the diagnosis matrix at different levels. When AHP is applied, the 1–9 scale recommended by Saaty is used to score the importance of indicators, thus quantizing the indicators in the matrix. Table 26.4 lists the values on the scale and the meaning of each value.

Table 26.4 Values on the scale and their meanings

Values on the scale	Meaning
1	Two indicators are equally important
3	The former indicator is slightly more important than the latter
5	The former indicator is significantly more important than the latter
7	The former indicator is strongly more important than the latter
9	The former indicator is absolutely more important than the latter
2, 4, 6, 8	Mean of adjacent diagnosis
The reciprocal of the value	If the importance ratio between indicator i and indicator j is b_{ij} On the contrary, the importance ratio between indicator j and indicator i is $\frac{1}{b_{ij}}$

Table 26.5 Diagnosis matrix

Code A	Indicator B under Code A			
A_n	B_1	B_2	…	B_n
B_1	1	B12	…	B_{1n}
B_2	B_{21}	1	…	B_{2n}
…	…	…	1	…
B_n	B_{n1}	B_{n2}	…	1

If code A_n is related to factors B_1, B_2, B_3, …, B_n in the next level, then the diagnosis matrix is shown as Table 26.5, whereas B_{ij} represents the importance of B_i to B_j. The diagnosis matrix should meet the following requirements:

$$b_{ij} > 0, \ b_{ii} = 1, \ b_{ji} = \frac{1}{b_{ij}} (i, \ j = 1, \ 2, \ 3, \ \dots, \ n)$$

(2) Calculate the maximum eigenvalue and eigenvector

After the diagnosis matrix is designed based on expert feedback, the maximum eigenvalue λ_{max} and eigenvector w need to be calculated. Below are the calculation steps:

1. Multiple the elements in the diagnosis matrix by line:

$$\prod_{j=1}^{n} (aij)^{\frac{1}{n}} (i = 1, \ 2, \ \dots, \ n)$$

2. Standardize and normalize the vector:

$$\overline{w}_i = \left(\prod_{j=1}^{n} a_{ij} \right)^{\frac{1}{n}}$$

$$w_i = \frac{\overline{w}_i}{\sum\limits_{j=1}^{n} \overline{w}_i}$$

Whereas, $w = [w_1, w_1, \dots, w_n]$ represents the eigenvector.

3. Calculate the maximum eigenvalue:

$$\lambda_{max} = \sum_{i=1}^{n} \frac{(AW_i)}{nw_i}$$

Table 26.6 Average random consistency indicator

Order	1	2	3	4	5	6	7	8	9	10
RI	0	0	0.52	0.89	1.12	1.26	1.36	1.41	1.46	1.49

Whereas $(AW)_i$ represents the ith element of vector AW

(3)   Conduct consistency check of the diagnosis matrix

As the evaluation items are complex and recognition varies across individuals, the experts' diagnosis of importance could be subjective. There could be errors in the diagnosis matrix. Consistency check is therefore needed to tell if the errors are within acceptable ranges. Below are the checking steps (Table 26.6):

1.   Calculate the consistency check indicator:

$$CI = \frac{\lambda_{max} - n}{n - 1}$$

2.   Determine the average random consistency indicator RI.
3.   Calculate the consistency check coefficient CR:

$$CR = \frac{CI}{RI}$$

When $CR < 0.1$ or $\lambda_{max} = n$, the consistency of the diagnosis matrix meets the requirements.

To ensure accurate calculation, Yaahp is used for verification. After data about the diagnosis matrix is input, Yaahp shows the consistency ratio in real time. When a diagnosis matrix lacks consistency, the tool would label the cases that are in need of correction and make automatic correction, while reserving the experts' opinion as much as possible. This helps avoid random manual correction. The weight of indicators is obtained based on manual calculation and Yaahp correction. After inputing the data of all experts, the diagnosis matrix would be established. The weighted arithmetic mean of the experts' ordering vector is used to pool the experts' data. After conducting consistency check on the whole, the w_i, λ_{max} and consistency results are calculated, obtaining the weight and order of the Level I & II indicators (shown in Table 26.7).

To observe the distribution of weightings of secondary indicators in the system more directly, the histogram of distribution is made with Excel (see Fig. 26.3).

Based on the weighting of each index computed with the Analytic Hierarchy Process, the evaluation model for high school teachers' teaching reflection is compiled with the weighted average method:

$$S = 0.0338B1 + 0.0291B2 + 0.0462B3, 0.0555B4 + 0.0433B5 + 0.0484B6$$

Table 26.7 Weighting ranking of primary and secondary indexes for high school teachers' teaching reflection

Primary index	Overall weighting	Rank	Secondary indicator	Overall weighting	Rank
Teaching background	0.1091	4	Curriculum standard requirements	0.0338	10
			Understanding of teaching materials	0.0291	11
			Student situation	0.0462	8
Teaching preparation	0.1472	3	Teaching objectives	0.0555	6
			Points and difficulties	0.0433	9
			Design of the process	0.0484	7
Teaching process	0.3693	2	Teacher's teaching	0.1377	4
			Student learning	0.1631	2
			Classroom culture	0.0685	5
Teaching effectiveness	0.3744	1	Teacher development	0.1620	3
			Student development	0.2124	1

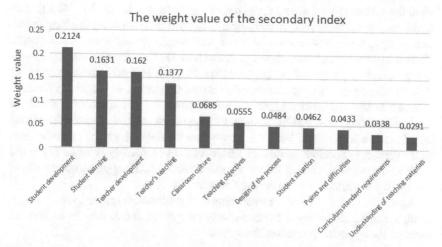

Fig. 26.3 Distribution of weightings of secondary indicators for high school teachers' teaching reflection

$$+ 0.1377B7 + 0.1631B8 + 0.0685B9 + 0.1620B10 + 0.2124B11$$

Hereinto, S is the total point of teaching reflection, and B_1–B_{11} represents points of secondary indicators "curriculum standard requirements", "understanding of teaching materials", "student situation", "teaching objectives", "points and difficulties", "design of the process", "teacher's learning", "student learning", "classroom culture", "teacher development" and "student development" respectively.

26.4 Establishing the Intelligent Evaluation System for High School Mathematics Teachers' Teaching Reflection

After defining materials for the corpus of high school mathematics teachers' teaching reflection, teachers and graduate students in College of Artificial Intelligence, Tianjin Normal University completed coding of the system, establishing the intelligent evaluation system for high school mathematics teachers' teaching reflection through Chinese word segmentation, stop word processing, TF-IDF computing words weighting, computing method of semantic similarity. The evaluation system can carry out an automated assessment of the reflective texts submitted by the user. The user logs onto the system and provides the reflective text required. After submission, the system reads the content of the text and transfer natural language therein into a formal structure recognizable by a computer, preprocessing teaching reflection by word segmentation and stop word processing, creating a text vector matrix. Then, the system calculates weightings of words by TF-IDF (Term Frequency-Inverse Document Frequency) method and generates the TF-IDF matrix, and thus, to better describe the degree of contribution of corresponding terms, highlight the function of terms in text-similarity computing, and improve the measurement accuracy of similarity among texts. Finally, through the computing method of similarity among texts based on primitives of HowNet, it compares the text with graded reflective texts in the corpus, to conclude evaluation results of the text, namely assessed grade and qualitative comment, and provide the same to the user. The application process of the intelligent evaluation system is as shown in Fig. 26.4.

Application is required after establishing the intelligent evaluation system, on one hand, to test the rationality and operability of the system, and on the other, to further describe the operation process of the system.

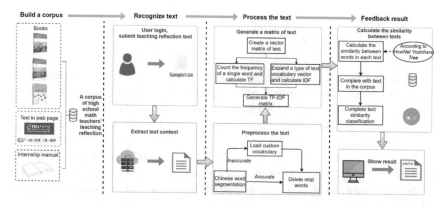

Fig. 26.4 The application process of the intelligent evaluation system for high school mathematics teachers' teaching reflection

26.4.1 Introduction of the Application Process of the Intelligent Evaluation System

In the application phase of the intelligent evaluation system, a total of 20 reflective texts as chosen as samples, including 3 texts of high school mathematics teaching reflections written by normal undergraduate and graduate students respectively, and 14 of ministry-level, provincial and municipal-level and county-level high-quality lesson teaching reflection on the One Good Lesson per Teacher platform. To guarantee the accuracy of the evaluation system, before evaluating with the system, three researchers are asked to grade and record the results of 20 reflective texts according to the evaluation index system and evaluation model. On this basis, the text is exported in txt. form to be applied in the evaluation system. the following is an example of the application process.

(1) The user logs onto the evaluation system by inputting the username and password.

(2) The user imports the reflective text to be evaluated. The system carries out automatically the text's word segmentation, stop word processing and word weighting calculation, and finally similarity comparison with existing texts in the corpus.

(3) Upon completion of the algorithm, evaluation results of the text are presented. The report of results consists of three parts including the address of text input, detailed content of the sample assessed and evaluation results, which include the grade of, and comment on the text. In this way, the intelligent evaluation of the reflective text is finished.

26.4.2 Analysis on Application Results of the Intelligent Evaluation System

Based on the application process above, 20 reflective texts chosen are assessed one by one, and results are recorded. After finishing the evaluation, the results of the system are compared with that of manual scoring as shown in Fig. 26.5.

The figure above shows that, 1 represents Grade A (excellent), 2 represents Grade B (Good), 3 Grade C (passing) and 4 D (failing). Overlapping points mean that manual scoring is the same as system evaluation, and others indicate differences between the two. The calculation accuracy is above 80%, indicating that this system can be used as a tool for intelligent evaluation of high school mathematics teachers' teaching reflections.

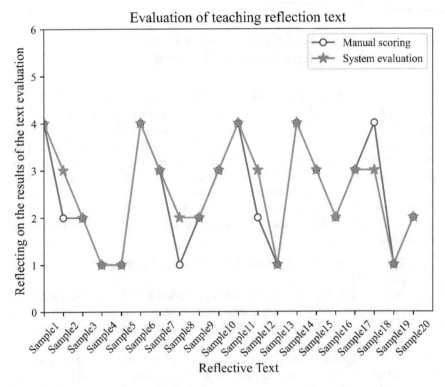

Fig. 26.5 Comparison of evaluation results

26.5 Conclusion

This paper integrates the CIPP model with the evaluation of high school mathematics teachers' teaching reflection, and follows systematic, scientific, oriented and feasible principles for establishing the evaluation index system. Through processes including index selection, definition of evaluation standards, application of Delphi method, and index amendment and examination, we conclude an evaluation index system consisting of 4 primary indexes and 11 secondary indicators and an evaluation model for high school mathematics teachers' teaching reflection. On these grounds, with AI as technological support, we build a corpus for high school mathematics teachers' teaching reflection. Based on the development of the new generation of information technology in the information age, we compile the intelligent evaluation system for reflective texts with Python, supported by AI professionals with coding and software development technologies. By comparing the similarity of the reflective text to be assessed with the corpus of teaching reflection, the system realizes automatic scoring for the reflective text. Further, through the application of evaluating different levels of reflective texts on the same subject, the operability and accuracy of the system are verified, with the accuracy being above 80%, indicating that it can be used as a tool for intelligent evaluation of high school mathematics teachers' teaching reflection.

By proper use of this tool, we can evaluate and assess the current situation and developing trend of high school mathematics teachers' teaching reflection more objectively and conveniently, and further, study and understand micro characteristics and macro trend of development of the same. With the help of result feedback, we may facilitate teachers' unification of "reflection" and "action", and thus promote their professional development.

Acknowledgements This paper was supported by the key project of the National Social Science Foundation of China (Project No. AFA170008).

References

1. N. Shi, G. Li, *Interpretation of Professional standards for Middle School Teachers (Trial).* (Beijing Normal University Publishing House, Beijing, 2013)
2. Central people's government of the People's Republic of China, the Central Committee of the Communist Party of China (CCCPC) and the State Council issued the Overall Plan for Deepening the Reform of Education Evaluation in the New Era. http://www.gov.cn/zhengce/2020-10/13/content_5551032.html. Accessed 13 Oct 2020
3. H. Zhang, H. Chen, J. Li, Construction of a model of checking teachers' reflection ability in "Internet+" era. J. Henan Normal Univ. (Philosophy and Social Sciences Edition) **47**(2), 143–150 (2020)
4. Y. Ren, Y. Feng, X. Zheng, Integration and innovation, intelligent lead—greeting the new era of educational informatization. China Educ. Technol. **1**, 7–14 (2018)
5. Y. Cheng, Design of test paper automatic correction system based on machine vision. M.A. Thesis, Shandong University of Science and Technology, Shandong, 2020

6. X. Yang, Z. Hao, H. Zhou, X. Zhou, Y. Li, A research on criteria for identifying teaching quality of open online courses in universities based on quality function deployment (QFD)—needs analysis of the value subjects. China Educ. Technol. **6** (2019)
7. G. Cheng, The impact of online automated feedback on students' reflective journal writing in an EFL course. Internet High. Educ. **34**, 18–27 (2017)
8. D.L. Stufflebeam, The CIPP model for evaluation: an update, a review of the models development, a checklist to guide implementation, in *Paper Presented at the 2003 Annual Conference of the Oregon Program Evaluators Network (OPEN)* Portland, Oregon
9. M.D. Singh, Evaluation framework for nursing education programs: application of the CIPP model. Int. J. Nurs. Educ. Sch. **1**(1) (2004)
10. A. Ge, J. Chen, G. Ji et al., Study on selection of public hospital performance evaluation system based on Delphi method. Acta Acad. Med. Nanjing **17**(3), 227–231 (2017)
11. F. Hasson, S. Keeney, H. McKenna, Research guidelines for the Delphi survey technique. J. Adv. Nurs. **32**(4), 1008–1015 (2000)
12. H. Fu, L. Zhang, C. Wang, Research of evaluation index system about the skeptical-mathematics key competencies based on the fuzzy-analytic hierarchy process. J. Math. Educ. **29**(1), 52–57 (2020)

Index

Printed in the United States
by Baker & Taylor Publisher Services